ANTI-APOCALYPSE

ANTI-APOCALYPSE

Exercises in Genealogical Criticism

LEE QUINBY

University of Minnesota Press
Minneapolis
London

Published by the University of Minnesota Press
2037 University Avenue Southeast, Minneapolis, MN 55455-3092
Printed in the United States of America on acid-free paper

Library of Congress Cataloging-in-Publication Data

Quinby, Lee, 1946-
  Anti-Apocalypse : exercises in genealogical criticism / Lee Quinby.
    p.   cm.
  Includes bibliographical references and index.
  ISBN 0-8166-2278-7
  ISBN 0-8166-2279-5 (pbk.)
    1. American literature—20th century—History and criticism—Theory,
etc.   2. Apocalyptic literature—History and criticism—Theory, etc.
3. Feminism and literature—United States—History—20th century.
4. Literature and society—United States—History—20th century.
5. United States—Civilization—20th century.   6. Postmodernism
(Literature)—United States.   7. Genealogy in literature.   I. Title.
PS228.A65Q56   1994
810.9'005—dc20   93-28600
                                                                      CIP

For Kate Mehuron
and in memory of Paul Pavel

Contents

Acknowledgments

I have been fortunate to have good friends with whom to share work in progress. Summers in New York City made it possible to have lively discussions with Pat Mann, Margaret Walker, Mary Katherine Wainwright, and Carole Cole about our respective projects. I have benefited enormously from their critiques of my work, reading and discussing theirs, and from their lively company. Tom Hayes's interest in my work has provided needed encouragement along the way. Some of the ideas that have found their way into this book stem from discussions about apocalyptic rhetoric that have occurred over more than five years. It has been especially rewarding to have Tim Landers as a sounding board for apocalyptic discourse as well as an astute reader of the Introduction and several chapters. Our discussions about cultural anxiety and hope, which helped to forge our friendship, were invaluable for helping me to think through issues of apocalypticism.

Hobart and William Smith Colleges provided support in two ways. Grants for gathering research materials were essential to the project and I'd like to thank Lisa Perhamus and Dana Osofsky for their research assistance as well as Stan Weaver and Fred Felten for their help in manuscript preparation. The support of my colleagues at the Colleges has been intellectually rewarding and emotionally sustaining, especially from Marie-France Etienne, Susan Henking, Eric Patterson, Daniel Singal, Deborah Tall, and David Weiss. I owe special thanks to José de Vinck, for his generosity in sharing his thinking about apocalypse and genealogy with me. I am indebted to his lengthy and perceptive commentary on several of the chapters, his genial insistence that I be more specific, and his cautions about my own apocalyptic zeal. Grant Holly's friendship has been particularly important to me during the period in which I was writing the last half of the book.

Special thanks to Biodun Iginla for his enthusiasm, advice, and editorial acuity. I also benefited from the initial readings of the reviewers for the press. Frances Bartkowski, Elayne Rapping, and a third, anonymous, reader provided both encouragement and astute critique of some of the arguments at an early stage. I also wish to thank Ann Klefstad for her copyediting.

As always, I write with my sons, Michael Miller and Paul Miller, in mind and heart.

This book is a memorial for Paul Pavel because many parts would not, indeed could not, have been completed without my having met him. Pavel died July 14, 1992. He was 67 years old, a psychotherapist, a Holocaust survivor, and an unusually wise and caring man. The last time I saw him was the week before he died of a heart attack. We talked at first about one of his cats, which was stretched just behind his chair. That wasn't unusual; Pavel had become known for his devotion to animals; it was even mentioned in Art Spiegelman's *Maus II*. But two things were different about this visit. One was that the cat was dying. It hadn't eaten, Pavel explained, for six days, only taking a little water and some liquid vitamins that he would place on his finger and then encourage down the cat's throat. The second difference was that, as we talked, the cat came over to my chair and curled up near my feet. I am allergic to cats and all the previous visits had begun with a ritual of Pavel rather playfully chasing two or three from his office and shutting the door to keep them out. But this one was dying and I had come to talk to him about death. And so the cat stayed and I even managed to relax a little, about it and the fact that it was dying.

I think I was able to relax for two reasons. One was because of Pavel's own calm. He had cared for this cat for fifteen years but he was accepting its death. The other reason was because his treatment of the cat reminded me of some comments he made in an interview on a video called "Living With Aids" that I had seen six months earlier. In the segment on that video titled "Thinking About Death," he observes: "Some people say that death is not the end, meaning death is a beginning." There is a pause, a slight smile, and then he remarks, "Well, I think it's an end." This is not uttered with dejection, nor delivered with any drama; it is simply in keeping with his next remark that "when you accept life, you accept death" and that "when one accepts, one relaxes." I am glad for this memory, and so many others of this remarkable man. His form of therapy, always more conversational than confessional, struck me from the outset as an enactment of the ideas I had been grappling with for the last few years, ideas about aesthetic self-transformation and an ethics of the flesh. Our conversations represent for me the meaning of nonapocalyptic thought.

I dedicate this book to Kate Mehuron. There's lots to say, but for now, let me just borrow some of the words from the end of Toni Morrison's *Jazz*: "Talking to you and hearing you answer—that's the kick."

Introduction
Apocalyptic Fits

Your country is desolate, your cities are burned with fire: your land, strangers devour it in your presence, and it is desolate, as overthrown by strangers.

Isaiah 1:7

"But everything isn't going badly."
Michel Foucault, "The Masked Philosopher"[1]

Approaching the Year 2000

U.S. society suffers from apocalyptic fits of two different kinds. First, there is the ready-made fit of an apocalyptic regime of truth that is dominant in the United States today. That is, the truth that has been made to prevail in the United States through a vast array of power relations is one that follows an apocalyptic grammar, semantics, and logic.[2] Conformity to apocalyptic truth is what brings on the second kind of fit, signaled by convulsions of fear and anxiety and paroxysms of hope for a new beginning. When Francis Fukuyama sights the end of history with the arrival of modern liberal democracy and New Haven residents spot the face of Jesus in a sycamore tree, the apocalyptic regime of truth gains momentum and scope.[3] As fundamentalist ministers and postmodern prophets register us closer to the millennium, apocalyptic anxieties over the end of the world and dreams of ultimate triumph will no doubt heighten, for the upcoming millennium is a prophetic year in apocalyptic thought. While according to the Chinese calender the year 2000 is long past, within the apocalyptic imaginary, the year 2000 promises to usher in history's final scene. Its enigmatic trinity of zeroes either promises cosmic embrace or threatens annihilation.

The hopes and fears associated with the end of the world are as likely to occur in nontheological discourse as in Christian millenarianism. While most analysts make a distinction between secular and religious forms of apocalypticism and millenarianism, the two forms are not so distinct. Carl Raschke, for example, offers such a differentiation by observing that the old millenarianism "could be understood only in the framework of traditional Christian belief. The new millenarian consciousness is basically political and secular." To my mind, this distinction (like my own use of the terms "religious" and "secular" on some occasions) is only useful provisionally in order to show the convergence of these two modes of apocalypticism. Politics has always been a feature of Christian millenarianism, and fundamentalist belief surely feeds nontheological perceptions.[4] The unusual elasticity of the term "apocalypse" facilitates this convergence of religious and secular attitudes and practices. Everyday usage of the term extends to images and ideas that are synonymous with cultural decline, urban chaos, and ecological devastation, and its range stems from evangelicals predicting Armegeddon to political officials calling for the United States to lead the way toward a "New World Order."[5]

It is vital to understand just how much the metaphors of biblical Apocalypse guide perceptions of everyday events for most people in the United States, despite the fact that relatively few actually read the Bible. Two Gallup polls from the fall of 1991 indicate how widespread certain apocalyptic notions are. An October poll indicated that 52 percent of the "typical" adults polled said they believed in the devil. A November poll reported that 47 percent of the respondents agreed that "God created man pretty much in his present form at one time within the last 10,000 years" while 40 percent agreed that "man has developed over millions of years from less advanced forms of life, but God guided this process, incuding man's creation."[6] These responses show that, even when people are not declared fundamentalists, they often hold to notions of divine origin and metaphysical evil. Even the overtly secular-minded speak of a nuclear blow-up, AIDS, rises in crime, and the greenhouse effect in apocalyptic terms. Media coverage of the events following the April 29, 1992, acquittal of four Los Angeles police officers accused of beating Rodney King often drew on images of apocalyptic fires and chaos to describe the burned buildings and broken windows of South Central L.A. Some secular apocalypticians, in concert with the fundamentalist sense of reaping havoc before harmony, regard worldwide devastation as a necessary step for a transformation in human consciousness.

Over the last few decades, Hollywood cinema has added entertainment to the mix. *Apocalypse Now* can be seen as a leader in the cinematic discursive field that depicts war as an end-time. More common and of longer standing is the cinematic fascination about life after technological destruction. As if enacting a repetition compulsion that simultaneously evokes and denies its sources of anxiety, such films tend to produce several sequels. From the series of *Planet of the Apes* films, first released in 1968 and then through the 1970s, to *Alien3* of 1992, one gets a sense of ever-dispersing denial of and despair over the end. Two of the most intriguing Hollywood apocalypse films from the early nineties, *The Seventh Sign* with Demi Moore and *The Rapture* with Mimi Rogers, are explicitly focused on the biblical book of Revelation. Their cinematic exegesis assumes as a plot device a supernatural divinity that brings about the end of time, but, by drawing on feminine apocalyptic figures such as the Harlot of Babylon and the Queen of Heaven, while targeting an audience familiar with feminism, both films focus on a woman to raise questions about human agency under apocalyptic duress.

It is understandable why apocalyptic rhetoric is used by so disparate a group of meaning-makers. Its images and symbols provide the kind of emotional drama we search for in trying to describe deep fear and widespread misery in the world today. For many, it is the only way to describe the horrors of the Holocaust, the destructive capacity of the U.S. bombings at Hiroshima and Nagasaki, or the devastation of bodies shrunken by famine. Apocalyptic prophecy is also the most resonant discourse in the United States today for expressions of hope and a sense of urgency about necessary changes in attitudes and behavior, for apocalypse is about celebration as well as destruction. The "revel" of the title "Revelation," the New Testament book of Apocalypse, reminds us of its announced promise that a new order is on the horizon. This view is endemic to the convergence of the theological and political in U.S. apocalyptic discourse. The nomination speech that Bill Clinton delivered at the 1992 Democratic Convention at Madison Square Garden drew on the puritan apocalyptic concept of a covenant in order to tap that effect.

I am not saying that this is all bad. Precisely because it is on tap in the United States, it is possible for apocalyptic ideas to aid struggles for democracy by exciting people toward activism. This is the force of Cornel West's warning about this country's failures in creating a multiracial democracy: "Either we learn a new language of empathy and compassion, or the fire this time will consume us all."[7] But even when apocalyptic imagery is used to fight racist suppressions of freedom, as with West's allusion to James Baldwin's warning, it runs the risk of displacing concrete political analysis. While advocating a new kind of leadership "grounded in grass-roots organizing that highlights democratic accountability," West's insistence that if we don't learn this lesson the fire will consume us all is the kind of hyperbole that undermines his own earlier analysis of local devastation. People in positions of privilege can, and clearly do, dismiss the threat to their own way of life as by and large inaccurate.[8]

At stake here are the relationships between power, truth, ethics, and apocalypse. In attempting to represent the unrepresentable, the unknowable—the End, or death par excellence—apocalyptic writings are a quintessential technology of power/knowledge. They promise the defeat of death, at least for the obedient who deserve everlasting life, and the prolonged agony of destruction for those who have not obeyed the Law of the Father. One does not have to succumb to apocalyptic eschatology to understand why end-time propensities imperil democracy: the apocalyptic tenet of preordained history disavows questionings of received truth, discredits skepticism, and disarms challengers of the status quo. Appeals to the Day of Judgment, the dawn of a New Age, even the dream of a cryogenic "return" to life, put off the kinds of immediate political and ethical judgments that need to be made in order to resist both overt domination and the more seductive forms of disciplinary power operative in the United States today and fostered by the United States in other countries.

Strictly speaking, Apocalypse refers to the Jewish, Christian, and Gnostic writings that announce what has already been predetermined: God's destruction of the world and establishment of a new order. Because their expressed desire is driven toward the future, these writings presume, yet do not themselves dwell on, their own narrative origin, as found in Genesis; they were composed centuries after its recounting of the divine creation of the heavens and the earth, Adam and Eve, and their fall. And although they dwell on the present by detailing the suffering of the elect and the iniquity of their enemies, Satan's accomplices, they are not themselves historical accounts in the sense that the two books of the Chronicles are. In its longing for the messiah, the savior of fallen humanity, the gaze of Apocalypse is riveted on the paradoxical vision of what will be: the end that is the beginning of eternity. The narrative focus of Apocalypse is the giving of the revealed word to the visionary prophet. Thus even though apocalyptic narrative is a story with a beginning and a middle and an earthly setting, it is a narrative that seeks to be nonnarrative, to get beyond the strictures of time and space.

Apocalypse understood in the strict sense dates from ancient history, and some scholars insist that this strict definition is the only proper way to approach apocalyptic attitudes and practices. One biblical historian who advocates this view argues that "apocalypticism in the full sense of the word, a balance of myth, method, and way of life, existed only for about 200 years, and formed a unique mentality" during the first two centuries C.E. Although he concedes that apocalypticism, because it is so "captivating," has "remained a constant theme" for many subsequent centuries, he takes issue with those who link apocalypticism with more recent and wider-ranging beliefs in the end of time and the dawn of a new age, stating that "the history of its reception has been the history of its constant dilution."[9]

That there are differences between the early form of apocalypticism and our own is a relevant historical point. But there are problems with the notion that the early form of apocalypticism is a "unique mentality" and that all subsequent forms are necessarily diluted versions of it. These particular assumptions are central to debates about apocalyptic writings and practices and are often found within discussions that do not otherwise adhere to the strict definition. The first assumption is that if something is unique then it is authentic, or, in this case, that the early form of apocalypticism was more "full-strength" than those that followed. This is not only misleading. It reenacts apocalyptic insistence on an originary moment. Such a view cannot account for why apocalyptic images, motifs, and fervor continue to be so compelling. The second assumption often

found in discussions of apocalyptic belief has to do with the notion of apocalypticism as a "mentality." To the extent that "mentality" is construed as a unified
mode of thought, predefined and continuous over time, and pure at its creation,
it logically follows that any changes in the idea will perforce be regarded as a
falling from grace. This too follows Apocalypse's footsteps.

Apocalypticism is not a single belief that can be gauged as full-strength or
diluted over the ages. It is better understood in the Foucauldian sense as a regime
of truth that operates within a field of power relations and prescribes a particular
moral behavior. By arguing that apocalypticism is a regime of truth I also draw
on Foucault's notions of discourse—but a caveat is in order: I want to avoid the
quasi scholasticism of the method defined in *The Archaeology of Knowledge*.[10] It's
then worth conceding up front the impossibility of fixing the parameters of a
given field of statements. It remains useful, nevertheless, to think of a discourse
as a "system of dispersion" of statements that define, designate, circumscribe,
and sometimes eliminate certain objects of its authority. Discourse is not the
same as language understood in the narrow sense as a transparent medium com-
municating a content. A discourse or discursive formation is constituted within
a social context, and that context establishes regularities or prescribed ways of
speaking that allow and disallow statements. Discursive analysis asks, "How is it
that one particular statement appeared rather than another?"[11] The discourse of
apocalypse has rules and conventions for establishing meaning, designating the
true from the false, empowering certain speakers and writers and disqualifying
others.[12] In short, rather than saying that contemporary apocalypticism is diluted, it makes more sense to say that it is a remarkably proliferative and persistent network of discursive and nondiscursive practices.

This proliferation and persistence is why it is accurate to use the term "apocalypse" beyond its scope of strict definition to designate a regime of truth that
has appeared over a long period of time and through a wide variety of statements, rather than insisting on it as a limited set of writings that appeared only
once in pure form with spin-offs for the last two thousand years. When viewed in
this way, what stands out is apocalypticism's perdurable appeal as a way of grappling with death, destruction, and eternity. The ancients aren't the only ones to
produce the truth of apocalypse, that is, to produce a mode of power/knowledge
that claims access to revealed and absolute truth about how the world will end
and who will survive it.

The modern history of this regime of truth has been expressed through three
modes of comprehending and narrating truth.

One of these modes is divine apocalypse. This is the discourse of religious
fundamentalists who see divine design and judgment as that which will bring on
the end of the world and provide a heavenly home for an elect group. It is also
the discourse of poetic visionaries such as Norman O. Brown, who, for thirty
years now, has heralded "Dionysian Christianity, an apocalyptic Christianity, a

Christianity of miracles and revelations."[13] And it is the discourse of New Age adherents who subscribe to a preordained planetary alignment that will bring a "mass ascension into new realms of consciousness."[14]

The second mode is technological apocalypse, which has two subcategories: technological devastation and technological salvation. The first holds technology responsible for human and world devastation, through such threats as nuclear crisis, environmental degradation, and mechanized dehumanization. The second position presents technology as the means whereby humanity and the earth will be perfected as a heaven on earth. Sometimes the two categories interlace in warnings of a harmonious but totalitarian world, yet holding out hope that from it will spring a new order.[15]

The third mode is ironic apocalypse, which is expressed through absurdist or nihilistic descriptions of existence. According to this discourse, there is an end to time, but no rebirth will follow. Time moves toward entropic inertia. A version of this view is sometimes identified as postapocalypse by its proponents. This is the dystopian view that history has exhausted itself. The irony is that we live on beyond morality or meaning.

These three modes comprise the apocalyptic regime of truth that dominates in the United States today. But apocalypse is not a single, unified regime of truth; quite the contrary. Although all three of these modes constitute apocalyptic discourse, they are often conflictual within a mode—as is the case between Norman O. Brown's Dionysian Christianity and Pat Robertson's fundamentalist Christianity. The different modes are also often at odds with each other, most notably the divine and ironic modes. And they frequently converge, especially the divine with the technological and the technological with the ironic. In other words, apocalyptic discourse is intensely contestatory in its claims for truth. But in its characteristic claims for the Truth, in whichever mode it is expressed, apocalypse is itself a totalizing production of knowledge.

Within U.S. apocalypticism, anxieties about and hopes for the end of the world as we know it and a new order of existence are commonly represented through the signifier "America." The convergence of general apocalyptic attitudes and a belief in the United States as the culmination of history is so thorough as to justify the term "American apocalypse." The status of "America" in the apocalyptic truth regime of the United States derives from the ways in which Puritan colonization made apocalypse a power/knowledge locus that prevailed even when English rule was defeated and separation of church and state was constitutionally mandated. Puritan magistrates and historians explicitly identified themselves as the elect, as "visible saints" in God's preordained war between forces of good and evil. They designated their society a "City upon a Hill," which obliged them not only to live according to divine plan but also to spread the word of the world's predestined and imminent end. Likening New England to the Israel of the Old Testament, they drew on biblical apocalypse both descriptively, to interpret events, and prescriptively, as a model of theocratic governance.

Because the Puritans so thoroughly adhered to the Bible, I want to turn briefly to the central elements of Old and New Testament Apocalypse that became dogma in Puritan apocalypse and have continued to hold sway over the last two centuries in the United States. One of the foremost features of Puritan apocalypse was its typological following of biblical descriptions of the present day as a time of supreme decadence, a wicked time deserving of God's unleashed wrath. Biblical apocalypse depicts the onset of great tribulation between nations, as in the Old Testament prophet Daniel's description of the battles between the four kingdoms (chapter 11) or Isaiah's account of the wars to befall Babylon (chapter 13):

> 9. Behold, the day of the LORD cometh, cruel both with wrath and fierce anger, to lay the land desolate: and he shall destroy the sinners thereof out of it.
>
> 15. Every one that is found shall be thrust through; and every one that is joined *unto* them shall fall by the sword.
>
> 16. Their children also shall be dashed to pieces before their eyes; their houses shall be spoiled, and their wives ravished.

In biblical and Puritan apocalypse, these disasters serve as signs for the holy, for apocalypse is also about how God's worthy people are to find their way to salvation. Among the worthy are the prophets who receive God's words and are bidden to pass them on to the chosen. Hence from Ezekiel (chapter 3):

> 16. And it came to pass at the end of seven days, that the word of the LORD came unto me, saying,
>
> 17. Son of man, I have made thee a watchman unto the house of Israel: therefore hear the word at my mouth, and give them warning from me.

God's warnings situate the prophet in time, emphasizing the importance to apocalyptic vision of linear time, as well as the way in which time is understood to be a totality. Apocalyptic time presumes a unity framed by a moment of origin and a moment of end. Old Testament apocalypse is fairly exact about the coming of the end-time, with calculations in days and weeks. Daniel records that Gabriel instructs him, "from the going forth of the commandment to restore and rebuild Jerusalem unto the Messiah the Prince *shall be* seven weeks, and threescore and two weeks: the street shall be built again, and the wall, even in troubled times" (9:25). Such precise determinations are not found in the New Testament; the Revelation simply announces that these things "must shortly come to pass" (1:1). But both Old and New Testament apocalypse focus on the nearness of the moment, a proximity that dramatizes the prophet's words and makes history a predetermined process that is reaching its culmination.

The culmination of history is to be enacted at Armageddon, in a battle between cosmic forces of good and evil. The Revelation of John in the New Testament details the suffering to be wrought from the clash of forces between the armies of heaven and hell. In the book of Revelation, Babylon is represented as a woman, "arrayed in purple and scarlet colour, and decked with gold and precious stones and pearls, having a golden cup in her hand full of abominations and filthiness of her fornication" (17:4). Her ruin is to be complete: "Therefore shall her plagues come in one day, death, and mourning, and famine; and she shall be utterly burned with fire: for strong is the Lord God who judgeth her" (18:8).

As devastating as this punishment is, apocalyptic writings also herald the triumph of the Kingdom of Heaven and the creation of a New Jerusalem, in which the holy—having suffered the acts of the vile sinners who will be condemned to "the lake of fire"—will be rewarded with eternal life. Crucial to this triumph is the coming of a messianic figure who is to lead the elect against the forces of evil by teaching them the way of righteousness through his own conduct and word. Jeremiah of the Old Testament records as part of his vision the following declaration: "Behold, the days come, saith the LORD, that I will raise unto David a righteous Branch, and a King shall reign and prosper, and shall execute judgment and justice in the earth" (23:5). The New Testament, which recounts the first coming of the messiah in the conception, birth, death, and resurrection of Jesus Christ, announces his second coming in Revelation as bringing about a "new heaven and a new earth" (21:1). Again employing feminine personification, the Revelation describes the New Jerusalem to be "prepared as a bride adorned for her husband" (21:2), thus connecting virginity, purity of soul, and eternal salvation.[16]

The sense of present iniquity, tribulation between nations, time coming to its culmination, the necessity of preparation by way of a prophet's warnings, the figurations of the cosmic forces of good and evil as feminine, the coming of a savior, and triumphant eternity—these are the tenets of biblical, Puritan, and "American" apocalypse. Although the Revolutionary War won independence from England and brought dramatic changes in law and governance, it did not eradicate apocalyptic ways of speaking. Instead, apocalypse turned nationalistic, as evidenced in the everyday parlance in which citizens of the United States refer to their nation as "America" and themselves as "Americans," thus sweeping together the diversity of two continents under their own national banner. Victory in the Revolutionary War was used to rekindle a sense of "America" as the culmination of history, the end of the old order and the beginning of a new existence. Alongside this continuity, however, came claims for the new nation as a place of rupture with history, a newly made lantern that would beam the doctrines of enlightened democracy to the rest of the world. Such postmillennial declarations of human betterment were bolstered by the technological productivity of the United States. Much nineteenth-century apocalypticism centered on achievements such as the railway and telegraph as signs of the beginning of human perfection. The concept of space as a new frontier, used by NASA officials and *Star Trek* enthusiasts alike, expanded this notion to include the universe and all its inhabitants. This sense of preordained expansion and progress was encapsulated in Ronald Reagan's address before the Republican National Convention at Houston in 1992 when he prophesied that "America's best days are yet to come. Our proudest moments are yet to be," justifying his hope by declaring: "We are an empire of ideals."

Of the three modes of apocalyptic practice in the United States, technological apocalypse has tended to predominate in the twentieth century. One version of technological apocalypse regards technology as a threat leading to an inevitable end, but this mode is more often accompanied by the possibility of thwarting the trajectory of destruction. The rhetoric of the 1960s New Left, for example, denounced U.S. war technology while simultaneously evoking the possibility of technology as the means for solving world hunger. While some define a desirable future as a place beyond technology (hence a return to a Golden Era of pretechnology), others posit technology as the means by which a future of abundance and comfort will be attained. On this view, technological prowess will extend human capabilities for the achievement of a total communications system and a defeat of bodily ills (and perhaps death). Both divine and technological expressions of apocalypse have been used in this century to revitalize a sense of "America" as a moral exemplar: a savior nation and a beacon of global democracy.

But utopianism has not been the sole feature of apocalypse in the British colonies and the United States in either its divine or its technological modes. Colonial apocalyptic prose and poetry included dire pronouncements of tribulation for deserving sinners. Slavery was a clear sign for many that the new nation was tapped for special suffering. As Thomas Jefferson remarked in *Notes on the State of Virginia* in regard to slavery: "I tremble for my country when I reflect that God is just: that his justice cannot sleep for ever: that considering numbers, nature, and natural means only, a revolution of the wheel of fortune, an exchange of situation, is among possible events: that it may become probable by supernatural interference! The Almighty has no attribute which can take side with us in such a contest."[17] Others regarded the telegraph and railway as ample evidence of demonic disruptions of nature. The frequency and extent of warfare throughout the twentieth century, as well as urban decay, economic decline, and increasing levels of personal violence, strike many as manifestations of an end-time. The Americanness of modern Apocalypse is particularly pronounced because of the

United States' use of the atomic bomb, worldwide nuclear arms sites, and extensive satellite surveillance systems.[18]

Today within the United States and in its representations abroad, the signifier "America" promises both millennial peace and harmony and military prowess and destructive force. In other words, contemporary U.S. apocalyptic discourse indeed differs from earlier versions, but it is no less real for that. Like the apocalypse of the first and second centuries and the apocalypse of Puritan colonization, the Revolutionary War, and the Civil War, twentieth-century apocalypse is a system of logic that understands mundane and momentous events in relation to the belief that the end of time is near. Unlike these earlier versions of apocalyptic expression, there is one key characteristic of twentieth-century apocalypse that was simply unthinkable in earlier eras: humanity's capacity to end the world. Although pre-twentieth-century forms of apocalypse have had any number of internal differences, they have all held the belief that God was the source of both revelation and destruction. Twentieth-century apocalyptic expression includes this concept of divine design but also includes the possibility of an accidental end brought on by technological prowess, which might occur in a flicker of time by a nuclear blast or by the gradual deadening of global warming.

In the twentieth century, belief in a technological disaster of irrevocable proportions on the horizon has fostered a double movement of anxiety and denial, characterized by an ironic stance in regard to human self-annihilation. Henry Adams was one of the first U.S. intellectuals to have coupled a sense of imminent apocalyptic *man-made* catastrophe with irony. (I use "man-made" here in the specific sense that Adams did; as Adams indicates, the burden of such dangers thus far resides with men.)[19] As Western calenders guide us toward the end of a millennium, postmodern cultural productions even more forcefully exploit this sense of ironic apocalypse. Director David Lynch, in films such as *Blue Velvet* and *Wild at Heart*, for example, boldly incorporates such irony into both utopian and distopian forms of apocalyptic cinema. On one hand, this kind of artistic experimentation helps dislodge apocalypse's insistence on its own uniqueness. Doomsday anxieties simply become banal. On the other hand, this insistence on the prevailing banality of everything, including fears about the end of time or the destruction of the environment, numbs people into inaction through its paralyzing sense of futility.

This sense of futility is every bit as dangerous to individual liberty as is the righteousness that accompanies divine and technological apocalypse. Apocalyptic suppressions of freedom (of thought, economic opportunity, sexual and affective relations, political action, and so on) are informed by two differing attitudes about the end of time. One attitude disposes people to join forces as righteous agents of a predetermined end. This leads to active suppression of conduct that does not fit with apocalyptic truth, as exemplified by the outlawing of homosexuality, or vandalizing and bombing abortion clinics. This sense of righteousness has been succinctly asserted by Randall Terry, founder of the antiabortion movement called Operation Rescue. As he put it in a 1992 television interview, "God put me on this earth for this hour, for this purpose." A slogan appearing on a U.S. flag in the fundamentalist meeting room where the interview was conducted neatly summed up his mission in terms of American apocalypse: "America shall be saved."[20] The second attitude, deriving from the irony found in twentieth-century apocalypse, inclines people toward a world-weary passivity. Although this stance doesn't lead to direct action against others, it too should be understood as a suppression of freedom. Operating through the stimulation of malaise and apathy, it renders people less inclined to political activity, despite their explicit acknowledgment of the need for social change.

Whether it is located on the right, the left, or in the center of the political spectrum, the apocalyptic self stands on a threshold positioned between an imminent end and uncertainty about the exact moment and means of that end. Agents of active apocalyptic suppression are spurred on by a sense of righteousness, whether they perceive themselves as acting on behalf of divine or of human justice. For them, the end of history as we know it is near, it will be accompanied by dreadful but deserved events, and the righteous will be saved. As the elect, they are to help bring the end about. In contrast, ironic apocalypse supplants agency with apathy. For those who hold this view, the end is near, it is probably unavoidable, it is not deserved by all but it will be suffered by all. Those who hold this knowledge are not the elect; they are merely among the unfortunate ones who will be here for the end.

These two attitudes inform the apocalyptic writings of the last quarter-century. A review of end-of-the-millennium publications shows Hal Lindsey as a leader in the field of the kind of apocalypse that fuels a sense of righteousness. *The Late Great Planet Earth* has sold over 25 million copies since its publication in 1970.[21] Lindsey's theological apocalyptic stance has a large following, despite his own glaring miscalculations. Even though predictive failure emerges as one of the most constant elements of apocalyptic prophecy, scholars of Christian fundamentalism indicate that the belief in an imminent apocalyptic cataclysm is held by 50 million U.S. citizens, including Ronald Reagan, a self-declared believer in Armageddon. "According to their theology, we are about to undergo a dreadful period of suffering (the Tribulation) in connection with the extraordinarily violent struggle between the forces of good and evil that is to precede the return of Jesus and the millennium of His peaceful rule."[22] This view is not limited to theological expression, however. Jesse Helms's congressional record is filled with the apocalyptic fury that guides Lindsey's discussions of cosmic struggles between the forces of good and evil. Nor is this view the prerogative of the political right. Anne Primovesi's *From Apocalypse to Genesis* documents a number of Green apocalyptic writers for whom "a cosmic war is being fought (some call it an 'Eco-war'). They are sure that if it is lost, there will be death, but are uncertain as to whether or not this will be preceded or followed by resurrection."[23]

Ecological debates have also been informed by the kind of apocalyptic stance that leads away from righteous action and toward alienated apathy. Such is the case, for example, with the writings of Bill McKibben, author of *The End of Nature*.[24] In McKibben's case, although there is an expressed hope that it isn't already too late, the sense of crisis overrides a call for ecological activism. While McKibben's and Lindsey's texts are strikingly different in their respective political persuasions, they echo each other ideologically insofar as they avow eschatological thinking. End-of-everything texts typically present a hostile or pessimistic view of radical politics. McKibben's apocalyptic apathy appears to be inadvertent, which makes it all the more telling. A sense of irony about a human-created ecological doomsday tends to override his righteous apocalyptic messages, which would otherwise elicit activism.

In the last few years, a more extreme version of ironic apocalypse has appeared, enjoying special vogue among academics in the United States, even though its chief spokesman, Jean Baudrillard, is French. For Baudrillard, postmodernist par excellence, the apocalypse has already happened. His writings are self-characterized as postapocalyptic, since "Everything has already been wiped off the map. It is useless to dream: the *clash* has gently taken place everywhere."[25] Despite his critique of contemporary apocalypse as anachronistic, Baudrillard is a quintessentially apocalyptic thinker in the lineage of Henry Adams. His already-too-late theme reinforces the antiactivist, apathetic stance of all ironic apocalypticians.

Know Apocalypse. No Apocalypse

There will be no announcement here of the end of apocalypse. But there will be invocation to struggle against apocalypse, to know its logic, to say no to its insistence on an inevitable end necessary for a new order, its infatuation with doom, its willingness to witness cruelty in the name of righteous justice, and its belief in an elect with access to absolute truth. Rather, there will an effort to seek, understand, and foster nonapocalyptic thought.

This book takes a stance of opposition to apocalypse, in all three of its modes: divine, technological, and ironic. *Anti-Apocalypse* has three goals: 1) to analyze the ways in which apocalyptic discourse and action thwart or prohibit exercises of freedom; 2) to better understand and provide support for struggles against apocalyptic vision; and 3) to highlight democratic practices that are nonapocalyptic. I call my effort genealogical, understanding genealogy to be an analytic approach that does not establish truth through the temporal and spatial narratives of the origin and end of history but rather through attention to the intricate details of discourses and practices and their inscriptions on bodies. I do not aim here to write a genealogy of apocalypse. Indeed, apocalyptic discourse superbly exemplifies Foucault's point that, even though a "field of discursive events" is "finite and limited," the events or statements "may, in sheer size, exceed the capacities of recording, memory, or reading."[26] Instead, considering my effort to be a contribution to that larger undertaking, which, like the writing of apocalypse, is the work of innumerable people, I provide here a series of genealogical studies of several instances of apocalyptic power relations and truth.

This book examines vastly disparate topics—jeanswear magazine advertisements, the Human Genome Project, contemporary feminism and philosophy, texts by Henry Adams and Zora Neale Hurston, Andres Serrano's photography, and radical democratic activism. The rationale for bringing together such a range of topics is to demonstrate what I referred to earlier as the elasticity of twentieth-century apocalypse. I want to show that the system of dispersal of apocalyptic discourse is a vast network of seemingly unrelated statements. The rationale for these particular topics is in keeping with the notion that genealogical critique is an exercise of thought that strives to problematize the limits of one's own subjectivity. I have tried here to rethink the literary and cultural texts that have most informed my own apocalyptic impulses in order to strengthen my means of resistance to them. These essays, or exercises in genealogical criticism, will probably not seem particularly personal to most readers, if by "personal" one means confessional self-revelations. Disclosure of that sort—the obligation to "tell all"—is itself apocalyptic, whether it occurs in a confessional or on a TV talk show. The essays are personal in the sense that they delineate the boundaries of my subjectivity. Given established social relations of gender, race, sexuality, religion, media, and so on, it is my hope that others will find this exploration, even when dissimilar to what they might pursue, relevant to their own subject formations and efforts toward agency.

For my understanding of genealogy, I draw from Foucault, not only because several of his essays specifically define genealogy but also because his writings provide some of the most important instances of genealogy at work. In "Nietzsche, Genealogy, History" he cites genealogy as pivotal for countering universal truth claims, for questioning totalizing myths of origin, and for showing the necessity of reading the body as a way of establishing the particular effects of history. As Foucault points out, reading bodies is a way of reading how history has been ordered; bodies record and hence make visible the effects of relations of power: "The body is the inscribed surface of events (traced by language and dissolved by ideas), the locus of a dissociated Self (adopting the illusion of a substantial unity), and a volume in perpetual disintegration."[27] Rather than claiming itself an impartial account, genealogy is a motivated reading of history, for its goal is to challenge the existing regime of knowledge precisely insofar as that knowledge lays claim to absolute and objective Truth. Foucault states it this way: "Genealogy, as an analysis of descent, is thus situated within the articulation of the body and history. Its task is to expose a body totally imprinted by history and the process of history's destruction of the body."[28] It's worth noting that Foucault strikes an apocalyptic chord himself here in emphasizing history's "destruction," a tendency that undermines his more important insight about history's embodiment.

The sources for genealogy are culturally available in what Foucault refers to as "subjugated knowledges." He argues that subjugated knowledges take two forms, one erudite but appropriated, the other popular but disqualified. The first form, the erudite, may be found in traditional scholarship—though not readily. Historical specificity is present but covered over by narrative unity, cultural generalization, and abstract theory. Nevertheless, it remains available to genealogical criticism, which has the charge of re-presenting the historically specific. In the case of the second form, that of popular knowledge, suppression has been made possible because its locality renders it vulnerable to more extensive networks of power/knowledge. Furthermore, the knowledge is made to appear (and may be) naive. In this instance, criticism's project is to return these disqualified knowledges to a more forceful level of opposition. Together these kinds of criticism constitute genealogy. In Foucault's words: "Let us give the term *genealogy* to the union of erudite knowledge and local memories which allows us to establish a historical knowledge of struggles and to make use of this knowledge tactically today."[29]

The seven essays brought together for this book have been organized to produce a countertext to the book of Genesis and the book of Revelation, the alpha and omega of biblical apocalypse. Part I seeks to replace biblical claims for the divine origin of everything with genealogical investigations of specific discourses. The first chapter traces the contours of two dominant twentieth-century fields of discourse—eugenics and jeanswear fashion—in order to demonstrate the workings of apocalypse (technological and ironic) in ostensibly secular practices. Fashion's overt play with continually changing surfaces and its use of postmodern irony may seem at odds with eugenic ideals of sameness. Yet the eternal state-of-being aspired to in apocalyptic thought resurfaces in eu(jean)ics, an interlocking technology of power/knowledge that promotes homogenized forms of subjectivity, values of mastery and control, and universalized Truth.

In the second chapter I focus on feminism as a practice that is both apocalyptic and genealogical. To call feminism apocalyptic in a book devoted to discrediting apocalypse is not to dismiss or denounce feminism, however. What I want to show are the ways in which feminist apocalypse can work to reverse the terms of masculinist apocalypse. I also want to show that feminism is not exclusively apocalyptic. Even though feminism's utopian impulses and doomsday urgencies may be understood as apocalyptic, feminism has from its inception also been a genealogical practice in its efforts to expose modes of oppression operating on and through women's bodies. Here I want to show how its genealogical insights have been and can be effective in countering the ways that apocalypse divests women of the means of self-determination. I focus on ecofeminism as one instance of a practice that is profoundly intersected by these two opposing tendencies. This location of feminism in relation to apocalypse and genealogy places it simultaneously within and at the limits of dominant culture. This is precisely where feminism can be most effective at this time: its genealogical work helps make possible a philosophy of the present (which I discuss in the following essay) while its apocalyptic logic encourages it to think and act on behalf of women.

The third chapter provides an overview of the ways in which a philosophy of everyday life challenges the tenets of apocalypse. I argue that genealogical critique is a necessary tool for a nonapocalyptic philosophy of the present. Philosophy understood this way dramatically recasts theories of power, truth, and ethics. Genealogically oriented philosophy questions the use of a general theory of power, seeking instead what Foucault calls "a new economy of power relations." Genealogical analysis of subjugated knowledges aids philosophical thinking about the status and value of truth. And a genealogy of ethics enables us to recognize subjugated modes of ethical conduct that have not been regarded as worthy guides.

Part II resituates the figures of Adam and Eve by focusing on twentieth-century conceptualizations of "man" and "woman." In these two essays I use genealogical literary criticism in order to demonstrate the ways in which apocalypse inscribes the body of a text (in the narrow sense of the word). Chapter 4 establishes the complexity of twentieth-century apocalyptic thought by analyzing a work that promotes both technological and ironic apocalypse, *The Education of Henry Adams*. I argue that this turn-of-the-century text manifests a form of apocalyptic thought that aligns itself with science and technology (rather than religion per se), a form that has become predominant as we near the turn of this century. As I indicated earlier, the *Education*'s irony introduced a new feature to the apocalyptic imaginary, one that has gained currency over the century. In some ways this irony offsets the eschatological momentum of apocalypse, but Adams's text resolves that internal tension through the Dynamic Theory of History, which not only restores a sense of the end of the time but also endorses men's control over women, the earth, and technology. This view is being resuscitated as we approach the year 2000, the year that Adams predicted would bring "every American who lived" the knowledge of "how to control unlimited power."[30]

Chapter 5 presents Zora Neale Hurston's anti-apocalyptic stance as a point of contrast to the apocalyptic vision that Adams offers. I analyze two works by Hurston, a folktale from *Mules and Men* and the short story "The Gilded Six-Bits," as countertexts to *The Education of Henry Adams*. Like Adams's text, Hurston's incorporate gender struggles, biblical themes, and humor. But unlike *The Edu-*

cation, the folktale and "The Gilded Six-Bits" draw on parody instead of irony to subvert utopian visions of a Golden Age of heterosexuality both promised and undermined by racist, patriarchal society. By reading Hurston's folktale and short story intertextually, I show how her use of humor challenges the race, sex, and gender hierarchies that are instated in the *Education*.

Part III turns to one of the typical ways in which "the end" is expressed in the United States in the 1990s: the end of "America" 's world domination. Instead of an end brought on by divine or technological fires of destruction, this view holds to the ironic apocalyptic perspective which sees history as exhausted, "America" a nation in decline. In a 1992 commencement address at Southern Methodist University, then-President Bush addressed this pervasive pessimism explicitly. "Much of the conventional wisdom these days portrays America in decline and its energy dissipated, its possibilities exhausted," he noted, but then ventured to reassure the demoralized. "These *declinists*, as they are called, will hate to hear it, but they're saying nothing new." "In the 1930s," he continued, "the *declinists* told us the Great Depression had made capitalism outmoded. Our victory in World War II put an end to that talk."[31] In keeping with the apocalyptic belief in technological salvation for the chosen and technological defeat for their enemies, Bush sought to assure his audience and the nation generally that "America" was indeed a world power to be reckoned with. How fitting that he chose to mark the declining days of his own administration with a deployment of U.S. military might called Operation Restore Hope!

Rather than joining those who would either deny or lament the decline of "American" empire, I close this book with a sense of hope that empire might in fact become a power formation of the past. The sixth chapter turns to the controversy that surrounded Andres Serrano's photograph *Piss Christ* as an occasion to introduce what I call "pissed criticism." I argue that the apocalyptic stance of the Christian-conservative alliance needs to be understood as an embodiment of power, in this case specifically in regard to the bodily function of urination, as well as the embodiment of institutional power in places such as museums and Congress. Genealogical analysis is used here to disrupt apocalyptic imaging of the body of Christ which, while acknowledging the flow of certain bodily fluids—tears and blood—invokes a perfected, hermeticized resurrected body. By focusing on a range of theoretical and visual representations of urination, I show how discourses that link urination to innate sexual difference have been used to sanction apocalyptic civilization and how counterdiscourses about urination can foster resistance to apocalypse.

The final essay then turns to the home as an everyday site of apocalyptic longing for heaven. This longing includes desire for an "American" homeland, or empire, that becomes more intense in correlation with the United States' loss of global control to multinational corporate powers. That desire for control over others is all too often expressed locally through violence against women and children, with homes functioning as closed-off spaces for battering and sexual abuse. Homes are a training ground for the apocalyptic regime of truth. But homes are also sites of resistance to apocalypse. I discuss the value of applying Foucault's concept of the heterotopia to home space, and I argue that the legacy of first- and second-wave feminism provides critical resources for current efforts to rethink power relations within homes. The analysis of homes as matrixes of apocalyptic power/space/knowledge needs to be fully integrated into social-political theory, which too often ignores the tactics, strategies, details, and complexities of power relations within homes. Such a focus provides a better understanding of the importance of current home-front struggles waged by gays and lesbians, feminists, African Americans, and activist groups who insist that homes must be places of liberty. Their resistance is itself a practice of freedom that combats the cruelties of apocalypse.

Part I
Genealogy Now

Chapter 1
Eu(jean)ics: The New Fashion in Power

Day 1: The Book of (Jean)esis

In the "always already" of postmodernism was Implosion. For the gods had said, let there be simulation.

And there was simulation. And the gods saw the simulation, that it was infinitely reiterable and so multiplied simulation upon simulation.

Sublime images moved upon the faces of media screens and computer monitors across the universe, spiraling into a precession of simulacra.

And the saturated relations of causality turned in on themselves.

And the gods said, Behold the Hyperreal.

And the gods said, let there be switching centers of Hyperreality. And Hyperspace came to pass. Mirrored images of passers-by merged with their materiality.

And the gods said, Behold the desiring subject in an economy of desire.

And the gods surveilled the firmament of advanced capitalism and saw that it was profitable. And they were beyond well pleased. Ecstasy on the seventh day.

Day 2: From Eugenics to Eu(jean)ics

Denim—for a while a signifier of New Left rebellion—is now an apocalyptic signifier of postmodern style. In the late 1960s, young men who rejected U.S. corporate power structure, bureaucratic impersonality, and military imperialism announced their politics by donning blue jeans, love beads, and tie-dyed T-shirts in place of the grey flannel suits of their fathers. Young women who joined the New Left and the feminist movement rejected the requirements of compulsory femininity by exchanging their bras, girdles, and garter belts for the same attire. The feminist challenge went too far for some who otherwise identified with leftist politics, though most were not as overtly ambivalent as Eldridge Cleaver, who designed codpieces for jeans in order to reassert sexual difference while rejecting class difference. On the other end of the political spectrum, the unisex look horrified the George Gilders and Phyllis Schlaflys, who knew full well that fashion and power formations are intricately related and that the class and gender hierarchies they condoned were under fire. But over the course of the seventies and eighties, with denim being touted as the fabric of choice for everything from designer casual wear to evening dress, and with simulated denim deployed on everything from school lunchboxes to checkbook covers, the New Left unisex challenge was thoroughly appropriated, though not necessarily to the ideological satisfaction of the Moral Majority.[1]

Jeanswear advertisements are a particularly illuminating vehicle for the study of cultural politics and late-capitalist power mechanisms for absorbing political challenge. Because jeans played so important a role in the political struggles of the New Left and seventies feminism, analysis of contemporary jeans ads gives insight into the machinery of media appropriation. Like the jeans themselves, the political values of the New Left have been spandexed, stonewashed, and bagged out. In addition to appropriating the politics of the New Left, many jeanswear ads relegitimize the sex, class, and race hierarchies that the New Left assaulted. Analysis of contemporary print ads used by leading jeanswear corporations shows how denim serves late-capitalist interests. Such analysis is useful for understanding appropriation, but that is a secondary concern of this chapter.

My foremost concern is the dominant technology of power/knowledge at the turn of the millennium. I explore how that technology operates through the production of a mode of homogenized subjectivity and a regime of apocalyptic truth that threaten the intricate diversity and variability of our existence. Intending both a pun and a deconstructive intervention, I call one of the predominant mechanisms of this current power/knowledge "eu(jean)ics." The pun incorporates the ways in which two initially distinct cultural logics and practices — eugenics and fashion — have come to be intersecting and mutually constitutive. Eugenic thinking, in other words, is not limited to supremacist views regarding selective breeding. In addition to driving scientific enterprises such as sociobiology, it feeds into a variety of other practices — such as the fashion industry. Fashion, in turn, informs the assumptions and values of contemporary eugenics. The convergence of genetics and fashion is strikingly evident in a September 1992 Harris poll conducted for the March of Dimes which shows that 43 percent of the 1,000 adults polled "approve of using gene therapy to improve babies' physical characteristics; 42 percent would approve it for improving intelligence."[2] The coinage "eu(jean)ics" thus overtly blurs phenotype (the total of an organism's morphological, physiological, and behavioral properties) and genotype (the state of an organism's genes), for that is one of the flaws of biological determinism. The belief that genes totally determine the life of an organism ignores variabilities induced by physical and social environment.

As the label "eu(jean)ics" suggests, my analysis draws from Foucault's conceptualization of power and Baudrillard's formulations of simulation. Unlike Baudrillard, I think that it is far too soon to "forget Foucault."[3] But it is also a mistake to dismiss Baudrillard's claims about the dramatic shifts in power operations that occur when media simulation becomes pervasive. This project therefore entails using Baudrillard's discussions of simulation in order to extend genealogical inquiry about contemporary power relations and resistance. What follows is an exploration of what I call the eu(jean)ic archive. By this I mean the ensemble of rules that allows for discursive and imagistic statements about genes and jeans to be made and to be judged true or false, legitimate or illegitimate.[4] I argue that eu(jean)ic rules inform and frame a commodified subjectivity and produce and reinforce the masculinist apocalyptic truth that prevails in advanced capitalist society.

Discerning how we are constituted as subjects within particular historical-cultural circumstances helps us combat impositions that endanger our freedom. In other words, my approach assumes that our subjectivity is not entirely determined nor entirely the product of free will. Instead, it assumes that existing power relations circumscribe us but are themselves subject to minor alteration and/or drastic change. This assumption runs counter to the philosophical determinism integral to apocalypse, whether it be manifest in the divine determinism of religion, in the genetic determinism of eugenics, or in the appearance determinism of the fashion industry. My project also aims to alleviate some of the political apathy or weariness that tends to pervade some strains of contemporary social criticism, particularly those that follow Baudrillard or the U.S. school of deconstruction. My analysis promotes the kinds of ethical-political activism that confront imposed limits on our freedom and strive for ways to empower people in relation to themselves as individuals and within political coalitions.

The eugenics movement was founded by Francis Galton in Britain at the turn of this century. As R. C. Lewontin, Steven Rose, and Leon Kamin explain in their important refutation of biological determinism called *Not in Our Genes*, the eugenics campaign made significant headway in both Britain and the United States during the first three decades of the twentieth century. While British eugenics focused primarily on class, the U.S. movement centered on race. For instance, in 1924 the United States Congress passed legislation that disproportionately restricted emigration from Eastern and Southern Europe; this legislation was based on testimony similar to that used by the Nazis. Lewontin, Rose, and Kamin provide the following overview:

> Testimony before Congress by leaders of the American mental testing movement to the effect that Slavs, Jews, Italians, and others were mentally dull and that their dullness was racial, or at least constitutional, gave scientific legitimacy to the law that was constructed. Ten years later the same argument was the basis for the German racial and eugenic laws that began with the sterilization of the mentally and morally undesirable and ended in Auschwitz. The claims of biological determinists and eugenicists to scientific respectability were severely damaged in the gas chambers of the "Final Solution." Yet forty years after Burt [Cyril Burt, of the infamous identical-twin research] and thirty years after the start of the 1939-45 war, Arthur Jensen resurrected the hereditarian arguments, uniting the British concern with class and the American obsession with race.[5]

Eugenics is one of several technologies of power/knowledge comprising the deployment of sexuality that Foucault describes as emerging in the nineteenth century. These technologies of power produce and manage both the individual and the social body by analyzing, classifying, and monitoring sexual activity and reproduction. He locates eugenics as part of a medical and political "project for organizing a state management of marriages, births, and life expectancies; sex and its fertility had to be administered."[6] Within this power formation eugenics provided and continues to provide guidelines for monitoring a middle-class lineage (which supplanted concern over aristocratic lineage with the emergence of the democratic nation-state). Foucault further argues that the "medicine of perversions" accompanied and merged with eugenics during the second half of the nineteenth century. Within this deployment or network of familial, educational, medical, therapeutic power relations, what is designated as "natural" is morally and medically sanctioned as normal, and anyone veering away from the so-called natural becomes a "personage, a past, a case history" categorized as abnormal, deviant, perverse.[7]

Foucault's discussions indicate the ways in which the technologies of power within the deployment of sexuality differ from the deployment of alliance, which was the dominant form of power relations before the eighteenth century. The deployment of alliance was associated with monarchical rule and the sovereign's right of death over his subjects. It was carried out through the law and enforced through bodily torture. In contrast to the deployment of alliance, the deployment of sexuality is a generative form of power, one that entices, rather than forbidding certain conduct. It is important to note that these new technologies glorified the natural and organic at a time when industrial production supplanted agricultural production. Hence, the rhetoric of enticement used by the deployment of sexuality involves an already nostalgic appeal to the natural. As I shall demonstrate, this appeal is often made through the "materiality" of denim.

The subjectivity produced through the deployment of sexuality is central to humanism, which defines a person as an individual with an interiority said to be discovered through psychology and disciplined through education. Such an individual is designated as an organic entity with inherent and inheritable traits improvable through eugenic management.[8] As radical critiques of the discourses of science have shown, this eugenically improvable self perpetuated a number of longstanding binary oppositions which privileged masculinity over femininity, mind over body, white people over people of color, and procreative heterosexuality over nonprocreative sexual practices.[9] As Michael Warner has argued, this subject formation is "heteronormative."[10]

It is worth noting once again that under the socioeconomic conditions of capitalism a given subjectivity is not necessarily, or even probably, produced coherently by the various technologies of power to which it is subjected. A good example of inconsistency among technologies of power integral to the deployment of sexuality may be found in late-nineteenth-century fashion's demand for a corseted female body. In this instance, fashion's localization of power in the body was at odds with the eugenic program of breeding healthy children, and yet the corset was crucial to the fashion apparatus of the bourgeois cult of motherhood which otherwise reinforced the the deployment of sexuality. An analysis of jeans-wear ads reveals similar contradictions among contemporary technologies of power. As nineteenth-century feminist critiques of the corset demonstrate, such discrepancies or ruptures in power/knowledge are potential sites of resistance to those formations.

Just as eugenics emerged from and bolstered a bourgeois social and political economy, so too eu(jean)ics derives from and promotes the social and political economy of late capitalism. In the contemporary era, state and medical management of middle-class lineage is being subsumed by the multinational corporate management of people all over the world. This is not to say that the class, race, gender, and sex hierarchies of eugenics have been abandoned, but rather that they are carried over through new formations of generative power. Nor is it to say that eugenics and the technologies of sexuality that took hold in the nineteenth century no longer operate. It is to say that they operate differently at the end of the twentieth century.

What has happened is that eu(jean)ics has been superimposed over eugenics without supplanting its mechanisms of power, similar to the way in which, as conceptualized by Foucault, the deployment of sexuality was itself "superimposed" on the deployment of alliance "without completely supplanting" it.[11] Furthermore, I would add, contra Foucault, that in contemporary U.S. society and around the world the deployment of alliance continues to operate through masculinist law and men's physical violence against women, even though I agree with him that biopower—the generative, normalizing power of medicalized sexuality—has supplanted it as the more culturally accepted deployment.[12]

As Baudrillard leads us to see, the power network of simulation is gradually overtaking that of the deployment of sexuality and is gradually supplanting it. But, as I have already indicated, despite Baudrillard's often brilliant descriptions of the postmodern scene, it does not necessarily follow that this scene is the only scene. In other words, these power networks do not become instantaneously pervasive, though the apparatuses of simulation surpass those of alliance and sexuality in the sheer speed in which they make such a system of power pervasive. The interpenetration of eugenics/eu(jean)ics was made visible in the 1980s, for example, in the songs of Tatiana and Johnny, a Latin American "teen" duet whose lyrics advocating "sexual self-restraint" were composed at the Johns Hopkins School of Public Health and used by the Agency for International Development.[13] The presumption and perpetuation of heterosexuality in their music video is also an indicator of the way in which the deployment of sexuality and simulation are currently intersected. Eu(jean)ics is but one of the mechanisms in the fashion technology of power in late capitalism, but an analysis of its semiotic specificity as a contemporary neocolonialist practice shows that it has been particularly resonant in the Americanization of the globe.

In conjunction with other postmodern technologies of power, eu(jean)ics produces a different subjectivity and a different regime of truth from that which had been predominant since the rise of humanism in the Renaissance. The humanist ideal of the autonomous individual with a core identity is supplanted by what Baudrillard calls "the schizo," who "is only a pure screen, a switching center for all the networks of influence."[14] Talking-head expertise takes a place beside, and possibly displaces, scientific authority in the dissemination of knowledge. Conception and pregnancy are refashioned through in-vitro fertilization and ultrasound imaging. Sexual contact occurs through telephone and video s(t)imulation. The shift from Victorian eugenics (and more generally the human sciences) to postmodern eu(jean)ics (and more generally fashion) is one in which the "natural" and "organic" overtly yields to the "artifical" and "simulated"; as Baudrillard comments, a "kind of non-intentional parody hovers over everything."[15] In short, eugenics is about reproduction. Eu(jean)ics is about replication.

As the medicalized body and the history of the deployment of sexuality are covered over yet again by new inscriptions of consumer culture, conduct deemed abnormal or perverse within eugenics sometimes becomes normative within eu(jean)ics, but when this occurs the challenge of the deviant, the transgressive, is diffused because it is simultaneously all-pervasive and "not real." Sterility emerges as a goal, for this is the era of suspect body fluids that threaten contamination. For eu(jean)ics, administering healthy bloodlines is less a matter of marriage and procreation and more a matter of purchasing items that either simulate youth or give death the look of kitsch. As both Baudrillard and the songwriter Paul Simon have put it, everyone is becoming "the boy in the bubble."[16] In the postmodern scene, the commodity is defiantly celebrated, artifice provocatively privileged, the synthetic parodically glorified.[17]

Day 3: Jean-Splicing

Contemporary jeanswear ads splice together the power axes of eugenics and fashion to create eu(jean)ics. This splicing makes for complex, often contradictory ideological assertions within single magazines and sometimes within single ads.[18] How is it that the messages of leftist social critique can so comfortably coexist with a reactionary relegitimation of homophobia, sexism, racism, and class elitism? Part of the explanation may be found in the fact that New Left iconography was *itself an appropriation* of two discourses iconically associated with denim, that of the natural and of rebellion. Because of denim's value as a durable cotton fabric suitable for work clothes, denim products have long served as metonyms for the natural, organic world, a nostalgic harkening to simple times when men were cowboys, women were in their kitchens, and nature was free of polluting chemicals. Thus the marketing of denim overlaps with the discourses of the natural that were integral to power concealments within eugenics.[19] As Stuart and Elizabeth Ewen have argued, what was introduced in the United States in the 1850s as an "unemotional, durable garb of miners and others among a newly mobile work force" became in the twentieth century "conspicuous within the moral landscape of media Americana."[20] Within three decades after Frederick Jackson Turner announced the closing of the U.S. frontier, Hollywood had made denim jeans a signifier of wide-open spaces and freedom.[21] The New Left's investment in natural clothes and its back-to-basics rhetoric and practices were a literalization of industrial capitalism's attempts to cover over the conditions of manufacture through appeals to nature.

Initially, this use of industrial capitalism's discourse against itself functioned as resistance, but this too was part of a New Left appropriation of denim, one that echoed the James Dean / Marlon Brando / Beat Generation scorn for affluent suburbia.[22] The civil rights struggles that were waged in the sixties did not *require* jeans, but as signifiers of rejection of bourgeois values blue jeans did advance New Left challenges. Yet, because of the nostalgic, romanticized, antiestablishment mystique of jeanswear, it did not take long for a leading denim company like Levi Strauss to recognize the market potential of the counterculture's uniform. At Levi Strauss the unexpected boom in 501 sales that followed the Berkeley Free Speech movement prompted a new campaign to tap what one Levi's advertising manager called "the tremendous creative energy generated in San Francisco at the time—flower power, modern graphics, psychedelic posters, the rock bands."[23]

This is what has occurred over the last twenty years: late capitalism has reappropriated the New Left's appropriation of the discourses of the natural and rebellion. In these processes of appropriation and reappropriation, meanings attached to the discourses of the natural and the rebellious are altered. All jeanswear ads begin from the premise, which may be located along the axis of eugenics, that denim is natural, true, pure. Yet, since by definition ads are simulations, depictions of the natural are already a product of the axis of eu(jean)-ics. As John Carlos Rowe has noted, "In a postmodern culture, the *representation* is always a *representation of a representation*, like the light on a computer screen that represents the hermeneutic and linguistic representation that belongs to scholarly discourse."[24] In other words, in terms of form, all jeanswear ads are a consequence of gene/jean splicing. Thematically, however, some ads splice in more images of the natural, and thus foreground eugenics, while others splice in more images of fashion artifice. The eu(jean)ic intersection of the two axes of power within jeanswear ads comports with what Baudrillard identifies as the last two "successive phases of the image"; in ads that accentuate the "natural," the image "masks the *absence* of a basic reality," while in those that accentuate "artifice" the image "bears no relation to any reality whatever: it is its own pure simulacrum."[25] Baudrillard's insight is aptly summed up in Levi's 1992 slogan for the loose-fitting 560s: "Everything basic . . . evolves."

Day 4: It's All in Your Jeans

This slogan of eugenics deconstructs its own resolute objective of genetic improvement when its pun implies that "it"—your sexuality, your identity—is all in your designer jeans. In the postmodern Americanization of the globe, fashion attains hyperreal perfection by recoding DNA (Denim Naturo-Artifice). This postfetishistic power field promises eu(jean)ic perfectibility by deploying signifiers of radical politics in service of simulated health, wealth, and sexual desire.

Benetton (1988)

Benetton's well-circulated Adam and Eve ad, found on urban billboards as well as in magazines in the late eighties, locates one point where eugenics and eu(jean)ics are spliced together in today's power networks. In Benetton ads, themes of global harmony and the promise of superior jeans go hand-in-hand. Yet such portrayals of global harmony cover over the fashion industry's sweatshop exploitation of workers. As Cynthia Enloe has demonstrated, Benetton in particular has led the way in maximizing worker flexibility for owner profits. By using subcontractors who employ women who work in their own homes or in nonunion workshops the company can keep wages lower than if they employed unionized workers for sewing.[26]

Although many of the conventions of submissive femininity are overturned in the Benetton Adam and Eve ad, the image also reinscribes masculinist hegemony. For despite evoking the unisex look of the sixties, the female model's jeans are suggestively unbuttoned while the male model's remain buttoned up. The concealment of her upper body by her jacket, ostensibly worn for the sake of discretion, draws attention to her partially exposed breasts. And of course it is still she who offers the apple.

Benetton's simulation of the scene of Genesis exemplifies the ways in which the eu(jean)ic system of power derives from, yet supplants the eugenic power formation. The differences can be seen in the subjectivity constructed within the ad. There is little to suggest an interiority for the Adam and Eve of a generation of postmodern teens. These models, like so many of their imaged counterparts, exhibit a self that is all surface. Adam's blank stare is a kind of imaged autism that recurs in a number of ads, especially those by Calvin Klein. By contrast, the new Eve is a playful temptress. Yet her enigmatic and knowing smile is equally a pose, in this instance a pose of transgression for fashion's sake. The biblical serpent as signifier of knowledge and pleasure, both the pleasure of knowledge and the knowledge of pleasure, is parodically replaced by a dimestore rubber snake—even Satan's subjectivity has been altered. As mere ornament, the serpent too becomes commodified but, in commodity capitalism's political economy of desire, pleasure bought is always pleasure deferred. The "degenerescence" of interethnic breeding, once so threatening to bourgeois ideals, no longer functions as threat in Benetton's world of "united superstars" where fashion's replication achieves worldwide homogenized subjectivity: jeanetic engineering renders that motive of genetic engineering obsolete.

Guess? (1988)

Does the imaginary territory of eu(jean)ics, like its eugenics counterpart, have a dark underside, always repressed yet endlessly evoked through the very denial of its legitimacy? Like eugenics, eu(jean)ics does indeed have its dark side—but not one that is repressed. Instead, the formerly repressed "pathologies" of eugenics are often hailed in eu(jean)ics. In other words, the power axis of eu(jean)ics legitimizes *both* the whitewashed scene of eu(jean)ic breeding and the dark-washed scene of sexual perversity. In the postmodern fashionscape of Guess?, images of artifice reign supreme. The sexism and racism of these ads is so overt and self-reflexive that it makes saying so virtually irrelevant. And to say that the models in these ads have no interiorized selfhood is merely to note the obvious, for they are more aptly described as floating signifiers of sadomasochistic desire.

This series is a post-Edenic celebration of simulated sexual coercion. That is, these ads present themselves as representing the site of pornography—and we as viewers become voyeurs. Both simulation and subordination are the themes of the first scene. Because of the mirror, we have a doubled image of a female model kneeling subserviently before the truncated body of a male model. The theme of doubling is carried out in the series of four scenes: this model appears in two of the scenes and a second model in the other two. In other words, the women are overtly portrayed as interchangeable. Only two of the scenes, the first and the last, show a denim product. In this one, the model wears a denim jacket; in the last, the second model wears the bottom half of the outfit. In the second scene, the second model appears in a velvet dress against a backdrop of expensive fabric. Her body position suggests an irresolvability: the positioning of her legs is simultaneously a pose of sexual availablity and a refusal of the presumed onlooker; her stare is both that of provocateur and frightened first-time call-girl.

As the third scene reveals, the man in question is a cross between a Mafia kingpin and Prince Ranier.[27] Within the Orientalist paradigm of white privilege, he is himself an Other, used here stereotypically to suggest sleaziness rather than oppositional politics. At the same time, he is a representative of the privilege of wealthy males. Although the male/female body positions of this scene ostensibly reverse the conventional gender hierarchy in ads—usually the woman is seated and the man is placed above her—here her body's pronounced cant, making a right angle, reaffirms that hierarchy. His outward glance as she hovers over him also reinforces the idea that this is an ad about voyeurism, ours and his. The fourth scene returns to the second model, now positioned on his lap in a conventional "sugar-daddy" pose. Again the traditional gestures of sexual differ-

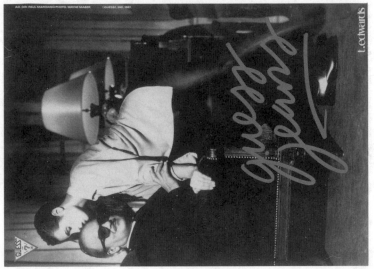

ence are parodied through reversals that relegitimize masculinist authority. The male model nuzzles her neck, a gesture that Erving Goffman documented as formerly reserved for women who would nuzzle children, men, and even objects. And she assumes the power of the outward gaze, again making us aware of ourselves as viewers/voyeurs, a device employed in experimental film as a way of diminishing the viewer's power of the gaze. Here, however, the woman's defiance of the male gaze is at the same time undermined by her place in his lap. There is also a possibility that she is looking at the other model, whose place she seems to have assumed. The doubling of the female models thus suggests a conventional pornographic triangle of two women sexually servicing one man. The fifth image, which generally appeared as a separate ad but contains the same models, more explicitly links the two women. This appropriation of lesbian politics evokes the possibilities of love and pleasure between women. But the framed image in the upper left-hand corner reframes a heterosexist paradigm.

In some Guess? ads, there is no jeanswear to be found. Only the Guess? insignia, an upside-down triangle — traditional symbol of female genitals — or the cursive inscription "Guess jeans" reveal the product.[28] This disappearance of denim is an indicator of the gaining force of eu(jean)ic simulation. The Guess? Delta of Venus trademark replaces the Sphinx's query with a postmodern fashion riddle: What goes on four feet in the morning, on two at noon, and on three in the evening? The well-Guessed subject.

Ralph Lauren (1988)

Ralph Lauren for Polo dungarees uses the rhetoric and imagery of the natural in the context of the overtly simulated to appropriate the style, not only of New Left politics, but also of Ur-jean company Levi Strauss. The traditional layout along an upper-left to lower-right diagonal begins the imagistic narrative with the backdrop of nature and moves down the page to the dungaree shirt and jacket and blue jeans, which, as the text informs us, "have been crafted in the spirit of an era when quality and durability were more important than fashion." From the "metal rivet and shank buttons to the triple needle stitching for added durability," these Ralph Laurens trade on the nineteenth-century patented inventions of a Jewish immigrant tailor that made Levi's the choice of miners, range hands, and factory workers. [29] In juxtaposition to these icons of nature and the working class, one finds signatures of wealth and aristocratic leisure — the silk tie, the natty pocket handerchief, the faithful pedigreed dog by his master's side, the confident gaze of the privileged male. The model's hands, firmly grasping the steering wheel of a luxury car, bear no traces of manual labor. Here, class conflict is readily resolved by uniting the sport of aristocrats and the coarse dungaree fabric of workers. The Polo insignia in the lower right corner neatly sums it up — in the eu(jean)ic fashionscape, one can simulate aristocratic breeding by playfully mimicking the working class.

Esprit (1987)

Just as Ralph Lauren appropriates a New Left critique of upperclass privilege while relegitimizing it, so too Esprit uses denim to appropriate feminist critiques of class, gender, and sexuality. The black strip that crosses the model's crotch, and which thus draws attention to, even while it disrupts, the viewer's focus on sexuality, reads: "Ariel O'Donnell San Francisco, California, Age: 21 Waitress/ Bartender, Non-professional AIDS Educator, Cyclist, Art Restoration Student, Anglophile, Neo-Feminist." This information makes the model into a real person, a socially committed one at that, by giving us the details that define her. On the right-hand page, the twelve discrete snapshotlike images, one with the model's face and the other eleven depicting parts of her jeans, decenter her subjectivity while conflating her identity with the details of her jeans. The text in the lower right-hand corner makes politics a matter of fashion by insisting, "Because denim and jeanswear are such social equalizers today you don't necessarily need silks and satins to be elegant. . . . This new elegance has become a *de*classification process that puts what you can do—your style and abilities far ahead of what you can afford. Now you don't have to be rich to be elegant." Esprit provides a eu(jean)ic ideal for liberals—you can be as elegant as a capitalist and as politically conscious as a proletarian, at middle-class prices.

Jordache (Billy and Lisa 1987)

The Jordache series that carries the slogan "BASICS because life . . . is not" gives a eu(jean)ics twist to the New Left's back-to-basics movement. In the Basics ads, the depiction of a natural landscape is displaced by the garish lights of an urban scene, and youthful rebellion becomes just another pose. Jordache boldly relegitimizes traditional dichotomies of sexual difference. Defiant teens Billy and Lisa are dressed in similar clothing, a gesture to the New Left unisex look, but gender differences are constructed through body posture and clothes arrangement. Lisa's skirt and her look of childishness, with her finger in her mouth, tousled hair, and off-the-shoulder, oversized jacket reinscribes a passive and dependent fifties femininity. And Billy's open shirt, which exposes his dog-tags and gold chains (along with his Brando / Billy Idol smirk), cocky hand-on-his-hip stance, and arm draped possessively around Lisa's neck celebrate macho masculinity defined in opposition to her (albeit excessively staged) vulnerability. Sexual difference is encoded by the differences in their handwriting: his thick, bold, phallic strokes report her feminine devotion while her neat cursive ones record rebellion against the authority of the bourgeois family. Jordache's indiscriminate mixing of fifties brashness, sixties antiestablishment anger, and seventies designer consciousness targeted an eighties generation of fashion(ed) teens.

Calvin Klein (1988)

Eu(jean)ics virtually splices out eugenics in the Calvin Klein sportswear domain. These men and women—perfect specimens of class privilege and race supremacy—are a eugenicist's dream, but that dream has been reached more by the dictates of fashion than by genetic engineering. Here the pastoral pretensions of eugenics have been relinquished for the golf-course artifice of a suburban backyard or exclusive liberal arts college campus. Appropriation upon appropriation: these are contemporary counterparts of the *Big Chill* ensemble cast, whose laments over abandoned political activism were diffused by *thirtysomething*'s weekly bouts of yuppie anxiety, (and eventually transmitted to the *Class of '96* and the residents of *Melrose Place*). In this twentysomething generation, there is little to suggest an interiority in keeping with nineteenth-century eugenic selfhood. Rather, these blank-screen faces, virtually interchangeable, all invested with the power of the outward gaze, are Baudrillard's schizos, subject to the "absolute proximity, the total instantaneity of things."[30] Although physical contact demarcates four opposite-sex couples from the remaining four figures, one woman and three men (a set of numbers that implies a variety of homosexual and heterosexual possibilities), in each case mirrored narcissism overrides the suggestion of sexual attraction to another. This is a eu(jean)ic simulation of desire as a thing unto itself, devoid of passion and reciprocal pleasure. In the eu-(jean)ic world, there is no referent, not even a masked one. Where there is no referent, there can be no pleasure—only cool, circulating, endless desire anesthetizing the senses through incessant stimulation.

Pepe (1989)

By the end of the 1980s, the genes/jeans pun was formally installed in the eu(jean)ic archive. As this ad for Pepe jeans indicates, the discourses of fashion and science converge to promise a fit between individual variability of body and genetic make-up. The small print running vertically down the left side provides a parallelism that simultaneously differentiates and conflates commodities, sex, and reproductive technology. Alongside the image of the blue jeans the ad reads: "Men's & women's jeans. Many colors & sizes. Available at Macy's & Bullocks." And alongside the genes images: "Men & women people. Many colors & sizes. Available through sex or test tubes." This emphasis on individualized fit is of course undermined by what must be stated yet not acknowledged in both cases: the prepackaging of genes/jeans.

silverTab (1991)

"As a species evolves, so must its jeans." What has also evolved in jeanswear ads is the advertisers' awareness of how to appeal to a heterosexual market while at the same time, as one marketing director has put it, not alienating gay consumers. As Danae Clark points out, this dual marketing strategy employs models who "bear the signifiers of sexual ambiguity or androgynous style. . . . Gays and lesbians can read into an ad certain subtextual elements that correspond to experiences with or representations of gay/lesbian subculture. If heterosexual consumers do not notice these subtexts or subcultural codes, then advertisers are able to reach the homosexual market along with the heterosexual market without ever revealing their aim."[31] Whatever sexual direction such an ad takes viewer pleasure toward, silverTab encodes the jeanome message clearly: higher evolution is evident through the ability of the male of the species to vogue.

Day 5: Designer Genes

Designer jeans/genes (1989)

Multinational monopolies of modes and codes of production produce a formidable economic-semiotic power/knowledge formation. As biotechnologies converge with the cultural logic of fashion, eu(jean)ics extends its capacity to become globally dominant. But it is vital to stress that genetics as a science need not be eugenically inscribed. Nor is it necessarily the case that fashion become a foundation for genetic medicine. The danger that I am concerned with here is that which occurs when eugenics and fashion gain apocalyptic momentum within the discourses and practices of genetic science and popular culture to produce the social reality of eu(jean)ics.

On the threshold of the nineties, the United States government announced the launching of the Human Genome Project, with a funding of $3 billion over 15 years through government and private sources. The goal: mapping every gene in the human body. It is worth noting how the announcement of the genome project was handled by mainstream media. For nonscientists, this is frequently the only information readily available. In the March 20, 1989, issue of *Time*, a cover story nostalgically entitled "The Gene Hunt" reported on the genome project. This article exemplifies the ways in which apocalyptic discourse informs the dominant modes of genetic thought, for a strident use of millennialist metaphors occurs throughout. The most modest statement of goals was voiced by Norton Zinder, chairman of the Human Genome Advisory Committee: "We are initiating an unending study of human biology. Whatever it's going to be, it will be an adventure, a priceless endeavor. And when it's done, someone else will sit down and say, 'It's time to begin.' " Zinder's comment provides a welcome contrast to the apocalyptic zeal of the others interviewed. Harvard biologist Walter Gilbert exuberantly states, "It's the Holy Grail of biology." And Mark Pearson, Du Pont's director of molecular biology, is no less fervent: "This information will usher in the Golden Age of molecular medicine." And George Cahill of the Howard Hughes Medical Institute: "It's going to tell us everything. Evolution, disease, everything will be based on what's in that magnificent tape called DNA."[32]

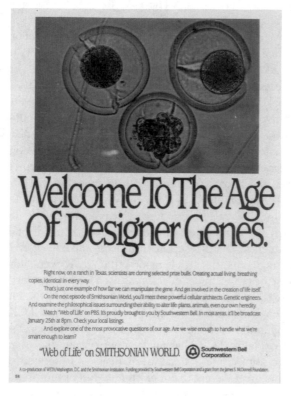

Welcome To The Age Of Designer Genes.

Right now, on a ranch in Texas, scientists are cloning selected prize bulls. Creating actual living, breathing copies, identical in every way.

That's just one example of how far we can manipulate the gene. And get involved in the creation of life itself.

On the next episode of Smithsonian World, you'll meet these powerful cellular architects. Genetic engineers. And examine the philosophical issues surrounding their ability to alter life: plants, animals, even our own heredity.

Watch "Web of Life" on PBS. It's proudly brought to you by Southwestern Bell. In most areas, it'll be broadcast January 25th at 8pm. Check your local listings.

And explore one of the most provocative questions of our age. Are we wise enough to handle what we're smart enough to learn?

"Web of Life" on SMITHSONIAN WORLD.   Ⓐ Southwestern Bell Corporation

A co-production of WETA/Washington, D.C. and the Smithsonian Institution. Funding provided by Southwestern Bell Corporation and a grant from the James S. McDonnell Foundation.

We might dismiss these claims as enthusiasms of the moment. But the focus on genetic problems dangerously ignores and displaces social causes of disease: toxic waste dumping, for example.[33] Furthermore, the quest for absolute knowledge and its violent consequences thus far have been too much a part of the history of the modern era to chalk up such hyperbole as merely excitement generated by the funding of so large and ambitious a project. Part of the problem derives from the way in which the "everything" of abstract conceptual models is both reductive and prescriptive. As Baudrillard observes,

> Abstraction today is no longer that of the map, the double, the mirror or the concept. Simulation is no longer that of a territory, a referential being or a substance. It is the generation by models of a real without

origin or reality: a hyperreal. The territory no longer precedes the map, nor survives it. Henceforth, it is the map that precedes the territory— PRECESSION OF SIMULACRA—it is the map that engenders the territory.[34]

The mounted trophy of genetic perfection sometimes threatens—and sometimes promises—to guide the "gene hunt." The *Time* article (drawing on the explanation of Mark Guyer of the Human Genome Office) puts it this way: "Eventually . . . people might have access to a computer readout of their own genome, with an interpretation of their genetic strengths and weaknesses. At the very least, this would enable them to adopt an appropriate life-style, choosing the proper diet, environment and—if necessary—drugs to minimize the effects of genetic disorders." And James Watson makes the ultimate eu(jean)ic statement: "We used to think our fate was in our stars. Now we know, in large measure, our fate is in our genes."[35]

These kinds of deterministic statements, made by renowned scientists and widely disseminated through the media, threaten our freedom in profound ways—as will genetic research itself, as long as it employs principles of masculinist objectivity and apocalyptic truth.[36] Another mainstream magazine article on such research, this one in *U.S. News and World Report*, entitled "The Amazing Gene Machine," reveals genetic research's propensities for determinism, for example through the elimination of certain genetic traits deemed undesirable. Discussing polymerase chain reaction, a process capable of rapidly producing copies of DNA fragments, the article reports that "PCR even allows genetic testing for many diseases to be done on embryos used for in vitro fertilization before they are implanted in the womb." It further explains that the Human Genome Project "has been rejiggered so that all researchers can use PCR as a common tool in analyzing and describing the many strands of human DNA."[37] And, as the article also explains, PCR "has made geneticists unlikely partners with detectives trying to solve crimes." Such mechanisms of genetic tracking pose both great hope for and great danger to our existence. Just as multinational control of the fashion code produces jeans uniformity, so too conglomerate control of DNA research may well gravitate toward gene uniformity.

Again, the claim here is not that modern genetics and natural science in general are necessarily geared toward eugenic domination, though its history certainly bears witness to racist and heterosexist scientific theories and practices. It is rather that apocalyptic logic is often an organizing principle of scientific thinking. The forms that apocalyptic science take include masculinist objectivity, reductionism, dogmatism, desire for mastery, and a belief in finding the Holy Grail of knowledge. Genealogical feminist theorizing about science has countered this apocalyptic determination. Donna Haraway has argued, for example, for "a doctrine of embodied objectivity that accommodates paradoxical and critical feminist science projects: Feminist objectivity means quite simply *situated knowl-*

edges."[38] Feminist objectivity, she points out, carries with it challenges to the mind/body split and the belief in transcendent truth characteristic of masculinist science; situated knowledge "allows us to become answerable for what we learn how to see."[39] And as Evelyn Keller argues, masculinist science is not all there is, although its practice has been to exclude and/or marginalize methodologies that don't comport with its assumptions and values, and it has certainly been disproportionately funded. Keller has shown how, despite such inequities, the work of such scientists as Barbara McClintock stands in contrast to the hegemony of masculinist science. McClintock's findings on transposition attest to the importance of refusing to adhere to abstract models and central dogmas.[40]

Day 6: Combating Technoppression Through Jeanetic Drift and Retrovirus Invasions

h.i.s. Blues (1990)

In the first year of the final decade of the twentieth century, proclamations for "American" victory and the New World Order were made in the world of fashion as well as in the world of military politics. This ad by h.i.s. appropriates and reproduces the patriotic fervor that swept through U.S. media coverage of the Gulf War. Just as with the 1954 erection of the famous monument to the conquerors of Iwo Jima, the effort to recapture an era of "American" victory requires the evocation of the World War II glory days. In this depiction, the soldiers of jeanetic prowess are all white, in striking contrast to the statistical ratio of people of color in the U.S. armed forces. (Is the missing sixth "Marine" Ira Hayes?) The figure whose face is completely turned away from the camera appears to be a woman, differentiated from the others by a belted shirt with armholes large enough to reveal a suggestive glimpse of black lace. Through its repetitions and its notable differences, this ad reveals the intersections of eugenic ordering and eu(jean)ic reordering: it is a simulation of a monument that was itself modeled after a staged photograph that followed an earlier photograph marking the moment of the initial flag-planting. So too, the New World Order is constructed around an Old Order of Things, with race, class, gender, and sexual hierarchies being reestablished along with the flag of eu(jean)ics. But the New World Order simultaneously announces its pride in achieving a level of artifice that one-ups the historical moment: Do Iwo Jima with Club Med style.

It may be that Baudrillard's speculation will come to pass: "Once everything will have been cleansed, once an end will have been put to all viral processes and to all social and bacilliary contamination, then only the virus of sadness will remain, in this universe of deadly cleanliness and sophistication."[41] But in the meantime, a radical politics can't be content to stand by and wait to see what the future will bring or risk inducing it prematurely by jumping ahead to the year 2000, as Baudrillard has parodically suggested. Baudrillard's demonstrations of the speed of hyperreal transformation notwithstanding, the operations of advanced capitalism do not expand monolithically but rather create, within the first world as well as in the third, socioeconomic conditions that range from early industrial sweatshops to computerized factories.

So what does this mean for radical politics? It means that we cannot afford to shelve Marx, forget Foucault, or ignore Baudrillard, because at least three power formations coexist in the United States and around the world. Interestingly enough, all three are put in operation in the ad for h.i.s. jeans:

1. The deployment of alliance, which operates through physical and legal constraint and seizure of bodies. Despite Foucault's arguments that this deployment has virtually been supplanted by the deployment of sexuality, Marxist, feminist, black, and gay critiques have shown how the law, military operations, and physical abuse are ever-present forms of domination. This deployment operates through the sovereign's (and his lesser counterparts') "right" of death over others. Its enactment is reg-

istered through street violence, abuse within homes, and the body count of civilians and soldiers in events like the Gulf War.

2. The deployment of sexuality, which, as Foucault argued, operates as a generative power through a myriad of surveillance techniques, including the police, education, medicine, the family and the military: This deployment operates through formations such as eugenics. Its primary dividing category is "normal/abnormal." It sexualizes and medicalizes bodies, dividing them into "naturalized" categories of race, sexuality, and gender. Rather than threatening death, this deployment promises life. This is bio-power, the regulation and management of the body.

3. A deployment that I call "technoppression": As I have shown here, this power formation operates through such means as the multinational economic-semiotic fashion complex and the Human Genome Project. Technoppression produces the hyperreality that Baudrillard has described, where "there is no longer any instance of power, any transmitting authority—power is something that circulates and whose source can no longer be located, a cycle in which the positions of dominator and the dominated interchange in an endless reversion which is also the end of power in its classical definition."[42] Technoppression operates through the binary "perfective/defective."

What my analysis of eu(jean)ics suggests is that a radical politics needs to intensify the struggle against technoppression without ignoring or becoming complicitous with the deployments of alliance and sexuality. In other words, each power formation requires different strategies and modes of resistance. The stakes are high. One way to think about the implications of the differences among these power formations is to consider the example of Venus Xtravaganza, whose story is depicted in Jennie Livingston's film *Paris Is Burning*. She and the other family members of the House of Xtravaganza, along with the other Houses and their voguing competitions, challenged the deployment of sexuality's insistence on binaried gender. Their performative of the hyperreal shows how one network of power relations can offset another. In this case, simulation offered Venus ways to shed masculinity and don femininity at will, in contrast to the static polarity of gender difference in the deployment of sexuality. But it was the domination of physical assault in the deployment of alliance that killed her.

Although there is little reason to be sanguine about the present, there is no reason to despair either. The last two centuries are testimony to resistance politics against the deployments of alliance and sexuality. The three great liberation movements of the nineteenth century—abolitionism, feminism, and labor—emerged in the historical intersections between the well-entrenched deployment of alliance and the developing deployment of sexuality. The outlawing of legally condoned enslavement and physical brutality are markers of successful resistance to white supremacist patriarchal powers of alliance. In the twentieth century that work has continued in third-world revolutions, feminism, black liberation, gay and lesbian liberation, ecology and animal rights movements, and struggles against child abuse. The struggle against physical violence and death continues (and must continue) in rights movements. Over the last century, people have also resisted forms of regulation that operate in domains other than the law and without outright physical violence, those occurring in education, medicine, and psychiatry, for example—the regimes of disciplinary power or biopower. Resistances against the deployment of sexuality are found in alternative clinics, in revisions of the literary and philosophical canon, as well as in the establishment of such innovations in education as women's, African American, and gay and lesbian studies, and in changes in the definition of the family.

What kinds of resistance emerge within the power relations of the third formation, the deployment of technoppression? I want to suggest three forms this resistance might take—indeed, is already taking. One form might be called jeanetic drift, insofar as new forms of subjectivity are being constructed through the operations of simulation. Jeanswear ads attest to this. What I have called jean splicing necessarily disrupts the technology of power associated with eugenics insofar as it suggests a self without a pregiven interiority. In the splicing together of eugenics and fashion, Luciano Benetton, Georges Marciano, Calvin Klein, and other eu(jean)ic engineers may produce a random fluctuation in the jeanetic code. When desire becomes this "uncanny," it risks becoming mutant, and the survival of a mutation is always in question, for the uncanny desire for replication may embalm itself in redundancy. And it might also be the case that, as the precession of denim spirals into pure simulacra, different chance encodings will occur, ones that render eu(jean)ics susceptible to its own late-capitalist efforts to sterilize everything. This is a Baudrillardian "response."

But why simply wait and see? Such ruptures in subjectivity are also events that radical politics in general and radical cultural workers in particular might *capitalize* on. After all, appropriation is not a one-way system. Reappropriation is, therefore, a second form of resistance to technoppression. If we regard the eu(jean)ic break in the ".genetic" code of humanism as a site of resistance, then ads and other domains of postmodern cultural production become a place to retrovirally recode for, in Foucault's words, a "different economy of bodies and pleasures."[43] The "pure screen switching center" of eu(jean)ics may be the fastest-spreading form of subjectivity to emerge within the postmodern era, but it is not the only one. Nor is it entirely unified. Part of the task of radical politics thus becomes the promotion of new forms of subjectivity that continue the break with humanist subjectivity while also resisting subjection to and by the powers of hyperreality. Radical media production, in AIDS activist films such as *Voices from the Front*, for example, which is also made readily available and more affordable through video distribution, exemplifies this form of image counterproduction. [44]

In addition to these first two strategies, it is worth attending to an ethical response to postmodernity's technoppression. Foucault's late essay "What Is Enlightenment?" presents the idea that a modern aesthetics of existence could be one such counterethic. In this work he describes a philosophical ethos of self-stylization, an ethos founded on a "principle of a critique and a permanent creation of ourselves in our autonomy." [45] One of the points I have wanted to make in this essay is that self-stylization challenges the fashioned selfhood of eu(jean)ics. It counters the eu-(jean)ic ideal of commodified selfhood by proposing an aesthetic elaboration of self, a labor on oneself as a work of art. Whereas eu(jean)ics strives for a subjectivity founded in truth that is global, universal, homogeneous, and fixed, even as it simulates change by reaccessorizing those old fashion standbys, an ethos of self-stylization uses local, particular, and heterogeneous truths as a means of unfixing hierarchicalized subjectivities. As such, it is an oppositional ethics engaged in specific transformations rather than totalizing programs.

Foucault's challenge to the "blackmail" of Enlightenment philosophizing—namely, that one must be either " 'for' or 'against' the Enlightenment"—may also be applied to postmodernism and to the three strategies against technoppression on which I am focusing. For it is of little value to declare oneself either "for" or "against" postmodernism, either reveling in its relativisms or decrying its amoralities. First of all, postmodernist simulation is neither completely unified nor centrally controlled—hence the rationale for acknowledging the Baudrillardian insight of pushing a system to its limits. Second, late-capitalist appropriation is a sign of radical resistance's impact—that's why the second strategy of ongoing reappropriation makes sense. And, third, it is vital to see that *both* the hegemonic, fashioned subjectivity of late capitalism *and* the counterhegemonic subjectivity of self-stylization are made possible by the material conditions of the present day. Whereas eu(jean)ic subjectivity is the embodiment of those conditions, a political ethics of self-stylization is as well. But that does not mean the struggle is over before it is begun, as the weary voices of too many straight white male theorists seem to suggest. What it can mean is that self-stylization is "at one and the same time the historical analysis of the limits that are imposed on us and an experiment with the possibility of going beyond them." [46]

Day 7: The Book of (Jean)esis, Cont.

In the interstices of hyperspace, there dwell freedom fighters.
At times their words surface through the din of white noise.
For they have written: "There's no such thing as a central dogma into which everything will fit."

They have written: "For postmodern Pangloss, a multiplicity of causes compete with a variety of effects, so we had best make the best of everything in the only possible world."

And they have also written: "There is a reality *that one cannot not know*. The ragged edges of the Real, of *Necessity*, not being able to eat, not having shelter, not having health care, all this is something that one cannot not know."

And they have written: "Where there is power, there is resistance."

And they know that this story was not finished before it started.[47]

Chapter 2
Genealogical Feminism: A Politic Way of Looking

One must probably find the humility to admit that the time of one's own life is not the one-time, basic, revolutionary moment of history, from which everything begins and is completed. At the same time humility is needed to say without solemnity that the present time is rather exciting and demands an analysis.

Michel Foucault,
"How Much Does It Cost for Reason to Tell the Truth?"[1]

This chapter reflects on feminists pursuing coalition both with each other and with other radical activists. In terms of practical politics, coalition is one of the most crucial means for combating male-dominant power relations and the apocalyptic logic that serves as an apologia for male dominance. Yet an ever-increasing diversity of feminist practices raises doubts about the viability of coalitions among feminists who are philosophically distinct and sometimes opposed. A catalogue of feminist practices of the last two decades would include entries for black, cultural, deconstructive, ecological, lesbian, liberal, materialist, psychoanalytic, semiotic, socialist, and third-world feminisms, and no doubt others that I have failed to mention, including a whole string of proper-name feminisms, such as Foucauldian, Lacanian, Marxist. Such differentiation is important because it honors the feminist principle of self-determination. Each of these forms of feminism has its own unique values, strengths, and self-reflexive narratives coming out of differing traditions. But the trajectory of differentiation also fuels infighting that weakens feminist opposition to male dominance.

One way to counter such infighting and enhance coalitional possibilities is for feminism to become more genealogical. As a method of analysis that seeks to "establish a historical knowledge of struggles and to make use of this knowledge tactically today," genealogy ascertains the means by which any given truth overextends its domain by claiming universality.[2] By refusing the "certainty of absolutes," genealogy emancipates and enfranchises the knowledges that have been disqualified for voicing uncertainty about or challenging outright those absolutes.[3] Genealogy attempts to put on display the places where force relations dig

31

in, below the surface of the skin, not quite visible yet making themselves felt, governing behavior, posture, gesture, becoming the truth of one's being. Genealogy exposes how that truth appraises certain behaviors and relationships as sinful or abnormal and designates others as virtuous or proper.

Genealogical feminism is a stance that endorses feminist coalition as paramount for fighting the force relations of masculinist apocalypse. Proposing that feminism become more genealogical is not to ignore the differences between feminisms that have taken shape out of specific concerns over race, class, sexuality, and so on. It is, rather, a way of accenting the genealogical momentum already integral to feminism that acknowledged those differences in the first place. A genealogical approach strives to situate feminist knowledges by ascertaining what distinguishes one form of feminism from another, hence clarifying the lines of demarcation between, say, semiotic and socialist feminism.[4]

Even more than drawing discursive boundaries (the defining characteristic of an archaeology of knowledge), genealogy examines the interrelations of power, knowledge, and the body. Because feminism's raison d'être has been to fight masculinist power/knowledge's domination of women's minds and bodies, it has always been genealogical in a second sense, that is, in discerning the configurations of power relations oppressive to women. This feature of genealogical analysis is pivotal in enabling feminist coalition because it illuminates shared targets of power relations that might otherwise be overlooked. Lesbian and psychoanalytic feminisms, for example, though often engaged in heated debates with one another, both emerged from and operate against the technologies of power integral to the deployment of sexuality.

Although feminism has always been genealogically engaged, neither historically nor currently can it be claimed that genealogy is a primary feature of feminism. Affixing the term "genealogical" to feminism has the effect of emphasizing certain apocalyptic features that have been integral to feminist discourse, namely, its claims for universal truth about man and woman, its arguments for a single origin of patriarchal oppression, its versions of anatomy as innate character, and its utopian visions of a harmonious matriarchal past and a future free from all oppression. At times, U.S. feminism has taken on strident messianic tones, as in the nineteenth century with Margaret Fuller's concept of the Virgin Mother of the new race, or, within our own time, Starhawk's revival of goddess worship.[5] Feminism has often dreamed the possibility of an absolute defeat of the patriarchy and a utopia of human harmony.

But feminism—Fuller's and Starhawk's texts included—has also always offered a feminist politics of everyday life, in such practices as nineteenth-century educational and legal reforms and twentieth-century rape crisis centers and daycare initiatives. These local struggles and disqualified knowledges are precisely what provide genealogy with historical knowledge about women's lives that had been wiped from the slates of masculinist scholarship and common sense. And this too has galvanizing power. The practice of genealogical feminism is thus constituted through this paradox: at this historical juncture, struggling against the determinants of our gendered subjectivity entails acknowledging both apocalyptic visions of the future and genealogical scrutiny of the present day.

The history of apocalyptic thought carries this paradox as well. Judeo-Christian apocalyptic writings themselves have a double movement that feeds an ambivalence that I want to exploit rather than conceal. In foretelling the future, apocalyptic literature tends to divide between two different kinds of millennia. One envisions a thousand-year reign of the elect prior to the final judgment. The other sees a thousand years of struggle against satanic forces as a preparation for the coming of the messiah. Whereas the first, at least as far as the believers are concerned, welcomes the apocalyptic moment that brings on the millennium, the second emphasizes the struggles of the elect in advancing toward the apocalypse. This second form has given rise over the centuries to a number of radical political movements that have insisted on universal education and have challenged family and governmental hierarchy. Some visions of apocalypse, like those of the Familists and the Ranters of the seventeenth century, for example, may even be seen as precursors of feminism.[6]

Even though this book takes an antiapocalytic stance, I am not arguing that feminism must be "cleansed" of its apocalypticism. In fact, I am arguing that such a cleansing is not possible—nor is it entirely desirable. As I have already pointed out, in the West generally, and in the United States especially, apocalyptic thought has always run deep and wide. Feminism has always found itself struggling on behalf of women in the context of masculinist apocalyptic discourse. To some extent, feminism must meet apocalypse on its own ground in order to be heard. And let's face it—feminist apocalypse is rhetorically powerful and has moved women to social action. It is also the case that, even when feminist discourse is manifestly apocalyptic, it is *not* synonymous with masculinist apocalypse. Unlike masculinist apocalypse, feminist apocalypse strives on behalf of women's self-determination.

In putting these terms together by using "genealogical" as an adjective for contemporary feminism, I am trying to emphasize simultaneously the diversity of feminisms as well as the coalitional political cause that, even when inconsonant, they nevertheless share: opposition to myriad forms of masculinist oppression.[7] Therefore, rather than putting genealogical feminism forward as one more item on a list of many feminisms, I use it here as an umbrella term to describe contemporary feminism's actual and potential coalitional practices. I should hasten to say that an umbrella term is not a master narrative but a concept that embraces a number of different elements; in this case, it is a concept that might serve, like an umbrella, as a temporary protective device.[8] Because apocalyptic claims for certain and total Truth create a climate of cultural oppression for women, it's worth having a coalitional "umbrella" on hand.

The many feminisms that have been forged can gain strength and protection by joining forces in coalition against various forms of women's oppression, which, as I have argued in the previous chapter, operate on three differing power registers, ranging from men's physical domination to masculinist imagistic simulation. To the extent that such coalition partners acknowledge each other as distinctive while they engage as temporary allies, they encourage genealogical thought. Thus, as a term, "genealogical feminism" has far more than linguistic economy at stake. It has a political rationale. For the moment—for this particular moment of the 1990s—contemporary U.S. feminisms occur in a decade increasingly defined in apocalyptic terms. Apocalyptic thought treats feminism as monolithic in an effort to contain it. But genealogical feminism defies that effort as a coalition of diverse political concerns. The purpose of this chapter is to show the merits of genealogical feminism as a *perspective* that is becoming a *practice* that might well become a *movement*.[9]

Contemporary Feminism: At the Crossroads of the Apocalyptic and Genealogical

The first evidence of the effects on feminism of end-of-the-millennium thinking occurred in the media's postfeminism declarations in the 1980s. Events of the early 1990s, however, made it clear that it was premature to predict, lament, or hope for feminism's demise. Although the assault on feminism was demoralizing, feminism not only remained alive but was able to act with vitality. Despite the serious backlashes that Susan Faludi has so forcefully documented, her book *Backlash* provides ample evidence of contemporary feminist counterstruggle.[10] The emergence of so many forms of feminism over the last decade is a register of that vitality.

By 1992, the media had switched claims, declaring the "Year of the Woman" to have begun. Opening with a feminist-educated public outcry emerging from the Clarence Thomas-Anita Hill hearings, picking up momentum with the William Kennedy Smith and Mike Tyson rape trials, and reaching headline status during the summer and fall presidential and congressional campaigns and elections, this characterization shows that even while acknowledging that feminism is still kicking, the media remains complicit in masculinism by submitting slogans where careful examination and analysis is due. Such claims and counterclaims demarcate the precarious space occupied by feminism under conditions of contemporary capitalism, which has increased the poverty of women and children, renewed suppressions of sexual freedom, and enhanced male control of technology. The discrepancy between the everyday oppressions of women and media sloganeering also establishes the necessity for feminists to continue fighting against each of the three deployments of power: against men's violence in the deployment of alliance; against gender inequities in the law, pay, job opportunities, medical attention, sexual expression, education, and child care in the deployment of sexuality; and against masculinist production of images and slogans in the deployment of technoppression.

These media flip-flops also indicate that contemporary feminism is not identical to the feminism that emerged out of the New Left in the late sixties and early seventies. The designation "genealogical" is a way of differentiating current feminism from its second wave, just as second-wave feminism differentiated itself from nineteenth-century and early twentieth-century feminism's goals and values. Calling feminism genealogical thus heralds a third wave of feminism with an enhanced potential for gaining power from coalitions within its own diverse ranks as well as with other political groups. This coalitional effort includes feminists who adhere to first- and second-wave principles. In other words, each of the three waves has defining principles and they are concurrent. For a variety of reasons, not the least of which is the far more extensive communications and travel systems of the postmodern era, the third wave of feminism far exceeds the first two in coalitional opportunities. And this capacity in turn carries the possibility of the third wave subsuming the first and second, of becoming a feminist tidal wave.

Let me concede at the outset that my use of third-wave rhetoric—bringing with it the possibility of a something else, even forecasting it—reiterates the ways in which feminism necessarily functions within the context of apocalyptic thinking. Dividing history into three epochs is a characteristic of one strain of apocalyptic thought and no doubt why referring to feminism's third wave makes sense; the term itself came into prominence upon Bill Clinton's 1992 defeat of George Bush. The apocalyptic tradition of three grand historical epochs holds that the world progresses toward the end of time in correlation with each member of the Trinity. Accordingly, history moves from the age of Law to the age of Love to the age of Spirit.[11] I would have a hard time convincing myself that world history had passed through the age of Love, but why not use the structure of the old story to tell a new one? Why not proclaim a new surge of power carried along by a third wave?

As a coalition of political-ethical practices within an apocalyptic era, genealogical feminism has double impulses of utopian dream and ongoing struggle. In recognition of this, Catherine Keller has argued that a "deliteralized, deapocalypticized eschatology can better serve the feminist project of a socially and historically responsible ecocentrism." Drawing on the continuing power of end-of-time thought and focusing on the environmental devastation of our time, she calls for an ecologically motivated "eschatological consciousness" which proclaims "the opening of the sacred community to be realized now, though its fuller realization is still in the future."[12] Although my own inclinations are to depart from Keller by emphasizing a deeschatologized stance as well, feminism as currently practiced is not an either/or proposition between radical action and eschatological appeals. The argument of this book is that *both* of these approaches constitute a foundational coalition of genealogical and feminist opposition to masculinist apocalypticism.

This is not a call to pluralism. Rather, it is a genealogical assertion: feminism has a legacy of eschatological, essentialist, and universalist thought and is in that sense apocalyptic. The most crucial point to stress is that feminist apocalypse has often been a powerful force for resistance to masculinist oppression. Thinking about feminist apocalypse genealogically provides insight into the essentialism/antiessentialism impasse that has beleaguered feminism over the years. Part of the fervor of this argument comes from both sides holding onto an apocalyptic notion of truth—two certainties in head-on collision. Even this many years after Diana Fuss's illuminating demonstrations of how the "bar between essentialism and constructionism is by no means as solid and unassailable as advocates of both sides assume it to be," essentialism remains a term still uttered in a tone of contempt.[13] In academic settings, it retains the capacity to stop a speaker in her feminist tracks. But I have also been on both sides of the philosophical divide, since I came to feminism as an essentialist—or, more acurately, *because* of its essentialist assumptions and utopian end-time visions. And although I no longer espouse essentialist human nature or hold eschatological assumptions and do not adhere to universalist truth claims, I agree with Fuss that the language of essence is not inherently reactionary. She shows through differing examples of how essences function in discourses of race, gender, and sexual practice that various essentialisms have been politically forceful.

Moreover, religiously motivated race essentialism, even when quite explicitly apocalyptic, has at times been deployed in the exercise of radical politics. As bell hooks observes in regard to Septima Clark's engagement in sexual politics, religion was "the source of her defiance. It was the belief in spiritual community, that no difference must be made between the role of women and that of men, that enabled her to be 'ready within.' To Septima Clark, the call to participate in black liberation struggle was a call from God."[14] Clark's political actions demonstrate the complex interplay of eschatological vision, essentialist race assumptions, and feminist insistence on equality. Liberation theology bears further witness to the ways in which essentialist, eschatological, apocalyptically motivated activism has challenged masculinist, militaristic domination.

I am arguing, then, that feminism, even when oriented genealogically, will by definition always be implicated in apocalyptic desires for the end of (masculinist) time and the transcendence of (masculinist) space, including the space of the innately gendered body. Feminism can be, however, (and often is these days), *anti*-apocalyptic insofar as it is anti-essentialist, anti-universalist, and anti-eschatological. That stance of overt opposition to apocalyptic logic marks a shift in perspective for feminism, one that alters its own features. Whereas first-wave feminism was made culturally possible by the construction of the logical category "woman" and second-wave feminism by the construction of the logical category "women," third-wave feminism has shifted its subject category from woman and women to feminists. This genealogical way of looking was in part made possible by the deconstruction of the presumed unity and naturalness of both of the initial categories (the thought itself made possible from the ways that postmodern material conditions dislodge naturalized identities). Yet feminism also retains the naturalized categories of woman and women and wouldn't be feminism without them. As Denise Riley has put it, "feminism must 'speak women.' "[15]

A brief survey of feminist discourses shows that, in order to "speak women," feminism speaks in apocalyptic tongues, precisely because masculinism does. To understand why this is the case, it is necessary to situate feminist thought at its point of emergence during the West's humanist era. Feminist scholars of the Renaissance have shown an intense struggle in gender definition during that period of changing economic and ideological conditions, demonstrating the prevalence of a variety of conceptions of womanhood, some of which condemned women as vile, and some upheld them as virtuous citizens.[16] As far as these views might have differed, all stressed that women were differentiated biologically from men. But biologism alone didn't preclude women's participation in the civic sphere. It was the status accorded women's interiorized selfhood that either entitled them to act in the civic domain (if seen as morally the same as or superior to men) or justified their exclusion from it (if seen as inferior to men). In other words, the apocalyptic humanist notion of an unchanging and given core self held sway for both dominant, masculinist thought and resistant, feminist thought.

As secular thinkers gained power during the Enlightenment, a predominantly white, property-holding male citizenry increasingly argued for its right to governance premised on notions of a core self with inalienable rights and the redemptive salvation of providential history. Eighteenth-century feminism took shape in relation to these modes of power/knowledge integral to the formation of the nation-state.[17] Theorists such as Mary Wollstonecraft formalized Anglo-American feminism through the same eschatological appeals to "natural law" that colonial male revolutionaries used to argue their right to independence and self-governance. Her contemporary Phillis Wheatley, captured as a child in Africa and sold to Massachusetts Bay colonists, wrote of her right to freedom in terms of divinely ordained history. From the outset, feminist thought materialized through the apocalyptic conceptualization of humanist thought that was forged in the Renaissance and formalized in the Enlightenment.

Coincident with apocalyptic humanism's universalist notions, and sometimes serving as a subcategory of universalism, were essentialist concepts of sexual difference, again interiorized but often justified through anatomical differences reduced to binary difference. As a dividing practice, the rhetoric of essential sexual difference is found in biblical apocalypse, but it is also the case that it has been articulated quite differently over time and used to different effects by mas-culinists and feminists.[18] The type of feminist essentialism that took form in relation to the emerging deployment of sexuality during the nineteenth and twentieth centuries, for example, concentrated more on the inherent moral su-periority of women than on their right to juridical equality. And both of these differ from masculinist essentialist claims of women's innate physical, moral, and intellectual inferiority.

In the twentieth century, structuralism, as both an anthropological model and a philosophical perspective, took hold as the dominant theoretical formu-lation for power/knowledge formations. Although it was often touted as histor-icist, the structuralist perspective upheld certain apocalyptic concepts, including a universal human nature (albeit clothed in cultural motley), sexual difference, and cultural origin. Virtually all of the writings of the first wave of women's movements in the West, and much of those of the second wave, function as part of this duplex formation of power/knowledge insofar as they uphold a notion of a transhistorical core self even as they also uphold inherent sexual difference and patriarchal origin. These writings challenge varying oppressions of women, but they do so in the name of woman or her multiplied but still essentialized coun-terpart: women.

Antiessentialist feminist thought is recent. In the 1980s, terms such as "fem-inine," "masculine," and "experience," having served quite admirably for over a century as rallying cries of solidarity, suddenly became exemplary of the sticky trap of essentialism. Some sought to eschew such terms altogether, while others sought to shift what had been presumptions of natural experience unmediated by representation to thinking experience as socially constituted. In *Technologies of Gender*, Theresa de Lauretis provides an example of the latter approach in her transvaluation of the term "experience," which she defines as "a complex of habits resulting from the semiotic interaction of 'outer world' and 'inner world,' the continuous engagement of a self or subject in social reality." While her use of quotation marks around "outer world" and "inner world" suggests that those terms may still operate transitionally between essentialist and antiessentialist conceptualization, the absence of such marks around "experience"—in this context—is a way of signifying her claim as exclusively antiessentialist. To take an antiessentialist stance does not mean that one relinquishes a radical politics (the charge made on both sides of the debate), for, as de Lauretis further argues, if a social complex of habits is what "en-genders one as female, then *that* is what remains to be analyzed, understood, articulated by feminist theory."[19] Thinking of experience semiotically helps us understand social reality's gender categoriza-tions without accepting them as inherent and unchangeable.

Judith Butler's provocative *Gender Trouble* takes antiessentialism to its analyt-ical limits. Butler describes the "task of *a feminist genealogy* of the category of women" as one that traces the "political operations that produce and conceal what qualifies as the juridical subject of feminism."[20] And she acknowledges the risk to feminism as we have known it:

> In the course of this effort to question "women" as the subject of feminism, the unproblematic invocation of that category may prove to *preclude* the possibilty of feminism as a representational politics. What sense does it make to extend representation to subjects who are constructed through the exclusion of those who fail to conform to unspoken normative requirements of the subject? What relations of domination and exclusion are inadvertently sustained when representation becomes the sole focus of politics? The identity of the feminist subject ought not to be the foundation of feminist politics, if the formation of the subject takes place within a field of power regularly buried through the assertion of that foundation. Perhaps, paradoxically, "representation" will be shown to make sense for feminism only when the subject of "women" is nowhere presumed.[21]

Like de Lauretis, Butler pushes feminist thought away from apocalyptic foundations and toward genealogical inquiry and practice. It is significant that she calls her analysis *feminist* genealogy, for in contrast to Foucault's inadequate attention to how history is gendered, Butler points to the ways in which history (among other constructed ontologies) has been a record of gender congealments. One of the requisites for genealogy today, as I indicate more fully in the next chapter, is to articulate—in ways conscious of gender—history's inscriptions on bodies.

This overview of feminism's apocalyptic discourses and the more recent challenges to such ways of thinking by antiessentialist and genealogical feminists should be understood in the political context of longstanding resistance to male dominance. To sum up what I have claimed thus far: genealogical feminism—understood as a politics that is coalitional in its perspective and its practice—has been made possible through the twin legacies of apocalyptic and genealogical thought and activism. Because it embodies both apocalyptic and genealogical features, contemporary feminism will of necessity be a site of discursive battle around key terms such as "feminine," "masculine," and "experience." There is much more than semantic differentiation at stake in this debate: women's bodies are literally—that is, physically—on the line. But, as I want to demonstrate by focusing on ecological feminism from a genealogical feminist perspective, there is no way for either side to predict the future of either apocalyptic or genealogical feminist thought and practice. Resistance doesn't carry guarantees for outcome. What we have ample historical evidence for is the outcome of *masculinist* apocalyptic thought and action. And that is why a coalition of genealogical and apocalyptic feminisms is so crucial.

Ecological Feminism: A Mosaic of Resistances

Perhaps more than any other mode of feminist thought and practice, ecological feminism, often called ecofeminism for short, exemplifies the apocalyptic and genealogical impulses of contemporary feminism. I focus on it here because, both in poststructuralist and social ecology circles, ecofeminism is often dismissed precisely because of its essentialist and teleological assumptions. And it is the case that much ecofeminist discourse—like a great deal of feminist discourse in general—promotes an apocalyptic view that combines the drama of an imminent end with the fervor of utopian hope. While I agree with some of the criticisms that have been made about ecofeminism and reiterate my opposition to apocalyptic thought, the point is not to legislate its discourses and practices but rather to scrutinize their effects in order to guide our thought and action in regard to ecological and feminist issues. Action motivated by essentialism can provide resistance to many forms of oppression. But avowals of an eternal feminine can also simply renew age-old constraints on women. A genealogical feminist analysis of the practices of ecofeminism allows us to better understand these consequences. Such analysis is useful not only for debates within feminism but also for the ecology movement and the left in general.

By locating ecofeminism within debates on the left we can discern its interplay of totalizing thought as well as its resistance to that tendency. There are numerous instances within the left where calls for unifying thought are made in the name of coherence and practicality. Calls for the gathering together of diverse groups are certainly warranted; as I have been indicating, radical democrats do need to find ways to create coalitions—such as those the Greens have forged between ecological, feminist, socialist, and antimilitarist groups, for example. But we also need to be wary of moves toward orthodoxy and calls for unity, which is different from coalitional activism. As Foucault has pointed out, "things never happen as we expect from a political programme," for "a political programme has always, or nearly always, led to abuse or political domination from a bloc, be it from technicians or bureaucrats or other people."[22]

In other words, the move toward orthodoxy is complicitous with the tendency of power relations to become totalizing, often in the name of consensus; to authorize certain alliances and to exclude others; in short, to limit political creativity. Calls for and moves toward totalization have at various times been detrimental to both the U.S. ecology and feminist movements. Polarized debates between deep ecologists and social ecologists were so pronounced during the 1980s that building coalitions between these groups often became impracticable if not impossible. Within mainstream (predominantly white) feminism, this period was one of a gradual shifting away from a wide-based, multiple-isues movement concerned with women's bodies toward a narrow-based, single-issue focus on Woman's sexualized body. That narrowed focus on sexuality and pornography was divisive and tended to limit feminist debates to a simplified prosex/antisex polarity. Genealogical analysis helps show that a proliferation of resistances, not political programs, enliven political energy and make coalitions feasible.

In light of the splits that have taken place within the ecology and feminist movements, I would argue against calls for coherence, comprehensiveness, and formalized agendas. Furthermore, I would cite ecofeminism as an example of a coalitional practice that has combated ecological destruction and masculinist domination without (yet) succumbing to the totalizing impulses of hegemonic politics. The diverse and sometimes idiosyncratic practices of ecofeminism are not easily channeled into a coherent and comprehensive political program. Nevertheless, urgent calls for a shared vision have come from both within the movement (especially from the spiritualist ecofeminists) and from those adjacent to it (from social ecologists). Both camps seem to be calling more for an orthodoxy of adherence to their particular perspective than for a coalition of diverse groups with diverse views working in concert around specific issues. Predictably, their debates have polarized and stifled coalition, stalling at an essentialist versus anti-essentialist impasse.

Spiritualist ecofeminists advocate a reverence for nature that they believe prevailed in prehistoric times. They cite archaeological evidence to support the theory that women-oriented, agricultural-based, goddess-worshipping societies existed during the Neolithic period in the Mediterranean area and the Near East. These peaceful societies, they say, lived in harmony with nature, a harmony that was disrupted by nomadic invaders whose religions sanctioned war and domination. Spiritualist ecofeminists suggest that a return to harmony is possible through recognition of the power of the earth goddess. Pagan advocates such as Starhawk argue that nature rituals, goddess worship, and magic should be understood as political protest because they confront and strive to transform patriarchal power/knowledge. Thus, incorporated into this form of ecofeminism is the essentialist notion that women are inherently feminine, by which they mean emotional, nurturing, and in harmony with nature's cycles.

Critics of the spiritualist position argue that ceremonial activity has little political impact and that, even worse, it tends to replace activism. They point to the rapid appropriation of goddess imagery by consumer capitalism as one such example, arguing that spiritualists mistake wearing goddess jewelry for political action. Social ecologists voice skepticism about the Golden Age concept of history, labeling it romanticized if not downright faulty. The concern most often expressed is related to the issue of essentialism, which, as Janet Biehl argues in *Rethinking Ecofeminist Politics*, is simply biological determinism in a new guise.

Although I think the social ecologists are correct in linking biologism and essential femininity, their own arguments risk fueling antifeminist and even anti-women sentiment. Their facile dismissal of the spiritualists also tends to gloss over that perspective's important critique of the longstanding masculinist valuation of logic over emotion. In this regard it is worth recalling Michelle Rosaldo's observation that "feeling is forever given shape through thought and that thought is laden with emotional meaning."[23] And, finally, the emotion-versus-logic polarization misses the challenge to both camps that can be found in the kind of resistance put forward by Vandana Shiva in *Staying Alive*. Shiva has shown how rural women in India's Chipko movement have been motivated by their allegiance to the feminine principle, which she defines in recognizably spiritualist terms. Yet she challenges both camps by arguing that nature as an embodiment of the feminine principle can only be understood in light of the social construction of the categories of femininity and masculinity.

All of this is to say that ecofeminism works more effectively as it has operated thus far, that is, as a hodgepodge of resistances rather than as a coherent theory and program. Programmatic agendas fail to see that power is a "multiplicity of force relations," and that, to continue with Foucault's description, it is decentered and continually "produced from one moment to the next." Against multiple force relations, coherence in theory and centralization of practice make a social movement irrelevant, vulnerable, or participatory with forces of domination. As Foucault explains, decentered power relations require decentered political struggle, for "there is no single locus of great Refusal, no soul of revolt, source of all rebellions, no pure law of the revolutionary. Instead there is a plurality of resistance, each of them a special case: resistances that are possible, necessary, improbable; others that are spontaneous, savage, solitary, concerted, rampant, or violent; still others that are quick to compromise, interested, or sacrificial."[24] The strength of ecofeminism thus far has been to target abuses of power at the local level, in a multiplicity of places.

Two works from the 1980s that provide evidence of the impact of ecofeminist resistance politics are the anthology *Reclaim the Earth* and Anne Garland's *Women Activists*.[25] They stand in contrast to the predominant move toward othodoxy during that decade. Both texts are politically astute and emotionally moving testaments of feminist resistance politics—or what I call genealogical feminism—operating at the microlevels where power relations are exercised, yet with a vision for change that is often, though not inevitably, utopian. What we find throughout these texts is a recognition that struggling against specific force relations not only weakens the junctures of power's networks but also empowers those who do the struggling. They show that ecological feminism is, by definition, a coalitional politics that emerges out of the insight that exploitations of land, labor, and women overlap and sustain each other. For example, recognizing this overlap has led to factory workers and nonfactory working women concerned with the contamination of their breast milk and wombs to combine forces in struggles against chemical dumping. These texts cite instances of activists from industrial and developing nations working together against deforestation that endangers species and makes it far more difficult and time-consuming for many third-world women to gather fuel and fodder. They also reveal that toxic working conditions are most likely to occur among working-class and minority men and women who also have inadequate health care. And they demonstrate that compromises to our immune systems, which render our bodies vulnerable to a whole host of viruses, need to be fought through coalitions between AIDS activists, holistic health groups, and environmentalists against late-capitalist food industries and medical practices.

These kinds of awareness and activism show how feminism's struggles for women's freedom and ecology's struggles for planetary well-being have come together in a coalition called ecofeminism. Because of shared concerns for health and freedom, a "we" has been formed. This we has not emerged from the prescriptions of a single-minded political program; indeed these "we"s may or may not be self-consciously ecofeminist. As Foucault observed, coalitions for freedom are formed when a "we" emerges through shared questions rather than as a "we" "previous to the question."[26] The instances of activism and analysis recorded in these texts, and subsequent anthologies such as *Healing the Wounds* and *Reweaving the World*, reveal activists/theorizers speaking for themselves on their own terrains, discerning power's specific effects on them and conducting skirmishes against its operations. Ecofeminism as a resistance politics has a great deal to tell us about the uses and abuses of theory as a power relation. It suggests that theory in the interrogative mode—as opposed to Theory in the prescriptive or apocalyptic mode—asks difficult questions; that is, it asks questions that pose difficulties, even—perhaps especially—for one's own practices. In fact, the "we" of ecofeminism is most formidable in its opposition to power when it challenges its own assumptions.

In "Roots: Black Ghetto Ecology," Wilmette Brown demonstrates the value of such questioning by combining the political insights of the black civil rights movement, lesbian feminism, ecology, the peace movement, and the holistic health movement. Her analysis exemplifies the value of bringing together a genealogical approach to the exclusions of medical practice and the identity politics of race, gender, and sexuality. Rather than trying to synthesize these positions into a comprehensive, centralized vision, her analysis uses each to disrupt the assumptions of the others. Writing from a personal point of reference, she explains that she is "a Black woman, a cancer survivor," but is quick to reject the romance of the autonomous hero, so popular with the media, for "this is not 'the triumphant story of one woman's victory over cancer.' " Speaking as an activist who theorizes about her experiences, she states: "For me the issue is how to transform cancer from a preocupying vulnerablility into a vindicating power—for myself and for everyone determined to reclaim the earth.' "[27]

That transformation involves making visible the links among sex, race, class, and cancer. Brown points to the disproportionate incidence of cancer among the poor who are forced to take jobs with greater risks of cancer, to live in "cancer-prone cities," and who are least able to afford the exorbitant costs of medical treatment. These conditions are exacerbated for blacks, falling the heaviest on black women and children. Against the backdrop of an international and economic order that causes health hazards and a medical industry that reaps enormous profits from treatment, Brown brings into genealogical focus the political creativity, energy, and struggle of black welfare mothers who "brought about the first concessions from the American state of anything approaching free health care for poor people [Medicaid] and for elderly people [Medicare]."[28]

Brown's analysis of convalescence from the perspective of a black working-class lesbian feminist also explores the limits and limitations of the holistic health movement as defined largely by white middle-class heterosexuals. She shows how, despite its critique of the medical industry, the holistic health movement has also been myopic regarding race, class, and gender issues. First, its emphasis on consciousness-raising ignores the necessity of organizing to struggle against the military-industrial complex that produces cancer-prone sites. Second, holistic health assumes financial access to self-healing classes as well as the time, skills, and money to obtain healthier diets. Finally, the holistic health movement has too often ignored traditions of herbal remedies that have been practiced for centuries among people of color or, when it has learned from them, it has turned them into high-priced commodities. Her site of struggle — the geographic and bodily place from which she speaks — is the international women's peace movement, which she feels has learned to refuse "the sexist and racist assumptions and practices of the peace and holistic movements." Brown's analysis and activism exemplify a coalitional politics of resistance that runs counter to the will to totalize. Such a position challenges the apocalyptic tendencies within ecofeminism that are also found in the ecology and feminist movements from which ecofeminism derives.

As I noted earlier, the danger from the left is a dismissal of ecofeminism on the grounds that it is the worst instance of essentialist feminism. To be sure, this is not an idle concern. Gayatri Spivak worded the concern succinctly when she observed, "Essentialism is a trap. It seems more important to learn to understand that the world's women do not all relate to the privileging of essence, especially through 'fiction,' or 'literature,' in the same way."[29] And yet we can also witness examples of essentialist solidarity as a generative energy in postcolonial women's struggles. This is most likely what led Spivak to rethink her position and suggest the value of "the strategic use of an essence as a mobilizing slogan or masterword like *woman* or *worker* or the name of any nation that you would like," as long as that strategy also works "through a persistent critique."[30] The point of this revision is that essentialism in and of itself is less important than the particular uses to which it is put in any given set of power relations. I agree with Spivak on the desirability of persistent critique, but I would add one caveat that a genealogist always needs to consider: it is possible to find instances of essentialist politics with little or no evidence of such critique but which nevertheless have resisted hegemonic power.

The Green Belt Movement of Kenya illustrates how an inherently essentialist perspective can effectively marshal women's resistance. This movement demonstrates the power of thinking about nature as a feminine force with which women have special affinity. Movement leader Wangari Maathai writes, "We must inform and train the farmers—who are mostly women and often illiterate. . . . Farmers need to realize that they have to 'feed' the soil. Since peasant farmers have always depended on shifting cultivation, it is essential that they appreciate the need to work with Mother Nature and hasten her processes of self-healing and self-rehabilitation."[31] This grassroots tree-planting movement generates income for women, helps meet basic needs by providing fuel-wood and food, prevents desertification, and promotes a sense of community.[32]

What postcolonial power struggles against Western dominance demonstrate is that, whether in South Korean factories or Kenyan fields, and whether oppressed by essentialist thinking or fostered by it, bodies are a crucial site of power relations. Bodies are beaten, imprisoned, starved—or nurtured, housed, fed. In order to combat hierarchical power relations and create strategies of resistance, therefore, we need to investigate the effects of essentialist and antiessentialist feminist discourse and practice on the bodies and minds of people living in a particular time and place. The imposition of purist categories means the inability to see or hear what others have to show us and tell us about their lives and diminishes our capacity to understand what others have to say about our own circumstances.

Ecofeminism as a politics of resistance forces us to question the categories of experience that order the world and the truths we have come to know, even the truths of our radical politics, by confronting us with the truths of other women and men, differently acculturated, fighting against specific threats to their lands and bodies. Ecofeminism also extends this questioning to the anthropocentric assumption that only human beings have truths to tell. The cries of factory farm animals, the suffocation of fish in poisoned waters, the sounds of flood waters rushing over deforested land—ecofeminism instructs us that these are also voices to which we must listen. Heeding subjugated voices makes us better able to question our own political and personal practices. As Donna Haraway has pointed out, ecofeminists have been "most insistent on some version of the world as active subject, not as resource to be mapped and appropriated in bourgeois, Marxist, or masculinist projects. Acknowledging the agency of the world in knowledge makes room for some unsettling possibilities, including a sense of the world's sense of humor."[33]

The difficult questions that ecofeminism has advanced may well risk the end of its own practice as currently constituted, for, like any social movement, ecofeminism is inevitably a provisional politics, one that has struck a chord of resistance in this era of ecological destruction and patriarchal power. It may well risk the end of feminism as we have known it. In the meantime, a genealogical approach indicates that multiple forces of domination require multiple forms of resistance. A rejection of programmatic coherence does not mean that ecofeminist or other such political practices lack direction or cohesion. On the contrary, in turning attention to the ways that domination of the land, labor, and women intersect, ecofeminism underscores the need for coalitions that are both aware of gender hierarchy and respectful of the earth. If other terms and different politics emerge from that questioning and that struggle, then we can strive to place them in the service of new local actions, new creative energies, and new coalitions that preclude apocalyptic constraints on freedom.

A Genealogical Feminist Way of Looking: Scrutinizing Postmodern Cultural Production

The coexistence of yuppie apoliticism and local-level resistance politics like ecofeminism should be reason enough to question monolithic definitions and descriptions of the sociosymbolic field known as postmodernism. Yet a tendency to contain the meanings of postmodernism may be found among even leading poststructuralist theorists, for example, in Fredric Jameson's claims for a cultural logic of late capitalism, Jean-François Lyotard's disease metaphor of a postmodern condition marked by the disappearance of master narratives (which he applauds), and Jean Baudrillard's postapocalyptic trajectories of simulation fast producing a global Disney World. This is not to dismiss these theorizers, for each has contributed in crucial ways to an understanding of postmodernism. It is, however, to suggest that feminist practice faces new issues and circumstances that cannot adequately be addressed through monolithic views of postmodernism or through theories that ignore gender.

Some of these new issues and circumstances have been framed by apocalyptic discourse as cultural decline, signaling (or promising) that the end is near. For dystopian apocalyptic thought—divine, technological, or ironic—postmodern culture means the erosion of clearly defined sexual difference and the loss of authority of heterosexuality, the failure of the nuclear family and its replacement by a number of other family forms, and the fragmentation of unified national identity, as represented in challenges to English as the official language for U.S. education, for example. In other words, in dystopian apocalyptic thought, postmodernism is synonomous with loss—and this is correct for those who stand to lose their privilege. But to challengers of high-culture elitism, heterosexism, and homogeneous identity, these changes mean cultural enrichment, not decline. Other new issues of crucial relevance to women have been framed as technological transcendence. From a utopian apocalyptic point of view (in which the changes noted above may or may not be lamented), postmodernist achievements in technology promise an escape from the ills humanity has long suffered. One of the central problems to which feminism has consistently alerted us, however, is that technology has been and continues to be dominated by masculinist forces of power and wealth that maintain their profits and control through exploitation and surveillance.

In both its dystopian and utopian modes, apocalyptic thought insists on absolute and coherent Truth. From the perspective of genealogical feminism, this insistence translates into eradication of race and ethnic identity, of sexual choice, and of opportunities to earn a livable wage. Postmodern life is not simply dystopian or utopian. What is fragmentation of identity to apocalyptic thinkers may be an exhilarating experience of personal coming-to-voice for others. In other words, postmodernism is a field of social conflict between multiple forces, some operating to bolster the absolutist Truth of the elite, others seeking to dismantle it, and still others that generate free-floating fear, melancholy, and nostalgia.

Perhaps the term "genealogical feminism" can prove to be as cantankerous as the term "postmodernism" in resisting final definitions. For what is so provocative about the term "postmodern" is that, rather than serving dutifully as an explanatory and descriptive term, its proliferation of meanings enacts a refusal of the monolithic. As Dick Hebdige pointed out in the mid-eighties, the term "postmodern" applied to:

> the decor of a room, the design of a building, the diegesis of a film, the construction of a record, or a "scratch" video, a TV commercial, or an arts documentary, or the "intertextual" relations between them, the layout of a page in a fashion magazine or critical journal, an antiteleological tendency within epistemology, the attack on the "metaphysics of presence," a general attenuation of feeling, the collective chagrin and morbid projections of a post-War generation of Baby Boomers confronting disillusioned middle age, the "predicament" of reflexivity, a group of rhetorical tropes, a proliferation of surfaces, a new phase in commodity fetishism, a fascination for "images," codes and styles, a process of cultural, political, or existential fragmentation and/or crisis, the "de-centering" of the subject, an "incredulity toward metanarratives," the replacement of unitary power axes by a pluralism of power/discourse formations, the "implosion of meaning," the collapse of cultural hierarchies, the dread engendered by the threat of nuclear self-destruction, the decline of the University, the functioning and effects of the new miniaturized technologies, broad societal and economic shifts into a "media," "consumer" or "multinational" phase, a sense (depending on whom you read) of placelessness or the abandonment of placelessness ("critical regionalism") or (even) a generalized substitution of spatial for temporal co-ordinates.[34]

Postmodernism is, indeed, all of the above and more, which is why the term "postmodern culture" is something of an oxymoron. The unity presumed by the human sciences category "culture" breaks apart when applied analytically to the proliferations of meanings of postmodernism.

What I am referring to as genealogical feminism—which is both about postmodernism and a product of it—has the potential to be similarly proliferative. A proliferation of meanings thwarts impulses toward orthodoxy, in part because of its (con)fusions of the ontological and epistemological. The fusing together of architectural design, attitude, subjectivity, economic production, image simulation, and philosophical stance produced through this era's mass-media technologies cannot be adequately addressed through any orthodoxy that attends exclusively to any one category, whether class, or gender, or race, or sexual practice. Postmodernism's mixed bag of cultural practices calls for a mixed bag of strategies and tactics.[35] To the extent that genealogical feminism refuses the temptation to be a "pure" feminism and employs an "impure" range of differing, even conflicting, approaches, using an array of strategies and tactics, often to intervene with one another as well as against totalizing forces of domination, it can be invaluable for understanding and challenging those forces.

As I have argued, a genealogical gauge that discerns specific historical effects of antiessentialist and essentialist discourse and activism can provide genealogical feminism with a theorizing tool crucially necessary for a radical politics in the postmodern era. It is equally important that such a gauge register the ways in which the mass media blur distinctions that formerly seemed clear. As Meaghan Morris has argued, in "a mass-media society with mass-media cultures and mass-media politics, the relationship between *signifying* (rather than 'aesthetic') gestures and political ones may not be so clear-cut"; we have to confront "the effect that the study of media could have on our understanding of politics, and thus on the formulation of political actions; and finally, the question of what the relationship of artistic and cultural work to other kinds of politics might actually become if it were fostered rather than dismissed by a denunciative (and self-defeating) sectarianism."[36]

Two major media events separated by three years may be used to illustrate the complexities of postmodernism and a genealogical feminist way of looking: the 1989 Grammy award ceremony and the 1993 presidential inauguration ceremonies. The Grammy's honoring of Tracy Chapman and Bobby McFerrin as the leading performers of the year was particularly notable because of the dramatically disparate hit songs of these two African American singers/songwriters. In quintessential postmodern fashion, the Grammys rendered their incommensurate messages—"Talkin Bout A Revolution" and "Don't Worry, Be Happy"—commensurate. Media events like the Grammys provide us with a number of the features of postmodernism catalogued by Hebdige, including not only cultural and political fragmentation but the reassertion of sexism with a glitzy vengeance.

Since such media presentations are typical, we need politically attuned ways of looking at the media.

A genealogical feminist perspective provides analytical tools for repoliticizing what the media depoliticizes, and for politicizing what it offers as pap. The Grammy ceremony is a cultural practice that can be used to demonstrate the problematic of traditional social science conceptualizations of culture. Drawing from the space/time logic of masculinist thought, such conceptualizations assume a totality, a unified and bounded entity called culture, which when employed in analysis is itself totalizing. To work within the domain of the "science" of the social entails gathering empirical data about a given culture. An event like the Grammy awards may be used to show the impossibility of this endeavor, at least as traditionally undertaken, for there is no clear-cut cultural boundary to be had. Instead we have a global transmission of Americanized multinational meaning systems. Since Americanization includes the appropriation of third-world musics, the notion of bounded culture is further undermined. Compounding methodological difficulties for the traditional notion of culture is the breakdown of a high culture / low culture distinction, a distinction that fosters and perpetuates white patriarchal humanist values. The Grammy awards, which give tributes to everything from rock to classical music, blur this distinction.

Although the popularity of McFerrin's catchy tune was seen by some cultural critics as a form of psychological and political denial of the dire economic trends of the Reagan-Bush administrations, it can also be read genealogically as an announcement of spreading anxiety. A sense of the precariousness of contemporary existence is part of the material conditions that give rise to such a song. Despite the leveling of Chapman's messages of political struggle amid the trappings of show biz, her very inclusion provided a dialogism that genealogical feminists might accent. Her mode of dress—jeans, T-shirt, short dreadlocks—and athletic carriage oppose the dominant sign system of white femininity: on such shows, satins, silks, and brocades are displayed on corseted or emaciated bodies balancing masses of moussed hair on one end and stiletto heels on the other. Her songs expose the harm done by the dominant systems of white power, ranging from the systemic underemployment of blacks in the United States and the resulting crises within black families to the surveillance mechanisms of prison psychiatry. Against these forces of domination, alongside the spaces of "po-mo" coolness and exhaustion, her songs marked out the spaces of resistance also made available by the postmodern entertainment industry. Taken alone, such events as Chapman's Grammy appearance might not mean all that much in terms of feminist political transformation. But of course such events are not isolated occurrences. The offerings of the media, and other daily events, offer abundant opportunity for practicing genealogical feminist ways of looking.

Understanding the Grammys through a genealogical feminist perspective also helps us to discern what is at stake in the "Grammyfication" of the Presidency.

Volumes have been written about the ways in which Roosevelt exploited radio and Kennedy television to get their ideas across to the public. I would put the 1992 Bush campaign in line with this use of the media as a way of pointing to a difference between the Bush and Clinton campaigns. The edge that Clinton had over Bush was that while the Bush campaign still relied on Kennedy's media methods, the Clinton campaign far more thoroughly blurred signifying and political gestures. In other words, more than any other U.S. president, Bill Clinton is as much a product of the media as he is a producer of certain ideas and values through media. The several days devoted to Inaugural activities, ranging from pilgrimages to Monticello, Hollywood night in D.C., and the swearing-in ceremony and the balls, demonstrate that contemporary politics are a mass media practice. Just as the Grammys can so readily bring together Tracy Chapman's songs of political protest and Bobby McFerrin's songs of reassurance, so too Bill Clinton's inauguration brought together the People and the Stars, the violent streets of Washington, D.C., and the upward mobility of Hope, Arkansas. The point is not to lament the postmodern state of the union, but rather to become more astute about feminist and mass-media productions of meaning.

It is too soon to document the effects of feminist resistance and activism during the first few years of the 1990s, but it is possible to see ways in which feminism's third wave also blurs the lines between signifying and political gestures. It is also clear that this third wave gathers momentum through coalition—and loses it when sectarianism over race, class, and sexual differences reemerges. An example of both dynamics may be seen in the Women's Action Coalition, founded in January 1992. Originating out of New York City and with no men allowed, within six months New York WAC had 1,400 on its member list, with 300 to 400 women in regular attendance at the weekly meetings, and WAC groups forming in other major U.S. cities, as well as in Toronto. The goal of the coalition is to link issues of representation of gender, class, and color, reproductive freedom, health, and sexual choice as part of the larger struggle to combat violence against women.

WAC's logo, an eye encircled by the phrases "WAC is Watching" and "Women Take Action" gives double meaning to the compliment "You're looking good, girl." In the center of the logo's eye is a repetition with a difference. Rather than the infinite regress of the modernist aesthetic, which would have been a replication of the logo in the eye's retina, the center point is a blue dot with WAC inscribed on it, suggestive of the bull's-eye of a target. WAC's blue dot is a feminist appropriation of the blue dot used in the media coverage of rape trials to block out a woman's face while she testifies against a man charged with rape. The WAC retina thus receives the media's simultaneously disclosed and blocked image, but reflects that image back in altered form, targeting it with the message of women's action. In keeping with postmodernism's conflations of style and activist politics, WAC's logo declares that women who take action know how to look.

It's not easy being coalitional, however, as the history of WAC's first year demonstrates. Over the course of 1992, various chapters of WAC began to feel the strain of division, particularly around issues of race, class, and sexuality. In New York, attendance and enthusiasm at meetings declined as arguments over lesbophobia and class awareness increased; in Washington D.C., the coalition fell apart due to irreconcilable views of how to combat racism within the group. These events show both the vitality and the difficulty of coalitional effort. Regardless of what happens to WAC, one message comes through: a coalition is a form of re-cognition, a way of looking at differences as a form of learning how to organize differently. As such, genealogical feminism has what it takes to be the most significant "look" of the nineties. As a practice of coalitional diversity, it gathers its solidarity from essentialism; its changing tactical designs from semiotics and media; its countersurveillance struggles from 1980s resistance politics; and its self-stylization from poststructuralist ethics. Genealogical feminism is a way of looking at postmodern cultural production that gets beyond the lament of cultural decline sounded by cultural critics on the right and the left, from Dinesh D'Souza to Fredric Jameson. By scrutinizing modes of subjection and their forms of signification, a genealogical feminist "look" is at one and the same time a genealogy of the forces that subject us and an exercise in transforming them into forces of freedom.

Chapter 3
Philosophy Today: Not-for-Prophet Thought

We must ask ourselves the question, what is today? . . . One can say that it is the task of philosophy to explain what today is and what we are today, but without breast-beating drama and theatricality and maintaining that this moment is the greatest damnation or daybreak of the rising sun. No, it is a day like every other, or much more, a day which is never like another.

Michel Foucault,
"How Much Does It Cost for Reason to Tell the Truth?"[1]

Genealogy is to philosophy what prophecy is to apocalypse; that is, genealogical analysis is an enabling act for philosophy.[2] But unlike prophetic discourse, which reveals to people what they will do and should do, genealogy seeks to provide means for people to say what they have done and are doing. This fostering of local histories allows critical examination of how actions and events accord with norms of the day or clash with them. By showing not only how truths emerge from specific sites of power relations but also how those relations of power are embodied, genealogical inquiry is a prying tool by which philosophy can dislodge claims of prophetic truth. It exposes the means by which truth becomes martial law, the ways in which a regime of truth is established by subjugating or absorbing other ways of thinking. Genealogy shows how bodies are inscribed through relations of power, how boundaries of subjectivity have been penciled in and then traced over with thicker lines until they seem to have existed forever. Genealogy puts on display the making of moral or ethical values, revealing how certain values have been promoted by denying their manufacture, proclaiming them to be according to God and nature.

A genealogical approach to philosophy led Foucault to argue that "there is always something ludicrous in philosophical discourse when it tries, from the outside, to dictate to others, to tell them where their truth is and how to find it. . . . But it is entitled to explore what might be changed, in its own thought, through the practice of a knowledge that is foreign to it."[3] By these lights, far too much of philosophical discourse is ludicrous. Committed to finding and prescribing absolute truth and universal morality, a great deal of philosophical discourse fails to heed the particular truths of people's lives and dismisses as biased and partial the kinds of ethical judgments that are made in response to specific events, needs, and concerns.[4] Such a commitment is what leads me to characterize much of the practice of modern philosophy as apocalyptic, despite assumptions that our age is a secular one.

This characterization is in keeping with Derrida's observation that modern philosophy has "recently adopted" an apocalyptic tone. Although his deconstructions of the metaphysical assumptions of philosophy establish numerous longstanding links between metaphysical and apocalyptic discourse, he attributes this heightening in tone to nuclear-age anxiety. While I agree with both his observation and the reason for it, it seems to me that Derrida's own tone seems unduly resigned. In arguing that apocalypticism's "demystification must be led as far as possible," he asserts that demystification "is interminable, because no one can exhaust the overdeterminations and the indeterminations of the apocalyptic stratagems."[5] Demystifying apocalyptic discourse is no doubt difficult and success is not guaranteed, but from a genealogical perspective apocalyptic stratagems are not *necessarily* interminable. Belief in interminability is itself inflected with an apocalyptic flattening-out of historical change. Pronouncements of interminability also deter us from seeing or hearing the nonapocalyptic tones in modern philosophy.

Foucault argued that Kant's essay "What Is Enlightenment?" established a mode of philosophy geared to an "ontology of the present." In contrast to what took hold as the predominant mode of modern philosophy (which Kant also established), namely, the analytics of truth, an ontology of the present reflects on the present as a "field of possible experiences."[6] In tone and concept, an ontology of the present withdraws allegiance from apocalyptic discourse's predilection for origin and predesigned end. Instead of expounding universal values from some place of wisdom "outside" the social, such inquiry takes its momentum and its insights from resistances to dominant forms of received wisdom. Nonapocalyptic or genealogical philosophy seeks to illuminate instances of social struggle at work precisely because such struggles rail against the circumscriptions of a presumed given truth and the existing power relations that operate to maintain that truth. Nonapocalyptic philosophy's genealogical union of erudite and popular subjugated knowledges catalyzes the questioning of the determinants of its own thought; it wrestles philosophy loose from the constraints of apocalypse.[7]

This chapter draws on Foucauldian concepts to explore the ways in which certain "foreign" knowledges function as liberating strategies for philosophy. More specifically, I am using genealogy as the practice of a foreign or subjugated knowledge to change philosophical discourse "in its own thought." I begin by focusing on the ways in which an explanation of "what today is" applies to issues of subjectivity. Because Foucault's work dealt both extensively and variously with the history of subjectivities, I first provide an overview of his arguments about subject-formation as a way of characterizing contemporary configurations of subjectivity. I then offer some ways to think about other "foreign knowledges" in regard to the three axes of genealogy: power relations, truth, and ethics.[8] What I am promoting is a genealogical philosophy that opens up possibilities for subjectivity and thought and fosters nonapocalyptic forms of them.

The Subject of the Day

Philosophical accounts of what we are today and what people were in other days reject human-nature arguments by putting the construction of subjectivities at the forefront of analysis. In pointing to the three axes of exploration that comprise a genealogical approach—the axes of power, truth, and ethics—Foucault emphasized that each is understood in terms of subject formation. As applied to the concerns of this book, discerning how "we constitute ourselves as subjects acting on others" (the power axis), "as subjects of knowledge" (the truth axis), and as "moral agents" (the ethical axis), allows us to see the ways in which we have been culturally constituted as apocalyptic subjects.[9] Genealogical investigation of subjectivity forces open apocalypse's self-justifying categories of fixed hierarchy, absolute truth, and universal morality.

Perhaps the first thing to emphasize—because determinism is so often ascribed to Foucault—is that although Foucault shows the complex ways in which our subjectivity may be determined, he does not argue that we are without agency or entirely determined by these forces. The point of delineating subject-formations from past times and cultures was to demonstrate that human beings have *not* always been the same. Changes have occurred, therefore change can occur. It is understandable how the misconception of Foucauldian determinism came about; the drama and intricate details of Foucault's first works in particular contributed to the belief that Foucauldian analysis was synonymous with revealing iron cages of subjection. Nevertheless, even in the earliest texts and increasingly in the later ones, his argument is not that we are not free, but rather that freedom can only be exercised in relation to these determinants, or more accurately, in relation to the technologies of our culture.

In an essay discussing shifts of attention from power/knowledge analysis to ethics, Foucault outlines four major types of technologies, "each a matrix of practical reason," that might be analyzed:

1) technologies of production, which permit us to produce, transform, or manipulate things; 2) technologies of sign systems, which permit us to use signs, meanings, symbols, or signification; 3) technologies of power, which determine the conduct of individuals and submit them to certain ends or domination, an objectivizing of the subject; 4) technologies of the self, which permit individuals to effect by their own means or with the help of others a certain number of operations on

their own bodies and souls, thoughts, conduct, and way of being, so as to transform themselves in order to attain a certain state of happiness, purity, wisdom, perfection, or immortality.[10]

Whereas the first works, up to and including the first volume of *The History of Sexuality*, focus on technologies of sign systems (as discursive formations) and technologies of power/knowledge, *The Use of Pleasure* and *The Care of the Self* turn more fully to the technologies of the self, exploring ethics as a relation of oneself to oneself. It follows that, since subjectivities are themselves culturally produced, the ethical relation of self to self is also culturally specific and historically changeable.

Rather than formulating a universalizing theory of the subject, genealogical philosophy focuses attention simultaneously on subjection and subjectification. Throughout his first works, Foucault shows how an increasing specification of individuality is part of the ordering of things in the modern era. These works stress the ways in which people are *subjected* to power/knowledge relations. *Madness and Civilization* and *The Order of Things* demonstrate that the categorization of madness from the place of reason and the gathering of empirical data about individuals consolidates and extends human science networks of power/knowledge. Techniques of verbalization and disciplinary practices of the body classify and systematize individuals as well as the population as a whole. In the relations of power/knowledge produced by and productive of the human sciences, psychological, medical, familial, penitential, military, and educational patterns of behavior are established.

Discipline and Punish and *The History of Sexuality* further demonstrate that the formation of the sciences of the individual and their correlative techniques of surveillance and discipline constituted a decisive shift in the history of subjectivity in the West. This shift marks a movement away from the Christian imperative to renounce the self and toward the secular aspiration to discover the self. By taking human beings as objects of scientific study, the human sciences produced a new form of subjectivity that defines itself in terms of positive rather than renunciatory operations of selfhood. A genealogy of subjectivities, then, explores the ways in which these differing power relations are invested in the bodies and verbalizations of individuals. It also explores the resistances that individuals exert in relation to networks of power/knowledge.

As Foucault's four technologies indicate, the specification of individuality through technologies of power is not the only means by which subjectivity is constituted. Foucault's last work turns to the means by which people are self-constituting individuals and inquires into the freedom of the individual. In these texts, his attention is on subjectification. In both *The Use of Pleasure* and *The Care of the Self*, Foucault deals specifically with sexual ethics. Before his death he had outlined a more extensive project on the genealogy of ethics. In an interview discussing his work in progress, he points out that an "aesthetics of existence" predominated among the elite within ancient Greek society. Such an ethics necessarily opposes forms of power/knowledge—religious or secular—which prescribe patterns of behavior for individuals and the population as a whole. The idea that one's life is a work of art, that one's existence is a process of self-creativity, runs counter to both Christian prescriptions for the salvation of the soul and human sciences prescriptions for the normality of the individual.

Commenting that we "have hardly any remnant of the idea in our society, that the principal work of art which one had to take care of, the main idea to which one must apply aesthetic values, is oneself, one's life, one's existence," he notes, however, that practices of aesthetic selfhood never entirely died out, for such an ethics "reappears at the moment of the Renaissance" and a few episodes also occur in "nineteenth-century dandyism."[11] Despite explicitly espousing the idea that one's life might become a work of art, Foucault reiterates a longstanding feminist objection to the traditional valorization of Greek society: the Greek aesthetics of existence should not be seen as a Golden Age version of such an ethics. He points out that the "Greek ethics were linked to a purely virile society with slaves, in which the women were underdogs whose pleasure had no importance, whose sexual life had to be only oriented toward, determined by, their status as wives, and so on."[12]

According to Foucault's formulations, what most distinguishes the Greek ethics of an aesthetics of existence from a modern ethics of normalization is the way each constitutes the self. Each has its own technology of the self, or mode of subjectification. Arguing that the practices making up the Greek aesthetics of existence follow as a first principle the maxim, "Take care of oneself," he indicates that within this ethics an individual became an ethical subject through "the will to live a beautiful life, and to leave to others memories of a beautiful existence."[13] In contrast, the technology of the self in the ethics of normalization rests on the injunction to "know thyself" and entails a set of practices requiring that one divulge the truth of oneself. (Foucault argues that the Delphic instruction to "know yourself" was an injunction in ancient Greece that was understood within the context of care of the self but that in the modern era the context of the care of the self has disappeared.)[14]

Normalized subjectivity inherits something of Christianity's confessional mode as well as an acceptance of "external law as the basis for morality."[15] Thus the religious self of Christian asceticism, which defines itself in terms of membership in a divine community, fed into a secularized self of normality, which defines itself in terms of membership in a state society. For the purposes of this study, such a genealogy allows us to see one of the continuities of apocalypse: the apocalyptic subject of Christianity bears a truth relation to the apocalyptic subject of normality produced by the human sciences.

A schematic difference between these two technolgies of the self may be seen in their respective stances regarding the relationship between truth and self-hood. In the Greek aesthetics of existence, an important technique of selfhood is *askesis*, which is to be distinguished from Christian asceticism. In contrast to Christian asceticism's renunciation of self, Foucault defines *askesis* as the "pro-gressive consideration of self, or mastery over oneself, obtained not through the renunciation of reality, but through the acquisition and assimilation of truth. It has as its final aim not preparation for another reality but access to the reality of this world."[16] The means by which one can acquire truth and "transform truth into a permanent principle of action," according to this tradition, involves cer-tain practices or exercises that train one in becoming an ethical subject. The Greek word for these practices is *paraskeuazo*, which means "to get prepared" and applies to both meditation (*melete*) and physical training (*gymnasia*).[17]

In contrast to this active and ongoing concept of aesthetic self-formation, normalized selfhood is constructed through a concept of a preexistent interiority: one strives to discover and liberate the truth presumed to be within oneself. Foucault calls this notion of revealed truth a "hermeneutics of desire," arguing that it leads individuals "to focus their attention on themselves, to decipher, recognize, and acknowledge themselves as subjects of desire, bringing into play between themselves and themselves a certain relationship that allows them to discover, in desire, the truth of their being, be it natural or fallen."[18] The tech-nologies of disciplinary power—the family, the school, the army, the medical and psychological professions, eugenic programming—authorize themselves to act as agents of normalization by claiming knowledge about how to discover this "interiority" or essence. This is why genealogy must attend to the mutual invest-ments of disciplinary subjection and normalized subjectification.

It is worth pointing out that much Foucauldian theory, with Foucault's own texts providing little as exception, has not been sufficiently attentive to the ways in which these modes of subjection and subjectification have been differentiated by gender, sex, class, and race. Foucault's focus on subjection in terms of prisons, schools, and the army, and on subjectification in regard to the ancient Greek citizenry, would have been enhanced through a clearer understanding that his work conceptualizes the formation of dominant forms of masculine subjectivity. Such an understanding does begin to come into focus in *The Care of the Self*.[19] But too much Foucauldian theory remains focused on "the subject" as if it were neutral in terms of gender, sex, class, and race.[20]

Despite this tendency in Foucauldian theory itself, the Foucauldian emphasis on genealogy has been preserved and enhanced in some areas of academic en-terprise as well as in some nonacademic educational efforts, such as ACT UP's print and video libraries, and the Lesbian Herstory Archives, which have been established to ensure the circulation of countermemories. Within U.S. aca-demia, cultural studies emerged over the 1980s and early 1990s as one of the most vital sites of genealogical challenge. By drawing on the interdisciplinary women's studies and black studies programs of of the 1970s, cultural studies furthered their critiques of disciplinary knowledge by elucidating gender, race, ethnicity, and class as enfolded relations and investigating the power relations within and between what Cameron McCarthy has called the "differentially oppressed."[21] One of the key challenges that faces cultural studies as a philosophical practice is how effectively it will be able to cross over the established borders between community education and institutionalized academia.[22] Another is how well it withstands challenges from within its own ranks that necessarily alter its critical frameworks. Such a challenge has been made, for example, with queer theory, which, among other tasks, explores the heteronormativity of power/ knowledge formations, illuminating the ways in which a heterosexist hermeneutics of desire gets distributed through diverse social practices.[23] These genealogical approaches provide a corrective not only to humanistic philosophy's universalizing concepts of human nature but also to mainstreamed Foucauldian theory's tendency to discuss "the subject" as if it embodied a single identity.

Genealogy avoids such flattening-out of cultural identity through its concept of subjectivity as a complex of multiple, sometimes conflicting, discourses. Thinking about subjectivity as multiply discursive radically recasts apocalyptic philosophy's concept of universal human nature.[24] From the perspective of multiple discursivity, individuals are mixes of culturally dominant and marginalized discourses which not only alter in relation to each other over time but are also the materials whereby aesthetic-ethical transformation may be effected. These discursive juxtapositions that make up a subject might be thought of as a newspaper. At the risk of oversimplifying a longstanding philosophical discussion on signification, subjectivity, and agency, a newspaper analogy helps differentiate genealogical subjectivity not only from transcendental claims that presuppose metaphysical meaning, essential human nature, and authorial intention, but also from deconstructionist critiques of those claims.[25] As a genealogical approach to discourse, the newspaper analogy is here used to call into question assumptions about language's metaphysical origin and analogies between creativity and divine inspiration. But rather than following deconstruction's dismantling of correspondence between word and world, my use of the newspaper analogy is more concerned with questions about the conditions of possibility for discourse, publication credentialing, and the circulation of certified meanings. Thus the analogy calls attention to its own historical parameters; the newspaper is a product of the modern era and for that reason the analogy applies to modern subjectivity more suitably than that of the ancients. This is underscored by the most typical occasions that place ordinary individuals in newspapers, and thereby individuate them: announcements of birth, religious ceremonies, marriage, divorce, death, and crime. Moreover, the newspaper of the modern era is undergoing transformation and potential obsolescence because of postmodern technology. With this change comes a corresponding shift from multiply discursive subjectivity to digitalized subjectivity processed through electronic pathways.

For the present, however, newspapers are still prevalent and the analogy is still applicable to today's predominant subjectivity. Itself a repetition, a newspaper contains numerous and diverse image and print entries. Conventions ranging from the placement of the headings and the weather report to what ranks as front-page news are akin to the generalized subjectivity of a particular historical moment. Even though the number and classification of sections as well as the size of the headlines and the prominent placement of lead articles generally determine a given subjectivity's overall construction, its meanings alter with the attention directed to specific columns, features, and ads. And although the monopoly circulation of certain newspapers materializes hegemony, there are many ruptures and gaps that affect individuals and whole populations: striking workers refuse to get a newspaper out, a neighborhood dog runs off with the morning edition, print errors make a particular story illegible, small independent newspapers provide counterhegemonic news, the paper is simply not read. Finally, daily news is filled with counternormative information; virtually any newspaper, regardless of its ideological orientation, contains accounts of transgressive behaviors.

And the task of genealogical philosophy in regard to explaining this mix of overdetermined and contingent multiply discursive "newspaper" subjectivity? To reflect on its specific features, discerning the discourses and the technologies that produce them and rendering visible the power/knowledge relations that produce a given construction. Genealogy shows how, under totalitarian social systems, multiply discursive subjectivity is suppressed, certain discourses are forbidden, and the state's news is the only news deemed fit to print. It also differentiates biopower's life-managing seductions from fascism's domination, showing how biopower's category of "newsworthy" generates normalized subjectivity, divides populations into medicalized categories, and supports bureaucratic agencies that manage social behavior. Genealogy's resistance to both domination and biopower fosters social dynamics in which power circulates more readily, transactions and negotiations of meanings are more possible, a diversity of news stories and interpretations are seen as a necessity for the practice of liberty. As I have indicated earlier, simulation presents yet other problems of power/knowledge and subjectivity. In some instances, genealogy's countermemories might function most effectively to slow down the rapid flux of postmodernism, preventing the fragmented subjectivity that accrues from whirling perceptual shifts. Against all three forms of subject-formation, the genealogist might try to see what differences a cut-and-paste job makes.

Genealogical philosophical analysis attends to individual subjectivity as well. A newspaper reading of myself as a multiply discursive subject might be used here

to illustrate how an array of diverse cultural forces operates through both subjection and subjectification and provides sites of potential resistance to those in-
tertwined processes. Although my birth and baptism announcements in the
Tampa *Tribune* elliptically indicated that I was the third daughter of Miriam and
Tom Quinby who resided at 4118 Emperado Drive, and was baptized at Christ
the King Church, this was sufficient to inscribe my cultural text as white, female, heterosexual, Southern, upper-middle-class, Catholic. In the U.S. South
in 1946, this was a conflictual combination of privilege and marginalization. As
white and well-to-do, I grew up in surroundings of physical comfort. But being
female and Catholic bred high anxiety at every turn. It was not lost on me as a
child in the public elementary school system that Catholics were on the Ku Klux
Klan's hit list, along with blacks and Jews. In my own case, involvement in the
civil rights movement in the sixties arose out of what I perceived as a religious
and racial alliance against Southern bigotry. That's why I was so shocked when,
at Sunday mass at Loyola University in New Orleans in 1964, those of us who
had joined the SDS's sit-ins at local restaurants were denounced from the pulpit.
I began to reread the meaning of Catholicism in my life, quite literally going
over the same texts with new eyes in the act of what Adrienne Rich called re-
visioning.

Despite coming of political age in the sixties through civil rights and antiwar
activism, it took me much longer to revise column after column of normalizing
middle-class, gender, and sexual discourse. I did not join the feminist movement
until the late seventies, after gaining feminist knowledge through a divorce and
inadequate child support, which made it necessary to learn the discourses and
practices of food stamps and communal living. A graduate program in literature
that included Marxist and feminist analyses and a teaching assistantship (the
first "real" job I ever had) helped me to reevaluate capitalist, heterosexist cultural inscriptions. Retrospectively, I began to discern familial reinforcements of
normative gender and sexuality through requirements of household conduct,
clothing, manners, dating expectations, and so on. Not that those requirements
were all that clear-cut. Even though I had been reared according to the dictates
of Catholic girlhood, I was equally well-versed in the peculiar style of white
Southern femininity. Having fortified its values with adolescent enthusiasm as
an insatiable reader of *Gone With the Wind*, I had internalized an ambivalent desire to conquer men like Scarlett O'Hara, wanting to win them over and defeat
them at the same time. As a high school student, the Catholic school I attended
had enacted sexual difference through a spatial distribution that divided the
school into separate buildings for male and female students, separated by a quar-
ter of a mile. The expectations of the nuns and priests who taught us were that,
if we did not become nuns and priests ourselves, we would marry and procreate
in nuclear-family fashion. Yet the spatial distance fostered homoeroticism at
least as much as it did heterosexuality.

These conflicting discourses can create ambivalences that are hard to work out, to say the least. One of the reasons an aesthetics of existence is so appealing to me is that it provides ways of thinking about transforming ambivalences into less self- and other-destructive activities. Turning to different discourses is one way of bringing about such transformation because it fosters a rethinking of past practices, making more visible their modes of subjection. Reorienting one's attention (with the newspaper analogy still in mind) to what is called "filler," the bits and pieces of information buried amid the regular features, allows a kind of play between strictly ordered reality reports. Even so, the ambivalences themselves are not entirely detrimental to radical politics. To the extent that ambivalence encourages reevaluation of what is excluded as being transgressive behavior, it helps decenter biopower's force-fed normalcy. While my positioning in Southern, Catholic femininity still crops up to obstruct my feminist thinking (at moments that always manage to surprise me), its odd combinations of resentment and morality, as well as the homoeroticism of my Catholic educational experience (which I now like to think allowed me to see Scarlett as a source of desire for women), have also repeatedly served as a resource in forming alliances against masculinist, heterosexist power relations. As I have often discovered in discussions with other former Catholics, a foundation of religious fervor does at times convert into political activism. And, in my case at least, Catholicism undoubtedly contributed to the shock of recognition I had when I first came across Foucault's analysis of the deployment of sexuality and the construction of the Western subject as a "confessing animal."

The point of this personal account, given form by the newspaper analogy, describing multiply discursive subjectivity is to redirect the ways that philosophy seeks to comprehend a truth of human nature; such redirection necessarily includes this kind of self-discursive reflection. Crucially, a genealogical approach to subjectivity advocates what academic philosophy eschews: the philosopher's task is to help challenge existing modes of subjection and subjectification that constrain the practices of freedom. In keeping with this effort, genealogical exploration of the concept of multiply discursive subjectivity can contribute to the coalitional strengths of feminism and other movements for radical democracy. Such thinking bolsters ways of finding and forging affinities that are not exclusionary by gender, race, class, or sexuality. Multiply discursive subjectivity also yields a better understanding of the deeply entrenched personal obstacles that form walls between gender, race, sexual, and class identities; these walls have to be broken down or at least chiseled away for political coalitions to occur. One of the most crucial questions regarding issues of subjectivity for philosophy today involves subject formation through the deployment of technoppression. As my discussion of eu(jean)ics shows, the forces of hyperreality fracture identity and sever even provisional roots of interpersonal connection. The concept of multiply discursive subjectivity allows us to see ways to resist thoroughgoing fragmentation without reinstating a universal, deep-core concept of self.

Toward a New Economy of Power Relations

Apocalypse presents power as a top-down affair. It presumes omnipotence and hierarchy. It commands obedience. It justifies punishment of those who resist its dictates. It rewards those who follow them. Under certain social systems, this is the predominant form that power takes. Absolute monarchy and the Vatican, for example, are structured in accordance with principles of apocalypse. But what about post-sovereign power? And what of the limitations and dangers of assuming the operation of sovereign power when the structures of governance have been substantially altered? Despite crucial transformations in political, social, and economic relations, apocalyptic views of power tend to prevail among social philosophers and political theorists.[26] Such views see power as emanating from "above." Whether from a divine source, the state, the patriarchy, or teleological forces of history, this view defines power as something that is possessed by a sovereign source. It adheres to the nay-saying or "thou shalt not" model of power. And, insidiously, even if not intentionally, it provides the rationale for isolating and/or punishing those who refuse to obey the dictates of normality.

Against such assumptions of omnipotence and hierarchical control, Foucault defines power as

> the multiplicity of force relations immanent in the sphere in which
> they operate and which constitute their own organization; as the
> process which, through ceaseless struggles and confrontations,
> transforms, strengthens or reverses them; as the support which these
> force relations find in one another, thus forming a chain or a system, or
> on the contrary, the disjunctions and contradictions which isolate them
> from one another; and lastly, as the strategies in which they take effect,
> whose general design or institutional crystallization is embodied in the
> state apparatus, in the formulation of the law, in the various social
> hegemonies.[27]

According to this view, decentered power relations circulate within discourses and are embodied through disciplinary, surveillance, and regulatory practices, ranging from applying makeup as a daily routine to the testing of fetuses to insure their genetic "correctness." Even though these power relations are not to be understood as dialectical forces (as with a Marxist notion of economic structures), their microoperations do intertwine with consolidated, large-scale relations such as "production, kinship, family, sexuality."[28] Power relations are thus a network of microlevel operations and global strategies.

To hold exclusively to the "shalt not" theory of power is to be blind to the forces that entice or incite behaviors, to the kinds of fashioned longings so integral to eu(jean)ics. Seeing power exclusively as a top-down structure perpetuates apocalypse while allowing the operations of biopower full sway. Foucault argued that biopower, or the "calculated management of life," was an "indispensable element in the development of capitalism."[29] Although the state plays a role in administering these forces, their development as disciplinary agents — in schools, families, medical facilities, factories — far exceeds state control. Media operations constitute increasingly dispersed forms of biopower. A genealogical approach focuses on the ways in which these power relations are, quite literally, embodied. Attending to the sexualized, racialized, work-disciplined, and fashion-accessorized body demonstrates the ways in which power relations "materially penetrate the body in depth."[30]

The notion of power relations as generative reconceptualizes the assumption that power and domination are synonymous. Foucault argues that domination is better understood as antithetical to power relations. Under systems of domination, the social hierarchy is stable, fixed, so that despite necessary strategies of survival, possibilities of reversing the hierarchy are profoundly limited. Such is the case under absolute monarchy, slavery, patriarchy, and fascism.[31] It may well be the case that the defeat of *domination* requires a revolution. Struggling against power *relations*, in contrast, presumes an exercise of freedom and calls for myriad resistances. Following from the premise that power relations are multiple is a relinquishing of the goal of *the* Revolution. In place of that centralized model of the defeat of dominant power, Foucauldian theory posits resistances and transformations that are localized, partial, and co-extensive with the power relations themselves. Because they are "co-extensive with the social body," power relations are constitutive elements of subjectivity.[32] The subject can never transcend power relations (the utopian dream of apocalypse), since power relations produce subjectivity. But just as microlevel and large-scale operations become integrated into "global strategies," so too microresistances can integrate with "certain grand strategies" such as class or gender struggle.[33] And these resistances can alter, and have altered, hierarchical relations on both small and large scales.

In "The Subject and Power," in response to his own question "Do we need a theory of power?" Foucault states, "Since a theory assumes a prior objectification, it cannot be asserted as a basis for analytical work. But this analytical work cannot proceed without an ongoing conceptualization. And this conceptualization implies critical thought — a constant checking." If not a theory, then what? Foucault's response is to call for a "new economy of power relations." Turning again to "The Subject and Power":

> What we need is a new economy of power relations — the word
> economy being used in its theoretical and practical sense. To put it in

other words: since Kant, the role of philosophy is to prevent reason from going beyond the limits of what is given in experience; but from the same moment—that is, since the development of the modern state and the political management of society—the role of philosophy is also to keep watch over the excessive powers of political rationality. Which is a rather high expectation.[34]

Indeed, so high an expectation as to be attainable only by the philosopher as demigod. Recognizing this at least allows us to understand why apocalyptic philosophy has been so inadequate, even on its own terms, why it has so roundly failed to limit reason's tendency to stray beyond its experiences and to curb the excessive powers of political rationality. Foucault's comments on the practice of philosophy since Kant suggests that the task of forging a new economy of power relations entails relinquishing the role of state watchdog and replacing inquiry into power's internal rationality with analysis of resistances to power relations.

The new economy of power relations Foucault calls for is one that stems from the places of struggle.[35] These struggles, or resistances, will not yield eternal verities but they will help philosophy better comprehend contemporary relations of power. Such analysis begins with an investigation of philosophy itself as a form of power/knowledge, taking as one point of departure the forms of resistance exercised in feminist philosophy. Approaching philosophy genealogically as a discourse produced by and productive of knowledge within a field of power seeks to study philosophy through its conditions of patronage and the uses to which its ideas are put by philosophers, educators, government leaders, and so on. One deficiency that runs through mainstream political philosophy, as feminist philosophers have shown, is that power is typically theorized from the perspective of the status quo. The point I want to emphasize here is that when philosophy does not focus on resistances as the sites that make power relations visible, it is susceptible to serving the excessive powers of political rationality in maintaining biopower's management of society. To understand the operations of disciplinary power, for example, genealogical philosophy looks to the resistances of African Americans to racist anthropology, of feminists to procreative regulation, and lesbian and gay challenges to compulsory heterosexuality. To understand obstacles to living a good life, genealogical philosophy focuses on the protests of chemical lab or agricultural pest-control workers whose work conditions cause sterility and bodily contamination. To discern what prevents the development of ethical judgment in our society, genealogical philosophy considers teachers' strikes that protest the underfunding of schools beleaguered by bureaucratic procedures.[36]

The more philosophy approaches power relations from the perspective of these kinds of immediate struggles, the more it deabsolutizes philosophy. The result is a more discerning analysis of the totalizing forces that people have struggled against, one that more effectively isolates the exercises of power over bodies, one that more fully illuminates forces of individualization. The practice of this kind of analysis significantly alters the traditional philosophical discourse that seeks to know identity in a metaphysical sense. It also aids struggles for self-determination and greater liberty without enrolling people further in the management apparatuses of biopower. It is not that this kind of philosophy is never practiced. But it is too rarely heeded by government officials, academics, social theorists, or other philosophers. Genealogical philosophy recognizes that the most crucial question today is what is happening to us today. As long as philosophical inquiry disregards the material forces that penetrate our bodies, whether those forces beat us into submission, mold us into regulated fashion, discipline us into docility, or technologically fabricate us into cyborgs, it will follow the way of apocalypse.

Truth as the Insurrection of Subjugated Knowledges

Apocalypse presents itself as the revelation of absolute Truth. Assumptions held today about absolute Truth differ in correlation with the three modes of apocalyptic expression: divine, technological, and ironic. Exemplifying the divine mode, apocalypticians herald a messianic revelation of Divine Truth, which, as the trinity of Pat Buchanan, Ralph Reed, and Jesse Helms present it, includes the justified destruction of evil embodied by feminists and homosexuals. For technological apocalypticians, there may be no first or second coming per se, but there remains a belief in Truth, in the whole story. A displacement occurs. The end of the world acts as threat and incitement. For the "duck and cover" generation in particular, having grown up in an era threatened by the total destruction of the world, the end is to be avoided precisely by getting "there" first— "there" being the state of absolute knowledge. Technological apocalypticism seeks to arrive in time, before the end of time, and defends its efforts through the threat of the end and the promise of technological breakthrough. Ironic apocalypticism is laced with ambivalence about Truth. Having already arrived, there is no other option left but to look back in pity. But to look back at what? Even while dismissing as human folly the hopes of the others for a future event of revelation, their retrospection implies a finality that is itself a claim for absolute knowledge of history.

The promise of absolute knowledge is a promise of total control: control over nature's storms and droughts, nuclear destruction (the hope of a winnable nuclear war, the dream of safe dumping of nuclear waste), control of street crime, drugs, sexual "abnormalities," the "decline" of the family and its correlate in education, genetically transmitted "disorders," infertility, disease, threats to U.S. global supremacy, control over history itself. Sometimes this striving toward absolute knowledge is rewarded, and the chosen receive divine visions that provide a glimpse of what God knows. Sometimes it is said to require secrecy.

The experts, whether ministers, scientists, or government officials, must know what most people cannot or should not know.

What is the task of philosophy today in regard to truth?[37] How might a philosophy of the present be the undoing of apocalypse? From a genealogical perspective, the task of philosophy is to aid the "insurrection of subjugated knowledges."[38] As I indicated before, these subjugated knowledges include the erudite as well as the popular. One of the erudite knowledges that genealogical philosophy might promote against the cause of prophetic philosophy is deconstruction, even though it is in a number of ways antithetical to genealogy.[39] Deconstruction creates an anti-apocalyptic wedge that allows us to break open Truth. Linking the contemporary focus on the end of the world, as manifested in particular by the nuclear age's anxiety over absolute destruction, Derrida has argued that "deconstruction, at least what is being advanced today in its name, belongs to the nuclear age."[40] Such a view is in keeping with his general argument that deconstruction is intrinsic to logocentrism, that deconstruction's strategy of deferral of a fixed and final meaning owes its conditions of possibility to logocentric claims of absolute meaning. In this sense, deconstruction is a search for ways to intervene against final destruction as a final meaning, an intervention made possible by the possibility of world destruction.

When used with genealogical purpose, deconstruction is a valuable analytical tool for dismantling apocalyptic systems of meaning. But I would also stress that genealogy is the most effective analytical means to counter deconstruction's tendency to slip into a nihilistic void. This is not an inherent tendency of deconstruction, but a consequence of it that is gaining acceptance within disciplines that privilege ironic apocalypse. Against the purveyors of the absolute truth of no truth, genealogy demonstrates why, despite the fact that there is no intrinsic meaning, we have neither a continual free play nor a whirling abyss of meaning. Genealogical analysis clarifies who profits from the congealment of certain meaning—whether individuals or groups or social institutions.

Although deconstruction provides an important challenge to apocalyptic philosophy, it would be shortsighted to limit the search for subjugated knowledges to those that emerge within the confines of traditional, predominantly academic, philosophical discourse. As the previous chapter indicates, the numerous and various insurrectionary knowledges of feminism challenge many of the presumed universals upon which apocalyptic philosophy is erected. Feminism's insurrectionary knowledges avow the importance of drawing on one's particular situation as a way of understanding—partially rather than absolutely—the makings of the present as an everyday experience. These modes of knowledge challenge apocalyptic knowledge claims privileging certainty, abstraction, and reductive generalization. Serving as foreign elements within philosophy, feminism's inquiries about the everyday conditions of women's lives prompt philosophy to seek not abstract generalizations about human conflict but truths about why there are so many homeless women and children in the United States, about how a breast-fed baby got so high a PCB count, or why marriage laws apply only to heterosexual couples.

There are many such subjugated knowledges from which philosophy today might learn. Patricia Hill Collins points to the standpoint of black women in this regard, noting that "traditionally such women were blues singers, poets, autobiographers, storytellers, and orators validated by everyday Black women as experts on a Black women's standpoint."[41] Joan Nestle's work in collecting materials for the Lesbian Herstory Archives and her femme-butch reader, *The Persistent Desire*, document suppressed expression of countertruths about desire, gender identity, and love.[42] Getting the truth out about how to prevent the spread of AIDS without mandating sexual abstinence has been the effort of a number of individuals, such as Cindy Patton and Douglas Crimp, and groups such as the Gay Men's Health Crisis and ACT UP.[43] These knowledges constitute a multidirectional driving force against the regime of Truth produced in apocalyptic discourse and practice. The greatest potential for philosophy today resides in seeking out these subjugated knowledges, to explore what they say about philosophy's teachings and to use these countertruths to demystify apocalyptic Truth.

An Ethics of the Flesh as a Genealogical Aesthetics of Existence

The predominant mode of morality practiced in the United States today is a hermeneutics of desire. As Foucault defined it, this is a hermeneutics through which interiorized desire is deciphered. According to this system of morality, the attainment of the truth of one's being involves bringing to light the shadowy impulses of one's innermost self. Only in making one's inner truth visible can the snares of desire be suppressed or regulated into normality.[44] There are various ways for the truth of this desire to be revealed. For some, perhaps, pastoral confession remains the primary mode of self-disclosure. For adherents of this system, there is an obligation to speak truthfully about one's sinful desires to an intermediary whose training bestows more direct access to or understanding of the divine; in confession, one can cleanse the soul and receive forgiveness. For others, however, inner truth is linked so firmly with the secrets of sexual behavior and longings that the codes and means of expression in the deployment of sexuality remain indispensable for speaking truth. In this case, disclosing one's innermost desire is regarded as psychologically risky, and not to be undertaken without the expertise of medical and psychiatric professionals. Being forgiven is less important than becoming normal. For yet a great many others, the television or radio talk show meets the requirements of the obligation to confess. Forgiveness and/or acceptance are less at stake here than broadcasting one's personal truth to the multitude. The predilection for the "peculiar" on these shows indicates a limit-point to normalization: such display might stretch cultural tolerance more than it reinforces the deployment of normality. Furthermore, the credentialing process of the show's host is notably different from that of a minister or psychologist and issues of confidentiality have clearly been thrown by the wayside. Nevertheless, what remains the same is the compulsion to confess—indeed, to confess one's compulsions.

All three of these modes of confession—pastoral, therapeutic, and media—construct apocalyptic subjectivity. In their adherence to practices of confession, they constitute a subject who must speak truth by disclosing a desire that seems to creep into the very flesh that encases a "cleaner," less obsessive interior self. This concept of a self at odds with its bodily surround is foundational to a moral code that privileges spirit over body. The predominance of a hermeneutics of desire in the United States derives from the entrenchment of the Christian European tradition of the war between soul and flesh. In the past, religious practices of sexual abstinence and fasting were used to combat the appetitiveness of the flesh. This distrust of the body continued, and in some ways became more widely dispersed, through the deployment of sexuality during the nineteenth and twentieth centuries.[45] These days sexual abstinence and fasting are more likely to be regulated by fears of sexually transmitted disease and obesity, but distrust of the body remains prevalent, as does the acceptance of certain bodily acts as morally permissable and others as properly forbidden.

A hermeneutics of desire has held sway for so many centuries in part because the privileging of spirit over flesh has roots in Platonic philosophy as well as theological apocalyptic discourse. The most succinct statement of these principles in ancient philosophy may be found in the Symposium, where they are credited to Diotima's philosophy of love. Diotima explains how the seeker of wisdom may be initiated into the greatest form of love. As a follower of beauty, "and never of the ugliness," the seeker is to move from beauties of the body, to those of laws and institutions, and eventually to the "final revelation." This vision of the beautiful will not

> take the form of a face, or of hands, or of anything that is *of the flesh.*
> It will be neither words, nor knowledge, nor as something that exists in
> something else, such as a living creature, or the earth, or the heavens,
> or anything that is—but subsisting of itself and by itself in an eternal
> oneness, while every lovely thing partakes of it in such sort that,
> however much the parts may wax and wane, it will be neither more nor
> less, but still the same inviolable whole. (211b, emphasis mine).

This passage highlights some of the continuities of discourse between Platonic and Christian thought, indicating that some features of apocalypse are a convergence of these two philosophical approaches to truth. In *The Use of Pleasure,* Foucault pointed to Plato's philosophy as expressed in both the *Symposium* and the *Phaedrus* as a departure from the ancient Greek ethics of pleasure. Platonic erotics marks a "transition from an erotics structured in terms of 'courtship' practice and recognition of the other's freedom, to an erotics centered on an ascesis of the subject and a common access to truth."[46] This shift marks the formation of a hermeneutics of desire in ancient philosophy, which was taken up with greater force and punitive zeal under Christianity.

The extent to which a hermeneutics of desire devalues women may also be understood through this convergence of Platonic and Christian concepts of morality, inner truth, and desire. In the *Symposium*, Diotima ranks bodily desires below the spirit's "longing for immortality" by arguing that "those whose procreancy is of the body turn to woman as the object of their love, and raise a family in the blessed hope that by doing so they will keep their memory green, 'through time and eternity.' But those whose procreancy is of the spirit rather than of the flesh—and they are not unknown, Socrates—conceive and bear the things of the spirit." (208e-209a) Biblical discourse is vigorously disdainful of women's sexuality. Recalling the biblical representations of Babylon as a sordid, sexual woman allows us to see how theological castigation of the flesh has subsequently been justified through a gender politics that portrays women's flesh as especially impure.

If disdain for the flesh is of such long standing, we may well ask whether it is possible to hear the word "flesh" without also hearing the calamitous warnings of an Augustine or the sneering intonations of a Jerry Falwell. In a society devoted to images of lean perfection, is it possible *not* to be besieged with anxiety about having too much flesh? And given today's preoccupations with sexually transmitted diseases, is it possible to think of one's own flesh without shrinking back a bit, fearing the contamination from the touch of another? Shifting the focus, we may also ask: Is it possible to see bodily care and preservative love as primary virtues for everyday life? To value life-shaping activities over a simultaneously death-infatuated and death-denying apocalyptic moment of eternal oneness?[47] Is it possible—in contrast to technological apocalypse's drive for bioperfectibility and absolute immunity—to engage in ethical practices that strive for health and life enhancement while acknowledging sickness and death as part of life's course?

My view is that such alternatives are not only possible but already available. Practices that comprise this ethics are varied, but they come together in two ways: they stand in contrast to the confessional practices of a hermeneutics of desire, and they approach the care of the flesh or body as an ethical concern. The contemporary practices that comprise what I am calling an ethics of the flesh are today's version of an aesthetics of existence.[48] Unlike the apocalyptic hermeneutics of desire which calls for truth's incessant revelation from deep within oneself, an ethics of the flesh holds that truth is produced in conduct toward oneself and others. According to this ethical stance, truth cannot be revealed by divine revelation or decreed by law, because it has not already been established. Truth is in the making, as an exercise of freedom, and, as activity, can be witnessed. In this respect, an ethics of the flesh is akin to the Greek aesthetics of existence.

But an ethics of the flesh as a genealogical aesthetics of existence also differs from the Greek practice in many ways, most notably in its critique rather than promotion of elite male privilege. And whereas the Greek ethics focused on an individual's achievement of self-mastery as self-stylization, an ethics of the flesh focuses on relations of care between individuals as part of an individual's ethical art of living. In other words, although both of these ethics aspire toward an aesthetics of existence rather than accepting normalization as a goal, they differ in the way each defines the meanings of bodily existence and care. Crucially, the practices of an ethics of the flesh reflect feminist thought in ways that were not part of Greek ethics.[49] Rather than emphasizing self-control and austerity, as ancient Greek ethics did, this ethics upholds the longstanding feminist teaching that the interconnectedness, diversity, and vulnerability of life require acts of care and nurturance.[50]

An ethics of the flesh is also situated in relation to the disruptions and dislocations particular to postmodern life. The mechanization of the body integral to industrial capitalism and more recent cybernetic technological transformations blurs traditional bodily boundaries, numbs sensations, and displaces a sense of coherence through multiple and fragmented mirrorings or screen simulations. One way to respond to technological dehumanization is to mime it. Baudrillard offers a version of this in his enjoinder: "Let us be Stoics: if the world is fatal, let us be more fatal than it. If it is indifferent, let us be more indifferent. We must conquer the world and seduce it through an indifference that is at least equal to the world's."[51] Practices of an ethics of the flesh reject this approach. Such thinking is against the well-being of flesh and in line with apocalyptic attitudes that disdain the body and seek domination of the world. Baudrillard's call for "indifference" is symptomatic more of privilege than of oppression. As Sarah Hoagland points out, the more "understandable response to living under conditions of oppression, of dominance and subordination, particularly of heterosexualism," is a paternalistic desire to control a situation or events in order to relieve another's pain.[52] But she warns against paternalism because it reinforces rather than undermines these conditions. What she calls "attending"—that is, acting to lend support to and enable another rather than intervening on her behalf—is fundamental to an ethics of the flesh and, I am arguing, a far more effective challenge to postmodern dehumanization.

Furthermore, as is characteristic of the universalizing tendency of apocalypse, Baudrillard's "us" flattens out myriad responses to the world. He ignores what our flesh reminds us of—not all bodies are the same. An ethics of the flesh takes as a central problematic the very issue of bodily difference that apocalyptic discourse disregards as irrelevant to ethical decision making. Carol Gilligan's groundbreaking studies of gender differences and ethical deliberation emphasize that differing bodily capacities call for a logic different from the abstract, autonomy-centered logic that has prevailed as if all people were identical.[53] She points out that issues of choice, agency, and violence are not symmetrical for women and men when it comes to the issue of abortion. An ethics that emphasizes abstract justice and autonomy does not deal adequately with differences in bodies regarding reproduction. In the discourse of divine apocalypse, such an approach naively privileges life over death, denouncing abortion as murder, hailing birth as on the side of life, and ignoring quality-of-life issues stemming from poverty and undesired pregnancy. In the discourse of technological apocalypse, abstraction leads to an impasse over rights of the fetus versus rights of the woman; on this view, the only resolution available is to settle on one side of a binary between violence and nonviolence. One stance favors the rights of the fetus because aborting it is seen to be an act of violence; the opposition favors the rights of the pregnant woman because to coerce her into carrying the pregnancy to term is seen as violence to her. But, as Barbara Johnson remarks in regard to Gilligan's study of women who have grappled with decisions about pregnancy and abortion: "The choice is not between violence and nonviolence, but between simple violence to a fetus and complex, less determinate violence to an involuntary mother and/or unwanted child."[54]

An ethics of the flesh thus confronts violence to the body, seeing bodily pain and pleasure to be basic conditions of life. In contrast to both Baudrillard's ironic advocacy of indifference and divine apocalypse's endorsement of suffering in atonement for sin, ethicists of the flesh actively seek to relieve bodily pain or discomfort, whether it stems from direct violence or the dulling process of technological dehumanization. An ethics of the flesh is not merely reactive for it seeks to provide bodily pleasure and comfort. Nor is it reductive, for it does not equate all inflictions of pain with violent assault. One of the reasons that consensual sadomasochism is worthy of ethical inquiry is because it helps illuminate distinctions between an erotics of pain that confirms selfhood and an assault that thwarts it. One of the most sustained theoretical discussions of the flesh that is in keeping with principles of this ethics is Sara Ruddick's Maternal Thinking. Her "conception of the bodily" is "centered in birthing labor and the unique relation of birthgiver and infant," but it is confined neither to the biological act of giving birth nor to females.[55] Ruddick argues that the preservative love a birthgiver bestows on her infant is an ethical model that can and should be undertaken by others. The activities this ethical approach emphasizes are those that foster the body's physical, emotional, sexual, and cognitive growth, maintain its safety, and encourage its well-being. Ruddick acknowledges the fact that some mothers are violent; in other words, her ethics is not dependent on an essentialist view of maternity. What she is proposing is an extension of those practices that do cultivate preservative love as a way of diminishing violence. She argues that these practices are most frequently associated with mothering. The extension of these practices involves a politics of peace that renounces bodily assault—including warfare, murder, torture, sexual assault, and domestic tyranny—and celebrates preservative love as a primary virtue.

Whereas Ruddick's notion of preservative love centers on maternal practices, other proponents of an ethics of the flesh focus on personal care for self. These practices may be understood as preservative love of one's own body. They include bodily conduct manuals that advocate a daily regimen of healthy diet and exercise as a means of preventing illness, increasing stamina, combating depression, enhancing sexuality, and diminishing physical discomfort. Practices of self-preservative love should be differentiated from mainstream practices formulated by the growth industry of workout gyms and aerobics classes in the 1980s which emphasize fashion over physical well-being. Such attitudes toward the body present dangers of excessive exercise and diet that harm the body rather than preserving it. And they promulgate standards for bodily appearance and abilities that are directly harmful to wheelchair users, people whose body shapes don't correspond to the norm, or who are ill. U.S. culture's emphasis on physical attractiveness also interferes with sexual expression. As Sucheng Chan has pointed out, "beyond learning how to be physically independent and, for some of us, living with chronic pain or other kinds of discomfort, the most difficult thing a handicapped person has to deal with, especially during puberty and early adulthood, is relating to potential sexual partners."[56] As AIDS educators have shown, mainstream media representations sustain normative bodily standards by portraying people with AIDS as a cultural antithesis, depicting the AIDS body as ravaged, resigned to death, and sexually dangerous.[57] Rather than imposing a single standard on all—the bodily normalization endorsed by a hermeneutics of desire—an ethics of the flesh supports activities of preservative love of self.

Writings that inscribe an ethics of the flesh necessarily focus on care for people living with a debilitating disease. For the last decade, U.S. culture has poured its apocalyptic fears about bodily misery and death into a fear of AIDS. For that reason I want to conclude my discussion of the value of this ethics for contemporary philosophy by turning to Paul Monette's AIDS memoir, *Borrowed Time*. It eloquently and poignantly exemplies an ethics of the flesh as a genealogical aesthetics of existence. Monette details the dreadfulness and the beauty of caring for a loved one whose bodily energy is sapped, whose eyes can no longer see, whose flesh is diminished.[58] He recounts how he and his lover, Roger Horwitz, face death as a part of their joined life. Significantly, Monette specifically draws on Plato's *Phaedrus* as an affirmative expression of love and thus redefines Platonic tradition for an ethics of the flesh, recording how love's eyes see how beauty can "take the form of a face, or of hands" and the other things that are "of the flesh." Monette's memoirs preserve that beauty, and his grief, in words that become shared knowledge, showing how care for another is an activity of self-transformation that may be sustained in the self-transformation of writing.

Borrowed Time also makes clear why an ethics of the flesh must insist on governmental responsibility as crucial. Exorbitant costs of private medical treatment, inadequate funding for some medical personnel and huge profits for others, and discrimination against people with illness are obstacles to living according to the principles of an ethics of the flesh. Monette's memoirs register why this ethics is far more suited than a hermeneutics of desire to meet today's concerns about well-being. He helps us see that to turn away from the flesh is to turn toward the hierarchical power relations of apocalypse which justifies and often lauds bodily suffering in the name of eternal reward. Taking up such an ethics would lead genealogical philosophy to promote a social nurturance model that mandates adequate nutrition and shelter for all members of a society, provides affordable health care, and ensures community education about preventing transmission of communicable diseases.

Monette's textual commemoration of the final period of his lover's life makes visible an ethical relationship of care between men whose sexuality and love is condemned under apocalyptic strictures. This portrayal radically questions the principle of normalization that propels power relations in the deployment of sexuality. It also radically redefines the meaning of freedom and friendship. Monette's actions and writings reject the masculinist notion of freedom as escape from bodily need and responsibility to others. His activities of care embody the meaning of the word "friend," which brings together the Old English words for "love" and "free." His memoirs show that an ethics of the flesh loves the freedom of friendship as a collaborative activity of self-stylization. Monette's testimony helps us understand that philosophy itself gains sustenance by incorporating this genealogical aesthetics of existence into its practice.

Part II
The Re-Creations and Recreations of Adam and Eve:
Reading Modernist Texts in Postmodern Contexts

Against Prophecy

Tonight my wife turns to the wall troubled by death.
I say silly, joking things that do not comfort her
and go out closing the door and darkness in.

Rain drums down as it has for days.
I watch it run to the tips of palm leaves
where the drops pause to gather mass before falling.

Since we, too, pause, before falling, to gather mass,
the idea of not-being repels my wife's imagination
with its nothing-to-imagine—worse than the thought of being

buried alive. There is comfort in words like *millennium* and *messiah*
spoken last night by three rabbis in Jerusalem: news was
each dreamed the same dream that the end of the world was near.

I heard this while scraping spots of red and green paint
from the formica top of a desk purchased secondhand.
I felt, then, a need to love or defend the useless attention

I was giving to make its shabby surface uniformly white again.
Indifferent to prophecy, the refrigerator drones in the dark
like a common prayer; it keeps milk fresh—a principle by

which we abide as surely as we do the return of sunlight.
My wife is sleeping when I slip into bed, her eyelids
scratching the pillow secretly like a leaf trembling

in a breeze so slight that if you wet a finger
and held it in the air, still you could not tell
which direction it was coming from.

David Weiss

Chapter 4
Conceiving the New Man:
Henry Adams and the Birth of Ironic Apocalypse

*The new man could only be a child born of contact between the
new and the old energies.*

Henry Adams[1]

Henry Adams's life spanned the decades of the first wave of the women's rights movement, from its emergence in the 1830s through the legal and social gains of the late nineteenth century to the threshold of women's suffrage. But Adams was not a supporter of these gains for women. He disparaged women's struggles for equality as imitative of men's proclivity to settle for less. Adams argued that women were a superior force, capable of transcending the mundane and often corrupt goings-on of the political arena. Above all, he was puzzled at women's willingness to relinquish what he assessed as their greatest power: fecundity. In this chapter I explore that puzzlement and the way Adams attempts to resolve it through a logic of apocalypse, at various times in the divine mode, at others in the technological, and finally in the ironic. I read *The Education of Henry Adams* as the site of an intense power struggle involving men's social-political privilege and women's sexual and reproductive freedom.[2] Through genealogical literary analysis I demonstrate the ways in which this struggle within the culture at large was incorporated into the body of Adams's text—a textual body draped in robes of irony. This is relevant precisely because Adams's ironic apocalypse has become paradigmatic for twentieth-century apocalypse.[3]

In other words, reading Adams's text from a genealogical perspective brings into clearer focus the nature of current sexual and gender power struggles. As Michael Kimmel has argued, the years between 1880 and 1914 are similar to our own period as both are "moments in which gender issues assume a prominent position in the public consciousness, moments of gender confusion and the vigorous reassertion of traditional gender roles against serious challenges to inher-

ited configurations."[4] As we approach the turn of the millennium, the reassertion of masculinist hierarchy is being cast in terms of apocalyptic avowals of
(heterosexist) family values and the New World Order. Given the political
right's recharged impetus to restrain women's reproductive freedoms and restrict
sexual choices for gay men and lesbians, given the technological means to manage women's reproduction, and given allowances of environmental dangers to
health for the sake of economic gain, it is crucial to see how the logic of apocalypse can be used to marshal public opinion against democratic freedom.

Many of the *Education*'s warring positions are found within current feminist
versus masculinist debates.[5] Interestingly, Adams does not always take the masculinist side on these issues.[6] For example, he expresses ecofeminist values when
he challenges an unblinking faith in industrial development as progress. And his
attacks on the martial ardor of governments and nationalism's zeal for domination aligns itself with feminist critiques. On other occasions, however, he explicitly asserts derogatory views of women, as with the comment that "woman
seldom knows her own thought" (442). Most troubling—because it is more
subtle and more profound—is the way he reasserts mathematical calculation and
abstracted objectivity as prime epistemological and ethical values, thus refusing
the situated representations of the world produced by partisan subjects that genealogical thinking promotes. Since this reassertion ultimately glorifies mastery,
and is thus inconsistent with his own critique of domination, it is important to
see how irony functions to render these textual contradictions not only plausible
but compelling.

The *Education*'s presentation of such conflicting views makes it a quintessential modernist text. But, as I will show, its positioning of conflicting views is
overridden by an ironic containment of conflict. Such a movement characterizes
the modernist aesthetic, which poses conflictual realities but ultimately undermines that stance.[7] This type of modernism provides the groundwork for ironic
apocalypse, and serves as a reminder that the features of *modernism* within post-
modernism function to restore a totalizing vision while denying unity and totality
of vision. Adams offers an apocalyptic resolution in his Dynamic Theory of History. As he states it, "he was beyond measure curious to see whether the conflict
of forces would produce the new man, since no other energies seemed left on
earth to breed. The new man could only be a child born of contact between the
new and the old energies" (500). The *Education*'s concept of the new man ends
the text's struggle over gender meanings by granting full authority to a stridently
masculinist vision, and fully expects the new man will be an "American." This
vision has become stronger over the decades since Adams formalized it with his
eloquence. Its current articulations are notably less eloquent and its irony has for
the most part been reduced to a pervasive cynicism or a dull whine. What remains is the danger of the vision.

In order to show the historical emergence, discursive logic, and political consequences of ironic apocalypse, I have divided my argument into three sections. In the first, I discuss Adams's explicit response to the emergence of the new woman in the turn-of-the-century United States. The second section analyzes the ways in which the *Education*'s use of genres produces a masculinist narrative that engenders—indeed justifies—a turn to the redemptive concept of the new man. And in the third section, I show how this concept of the new man privileges modes of apocalyptic power/knowledge that pose dangers for women, children, and men who don't conform to white heterosexist values, and for the earth.

Adams and the New Women

Historians of the United States at the turn of the century mark that period of profound social and economic change as especially transforming for women's lives. For those who adhered to a society divided into separate spheres for men and women, these changes constituted a virtual breakdown of social order. For them, this order had been insured in part by women's innate moral superiority, which was in turn protected by their place in the home. During the 1880s and 1890s, working-class women entered the urban work force and middle-class women sought college education and professional careers in numbers greater than ever before. A large proportion of professional women maintained single lives, many sharing households with other women. These new women espoused women's right to careers and to the public spaces formerly reserved for men.[8]

The *Education* comments on the emergence of these new women and records Adams's unease with them in the following passage:

> One had but to pass a week in Florida, or on any of a hundred huge ocean steamers, or walk through the Place Vendome, or join a party of Cook's tourists to Jerusalem, to see that the woman had been set free; but these swarms were ephemeral like clouds of butterflies in season, blown away and lost, while the reproductive sources lay hidden. At Washington, one saw other swarms as grave gatherings of Dames or Daughters, taking themselves seriously, or brides fluttering fresh pinions; but all these shifting visions, unknown before 1840, touched the true problem slightly and superficially. Behind them, in every city, town, and farmhouse, were myriads of new types—or type-writers— telephone and telegraph girls, shop-clerks, factory-hands, running into millions on millions, and, as classes, unknown to themselves as to historians. Even the schoolmistresses were inarticulate. All these new women had been created since 1840; all were to show their meaning before 1940. (444-45)

The "true problem" Adams raises concern over, and about which he judges these women to be "inarticulate," is that of reproduction: "All these new women" were not breeding. He is certainly accurate in seeing the link between women's entrance into the public sphere and lower fertility rates. As John D'Emilio's and Estelle Freedman's review of studies on reproduction and sexuality indicates, the middle class in particular had made significant efforts and had attained considerable success in curtailing reproduction. They report that in 1900, "the total fertility of white American women stood at an average of 3.54, or fifty percent below the level of a century earlier."[9] The movement for voluntary motherhood had especially dramatic results for middle-class married women; in the 1890s, of those whose childbearing years were coming to an end, nearly half had only two or fewer children.[10]

According to Adams (and others at the time), this decline in reproduction rates boded ill for the species. His predictions reach a hyperbolic pitch when he claims that woman "had nothing to rebel against, except her own maternity" and that "if her force was to be diverted from its axis, it must find a new field, and the family must pay for it. So far as she succeeded, she must become sexless like the bees, and must leave the old energy of inertia to carry on the race" (446). Yet in response to the debates about whether species extinction might warrant state coercion, Adams takes the part of historian—whose job he insists must be objective rather than partisan: "No honest historian can take part with—or against—the forces he has to study. To him even the extinction of the human race should be merely a fact to be grouped with other vital statistics" (447). He characteristically frames the issue in terms of his personal helplessness:

> An elderly man, trying only to learn the law of social inertia and the limits of social divergence could not compel the Superintendent of the Census to ask every young woman whether she wanted children, and how many; he could not even require of an octogenarian Senate the passage of a law obliging every woman, married or not, to bear one baby—at the expense of the Treasury—before she was thirty years old, under penalty of solitary confinement for life; yet these were vital statistics in more senses than all that bore the name, and tended more directly to the foundation of a serious society in the future. He could draw no conclusion whatever except from the birth-rate. (447)

The touches of ironic humor in this passage suggest that such policies should be construed as excessive, not to mention oppressive. Moreover, Adams goes on to make the point that women themselves would ultimately decide this issue, or, as he puts it, that the "Marguerite of the future could alone decide whether she were better off than the Marguerite of the past; whether she would rather be a victim to a man, a church, or a machine" (447).

On first view, such a stance more closely echoes feminist demands for women to be able to make decisions about their reproductive capabilities than demands made by anti-birth control advocates in his time and antichoice proponents in our own. But then Henry Adams was more clever than Pat Robertson and Randall Terry combined. Closer scrutiny of Adams's formulation shows his view of womanhood to be much closer to theirs after all. The reference to Goethe's heroine critically undermines any decision women might make in their own behalf and expresses a desire for women to save men. The three paths of victimage follow what the *Education* designates as a chronology of women's history—a secularized, darkened inversion of the Ages of The Father, Son, and Holy Spirit—represented through a past of sexuality when Venus ruled, a period of allegiance to the Church when beauty and the Virgin reigned, and one moving toward a future "reserved for machine-made, collectivist females" (384, 446). The allusion to Marguerite, who redeems the very man who betrays her, retains a glimmer of hope that, even if women do "marry machinery," they will still prove to be men's redeemers. But for the most part, the hope for redemption through women is cast off with the belief that women's entry into the public sphere entailed an imitation of men, many of whom had already become "sexless." Adams represents such a fate as a tragedy, but, as he is quick to add, such a consequence would not be new, for "tragedy had been women's lot since Eve" (445-46).

While this clash between opposed feminist and masculinist discourses pervades the *Education*, the struggle becomes intensified around the issue of reproduction, as in this passage. Part of that ambivalence and intensity reflects the nature of the public debates at the time, but part is personal as well. Ernest Samuels has argued that Adams was profoundly disappointed that he and his wife never had children.[11] Whatever the reasons for the ambivalences, ambiguities, and even contradictions in these passages focusing on reproduction, a genealogical examination of them highlights the ways in which the propositions of the Dynamic Theory of History advanced in the final chapters displace overt discussion about women's reproduction and power relations between men and women while promoting an apocalyptic masculinist ideology.

Adams's proposition that history is a force beyond human intervention ultimately converts his ambivalence into advocacy of human submission to History, writ transcendent. According to this view, he may not like what is occurring, but he cannot prevent it, nor can anyone else. In regard to changes in women's social and economic status, for example, he manifests regret about women's entry into the public sphere while nonetheless deeming such a move historically inevitable. As he states, in America "the woman had been set free—volatized like Clerk Maxwell's perfect gas; almost brought to the point of explosion like steam" (444). The infelicitous metaphor of "perfect gas" to describe women's freedom expresses both the hope that women would be stable and constant and the fear of their becoming volatized and explosive.

As an advocate of separate spheres, Adams initially held out the hope that women would be able to transform the public sphere by exerting their morality in such a way as to feminize men, whom he considered the proper custodians of the public domain. The *Education* indicates that such feminization would help combat the two opposing tendencies characterizing men in the United States, whom Adams depicts as either dehumanized, having lost the capacity to respond to sensuality and beauty, or subhuman, too brutish to be feminized, like President Grant who "should have lived in a cave" (266). Ultimately the *Education* portrays Adams as giving up on the idea of feminizing men, since women were themselves becoming dehumanized.[12] Even the artists to whom he turned "as naturally as though the artist were himself a woman" (thus presuming all artists are men) were as ignorant of the mysteries of "female energy" as the rest (385-88). Citing as exceptions Walt Whitman and Bret Harte, "as far as the magazines would let him venture, and one or two painters" because they had understood "the power of sex" rather than sentimentalizing it as the rest had (385), he indicates that the forces of history were fast overriding such artistic sensibility. And although he portrays himself as having been especially responsive to beauty throughout his life, he says that as his "sixtieth year approached, the artist began to die" (350-51).

Appreciators of Adams's prose might disagree with the claim that the artist in him had begun to die, but the writings he produced from this time on are marked by a darker, more intense irony. Over the twentieth century, we have come to regard irony as the height of artistic sensibility. But we should be better attuned to the ways in which the dark irony of modernism operates in conjunction with white male elitist anxieties over urbanization, African American and women's rights, and immigration. In Adams's case, the use of irony made his masculinist advocacy of the new man acceptable to an intellectual elite. It also facilitated an acceptance of his apocalyptic claims. Adams's turn from art to science, from the Virgin to the Dynamo, from sensual nature to mechanized universe—a turn he depicts as both personal and historical—led him to ponder the possibilities in store in terms of apocalyptic inevitability. If the new woman was a sign of the times, then what of her counterpart, the new man? And how would Adams, as historian turned prophet, tell the story of the coming of the new man?

Formulating the New Man

The "Editor's Preface," composed by Adams but bearing Henry Cabot Lodge's name, opens the text with the problematic of literary form and historical narrative:

> The point on which the author failed to please himself, and could get no light from readers or friends, was the usual one of literary form.

Probably he saw it in advance, for he used to say, half in jest, that his great ambition was to complete St. Augustine's "Confessions," but that St. Augustine, like a great artist, had worked from multiplicity to unity, while he, like a small one, had to reverse the method and work back from unity to multiplicity. The scheme became unmanageable as he approached his end. (xxvii-xxviii)

As usual, Adams's self-deprecation should not lead to ready acceptance of his claims to failure. The *Education* may be read as a series of arresting experiments in literary form.[13] Its use of a number of literary genres and modes befits the subtitle Adams suggests, "A Study of Twentieth-Century Multiplicity," far more than the unitary "autobiography" affixed by an editor on the 1918 edition.

Nevertheless, there is significance to the admission that he was not altogether pleased with the work's literary form. Letters to friends are more specific regarding the difficulties of the task at hand. He commented in one letter, for example, that his message must be "sugar-coated," for the "nearer we can come to romance the more chance that somebody will read—and understand."[14] In another he conceded that he had "undertaken to do what cannot be successfully done—mix narrative and didactic purpose and style." Deciding that "a narrative style was so incompatible with a scientific or didactic style," he explains further, "I had to write a long supplementary chapter to explain in scientific terms what I could not put into narration without ruining the narrative."[15] Overall, the narrative of the *Education* does indeed depict the perilous journey of a romantic hero in quest of the holy grail of knowledge. Thus the "incompatibility" Adams refers to is not so much between romance and didacticism per se. Rather, it is more the case that the moral ideology of the romance is at odds with Adams's thesis regarding how forces of multiplicity prohibit heroism and certainty. But Adams's solution—the shift into a "scientific or didactic style"—recuperates the unity if not the narrative of romance, despite his stated commitment to represent multiplicity.

In this section, I analyze how the use of literary forms in the *Education* provides a play of meanings that is at times at odds with the "sugar-coated" and unitary frame of a romance but that ultimately employs irony to buffer a totalizing apocalyptic vision.[16] The text begins with allusions to an epic past, contrasts that to an ironic present, draws on the pastoral tradition, contrasts that to satire, shifts between satire, confession and anatomy, incorporates elements of the gothic novel and tragedy, and concludes in an ironic apocalyptic mode staged through an opposition between a dystopia and a utopia. I want to stress two points of critique in this genealogical literary analysis. First, these literary forms have a legacy of gender conventions that inform the *Education*'s many, sometimes conflicting, discourses. Second, the shift into supplementary scientific explanation puts a stop to the text's dialogical experimentation by defining the new man in overtly monological terms.

Adams himself and numerous critics have noted that the *Education* is a divided text.[17] Regarding what he designates as inherent oppositions signified by summer and winter, Adams remarks that the "bearing of the two seasons on the education of Henry Adams was no fancy; it was the most decisive force he ever knew; it ran through life, and made the division between its perplexing, warring, irreconcilable problems, irreducible opposites, with growing emphasis to the last year of study" (9). The view expressed in the initial chapter that "Life was a double thing" runs throughout the text (9). It is manifest in its devotion to and yet repudiation of beauty, its elevation of scientific explanation alongside declarations of uncertainty, and its espousal of silence in conjunction with urgings toward action (or reaction). Yet this acceptance of life as doubled does not mean that the text altogether repudiates resolution. Nor does it mean that dualism is its only structuring device. What it does suggest is that the text's narrative structurings and espoused resolutions are likely to carry the problematic of dualistic categorization.[18]

Genre analysis bears out Adams's philosophical disposition toward dualism. The initial dualism set up in the opening line is that of past versus present. The *Education* begins with allusions to an epic past through the evocation of the heroic deeds of Adams's ancestors and the other fathers of the nation. In contrast, time present, the course of his life — begun "under the shadow of Boston State House, turning its back on the house of John Hancock" — is the stuff of irony. Through irony, Adams portrays himself and his era as inferior to the epic warriors of the Revolution. Telling his story between the polarities of epic and irony formulates masculinity as divided into either victor or victim. Yet, as a self-deprecating *eiron*, Adams also suggests the superiority of self-consciousness and the creative prowess of the romantic ironist. And to the extent that his irony gravitates toward an apocalyptic vision, as it does with the concept of the new man, it resurrects epic — by convention a stridently male warrior discourse — and resituates it messianically in the future tense.

The past/present dualism is also linked to a binary gender opposition that associates the past of early childhood with a feminine sphere and the ongoing present of a maturing male with a masculine sphere. The opening pages of the *Education* evoke pleasures of fusion associated with the domestic scene and pains of separation associated with the public sphere. Adams reports that his first memories are of yellow from the sun streaming into the kitchen and the taste of baked apple, a gift to a sick child from a caring aunt (5). The first jolt he experiences within this pleasurable domain occurs when, upon his recovery, he is removed to a second, larger Boston house: "The season was midwinter, January 10, 1842, and he never forgot his acute distress for want of air under his blankets, or the noises of moving furniture" (6). This event foreshadows a more significant occurrence three years later when his childhood world is "suddenly cut apart—separated forever—in act if not in sentiment, by the opening of the Boston and Albany Railroad; the appearance of the first Cunard steamers in the bay; and the telegraphic messages which carried from Baltimore to Washington the news that Henry Clay and James K. Polk were nominated for the Presidency" (5).

Throughout the first two chapters, these dualities of sexual difference and separate spheres act in conjunction with seasonal and town/country oppositions. The use of pastoral and satiric modes helps frame traditional philosophical dualisms between body and mind. Drawing on the pastoral tradition to describe Quincy, Adams associates rural life with idyllic sensuality. Summer and the country represent a profusion of smells, textures, tastes: "To the boy Henry Adams, summer was drunken. Among senses, smell was the strongest. . . . Next to smell came taste, and the children knew the taste of everything they saw or touched, from pennyroyal and flagroot to the shell of a pignut and the letters of a spelling-book—the taste of A-B, AB, suddenly revived on the boy's tongue sixty years afterwards" (8). In contrast to this depiction of summer as a Dionysian season of fusion, a Golden Age of immediacy in which the letters of the mother tongue can be tasted, Adams employs satire to associate winter with the world that Apollonian fathers make. "Town was winter confinement, school, rule, discipline; . . . Town was restraint, law, unity" (7-8). He extends these dualities to include culture and cognition: "Winter and summer, cold and heat, town and country, force and freedom, marked two modes of life and thought, balanced like lobes of the brain" (7).[19]

Despite the fact that as a fourth child and thus of "less account" he was "in a way given to his mother" (23), as a male Adams is culturally obliged to leave her orbit and enter a different field of force in the public sphere. According to his telling, his entry into the sphere proper to his gender is the result of a battle of wills between a resisting boy wanting to remain at home and a firm and more forceful Presidential grandfather who demands his attendance at school. Significantly, the event occurs during summer, the ostensible time of freedom. Yet school is in session and attend he does (12-13). Giving his age as six or "seven at the utmost," Adams underscores the age of reason as a boy's formal move into the masculine sphere. But the nostalgic desire to reunite with the mother, to reenter the feminine sphere romanticized by the pastoral, remains and erupts as a textual return of the repressed in Adams's Dynamic Theory of History.[20]

Upon attaining the age of reason, Adams becomes variously an Augustine embarking on a journey of self-knowledge, a Swift satirizing the vulgarities of bourgeois society, a Carlyle studying the anatomy of alienation and spiritual rebirth, a Franklin pursuing self-discipline, and a Rousseau disclosing his virtues and vices to the world. These discourses of self span the field of canonized representations, which range from religious to secular, from devotional to damning, from interior revelation to exterior construction.[21] As for the goal of representing multiplicity, this plurality of discourses of self is the text's most successful expression of heterogeneity (although even here the models employed are preeminently white and male). Conversely, toward the end when the text most insists on the *fact* of multiplicity, it does so through a totalizing discourse.

The most profound point of contrast to these discourses of self occurs at the midway point in the work. Suddenly, a gothic mode takes precedence as nature becomes a dichotomized feminine force that follows the angel/demon duality so characteristic of nineteenth-century fiction.[22] We can witness this shift in the first paragraph of the chapter entitled "Free Fight," which describes the "charm of the Washington spring." Adams injects words of menace into a passage ostensibly devoted to recording his "delight" in the landscape:

> The Potomac and its tributaries *squandered* beauty. Rock Creek was as *wild* as the Rocky Mountains. Here and there a Negro log cabin alone *disturbed* the dogwood and the judas-tree, the azalea and the laurel. The tulip and the chestnut gave no sense of *struggle* against a *stingy* nature. The soft, full outlines of the landscape carried no hidden *horror* of glaciers in its bosom." (268, emphasis mine)

This is a far remove from the pastoral landscape of the Quincy chapter. Now, rather than the full presence of sensuality associated with childhood's summer and the intrusion of discomfort or pain associated with winter, Adams focuses on spring to intimate and yet deny a betrayal lurking within nature's promise to nurture. "No European spring had shown him the same intermixture of delicate grace and passionate depravity that marked the Maryland May" (268). That nature's combination of grace and depravity is unique to the U.S. landscape or to spring is far from Adams's point, for these hints of nature's destructive potential become the self-pronounced final lesson in his education, a lesson he learns surrounded by the European landscape in summer (287). It is a lesson that assumes a white/black hierarchy, manifest here in its observation that a Negro log cabin could "disturb," perhaps irredeemably, the beauty of nature. And it is a lesson that follows the masculinist concept of femininity in which womanhood is defined as both innocent and fallen, man's savior and destroyer. As Nina Auerbach points out, these oppositions within Victorian womanhood "are the many faces of a single image. The mobile and militant woman is the source of the placid self-renouncing paragon of official veneration; the demonic angel rises from the angel in the house."[23]

Adams's "last lesson — the sum and term of education" begins with the death of his sister following a chance event that threw her into ten days of "fiendish torture" from "lockjaw" (tetanus), after which she died. He recounts his emotional pain through metaphors of male powerlessness and female sexual vengeance, images of longstanding apocalyptic status that were reinvigorated for men of the Victorian era threatened by women's agency. These metaphors placed the onus of sexual power on women—at least rhetorically. Before his sister's death, he states, "He had never seen Nature—only her surface—the sugar coating that she shows to youth" (287). In "Chaos" Nature becomes a Lilith, a whore of Babylon, a vampire-harlot or she-demon who delights in torturing her victims, who, even when female, are described through metaphors of masculine suffering. To indicate his sister's courage, for example, he describes her as "a soldier sabred in battle" (288). In juxtaposing the image of her body, growing rigid with the "terrors of lockjaw," against the "rich and sensuous surroundings" that Nature has ostentatiously lavished on the Italian countryside, her body becomes an erect but wounded phallus, a symbol of male power victimized by the demonically feminine. "Nature enjoyed it, played with it," Adams writes, "the horror added to her charms, she liked the torture, and smothered her victim with caresses. Never had one seen her so winning" (288). Nature as witch, seductress, whore, is thus a castrating power—a phallic woman—that threatens to go on "sabring men and women with the same air of sensual pleasure" with which his sister was brought down (288).[24]

Against Nature's nightmare power, Adams represents himself as impotent, emasculated, the boundaries of his selfhood dissolved: "the human mind felt itself stripped naked, vibrating in a void of shapeless energies, with resistless mass, colliding, crushing, wasting, and destroying what these same energies had created and labored from eternity to perfect" (288). Nature strips him, humiliates him, and then sadistically annihilates him. Thus Adams's anger, grief, and frustration over his sister's death is displaced onto a demonically feminine Nature and directed back at him, rendering him powerless, unable to save her. Nature becomes an eroticized, death-dealing, feminized force responsible for human vulnerability to death.[25]

In the *Education* Nature is never again to be depicted as a solely innocent, nurturing feminine power, although Adams writes that he strove to recreate that illusion for himself. After his sister's death he describes the horror he experienced from witnessing Nature's "reality" through metaphors suggesting unease with the "reality" of an unclothed feminine body. He reports that he traveled to Mont Blanc so that he might recuperate, but for "the first time in his life, Mont Blanc for a moment looked to him what it was—a chaos of anarchic and purposeless forces—and he needed days of repose to see it clothe itself again with the illusions of his senses, the white purity of its snows, the splendor of its light, and the infinity of its heavenly peace" (289). And although "Nature was kind; Lake Geneva was beautiful beyond itself, and the Alps put on charms real as terrors" (289), he finds that once he has lifted this veil of Maya, he is neither able to re-cover the sight nor recover from it. The dichotomy in this passage between illusion and truth is played out metaphorically in the polarity between the charms of the veiled female body, which promise purity, splendor, and peace, and the terrors of the unveiled one, which reveal impurity, darkness, and chaos. Nature's reality (with civilization in tow) Adams suggests, is like a woman's unveiled body, an eroticized body that burdens the viewer with desire and dread, indeed, with a desire that is dreadful. And "before the illusions of Nature were wholly restored, the illusions of Europe suddenly vanished" with Europe's entry into "the full chaos of war" (289).

Following this outbreak of chaos, chapters 20 through 24, covering the years from 1871 to 1900, depict Adams as a tragic figure, even though these decades were his most productive in terms of publication.[26] Ever more an *eiron*, his tragedy lies in a series of failures of education. Dissatisfied with the standard educational system, "which could only lead to inertia" (303), he leaves Harvard. The triumph of capitalistic forces around the issue of the gold standard seems to mark the end of possibilities of further education. And then, as suddenly as his world fell apart with the death of his sister, he is wrenched from tragic decline at the World's Fair of 1900.

The first decade of the twentieth century begins Adams's education again. Correspondingly, the chapter entitled "The Dynamo and the Virgin (1900)" marks the beginning of another genre shift, from the tragic to the apocalyptic. The apocalyptic mode dramatizes the importance of the coming of the new man, making Adams in the great hall of dynamos the prophet at the moment of epiphany. With this shift, the internally dichotomized feminine power of gothicized Nature becomes the apocalyptic Force that he calls the "supersensual multiverse." Adams argues that an acceleration of force had actually brought about new energies. Over the centuries, "As Nature developed her hidden energies, they tended to become destructive," and during the century occupying the major portion of his life, the "stupendous acceleration" of these forces attained a qualitatively different status, ending "in 1900 with the appearance of the new class of supersensual forces" (486). This "supersensual multiverse" is one of the most problematic features of Adams's problem-raising account of education, for the concept of supersensuality in his Dynamic Theory of History supports sexual and gender hierarchies integral to apocalyptic discourse.

The Coming of the New Man

As the previous chapters indicate, the production of apocalyptic power/knowledge is a legacy of Judeo-Christian heritage, but apocalyptic thought has been neither unified nor continuous. It has emerged in strikingly different historical contexts and has taken dramatically different forms over the centuries, from the Old Testament book of Daniel, to the early Christian texts of Origen and Tertullian, the medieval writing of Joachim of Fiore, the seventeenth-century poetry of John Milton, the eighteenth-century treatises of Jonathan Edwards, the nineteenth-century political tracts of Karl Marx, and the twentieth-century nuclear Armageddon predictions of Hal Lindsey. Bearing in mind the vastly differing ideological directions of these texts, they are all nonetheless apocalyptic insofar as they envision an end to history as it has been known, attribute that end to a force greater than humanity, call for action in the name of a higher cause (metaphysical or political), and forecast a new era. Adams's version of apocalypse is one that introduces natural forces as the higher cause of transformation. This concept of nature begins from a mode of divine apocalypse but then shifts into technological apocalypse. In the *Education*, the forces of nature—or, in Adams's terms, the multiverse—collide with humanity's technological prowess. As I have said, the technological mode of apocalypse is one that has increasingly been invoked in the twentieth century. In Adams's case, technology poses such a threat that only a shift toward irony can accommodate his ambivalence toward the possibility of humanity's self-made destruction.

Adams dates his final phase of education from the Great Exposition of 1900, portraying himself humbled there before the new "symbol of infinity." At that moment, "the continuity snapped" (457) and the "Virgin's pilgrim" became the dynamo's champion.[27] He declares the era over in which the Virgin could be an evocative moral and aesthetic force. According to this narrative of the rise and fall of unity, both men and women were responsible first for creating that illusion and then for succumbing to it. His explanation, however, is not entirely consistent with this assertion, for it employs sexual imagery and gender stereotypes that subtly shift the burden to women and feminine power.

Initially the argument combines images suggestive of feminine disrobing and masculine ejaculation. "As history unveiled itself," Adams argues, associating history with the naked body of Nature he had witnessed upon his sister's death, "man's mind had behaved like a young pearl oyster, secreting its universe to suit its conditions until it had built up a shell of *nacre* that embodied all its notions of the perfect. Man knew it was true because he made it, and he loved it for the same reason" (458). But the "man's part in the Universe was secondary" compared to the woman's. Women bear primary responsibility for both the creation and the demise of the beguiling illusion of unity, for the woman "conceived herself and her family as the centre and flower of an ordered universe which she knew to be unity because she had made it after the image of her own fecundity" (459). According to Adams, then, the woman, even more than the man, is a parthenogenetic creator of unity. Her myth was so powerful that it even "compell[ed] the man to accept the Virgin as guardian of the man's God" (458). Woman is the master of illusion, man her gullible slave.

At this point in the text, the gender categories become unsettled and the sexual imagery violent. The confusions and reversals here (inadvertently) reveal the ways that heterosexism simultaneously constructs misogyny, homoeroticism, and homophobia. Adams indicates that although "neither man nor woman ever wanted to quit this Eden of their own invention" (459), history's accelerating forces could no longer be resisted even by woman's narcisstic unity. Returning to the image of the young pearl oyster, the passage shifts to an image of assault to describe the oyster's fate: "Although the oyster might perhaps assimilate or embalm a grain of sand forced into its aperture, it could only perish in face of the cyclonic hurricane or volcanic upheaval of its bed" (459). Violated by the grain of sand, man's mind accommodates the intrusive grain of sand by creating a pearl, but symbolically the pearl is an embalmed fetus. History—continuing to unveil itself—finally so disrupts the oyster's bed (a sick bed? a marriage bed? a Procrustean bed? bedlam?) that it, man's mind, can no longer survive the violence of the grains of sand forced into its "aperture." The next sentence suddenly switches to a feminine pronoun: "Her supersensual chaos killed her" (459). Blame for the upheaval of the oyster's bed is thus placed onto "her," explicitly assigning fault to a feminized Force for the metaphorical rape of man's mind, which, in the wake of this destructive chaos, expels humanity from its second Eden, a paradise of imagined unity.

Adams portrays himself as wishing in vain for a return to the old order of things: "As a matter of taste, he greatly preferred his eighteenth-century education when God was a father and nature a mother, and all was for the best in a scientific universe" (458). If the old model that Adams preferred was based on an ideal bourgeois family with humanity as the children of God and Nature, then his new model seems to be based on what the old one requires but denies: the sexual union of the father and the mother. Although Adams as Oedipal son represses knowledge of parental *jouissance*, the repressed returns with all the trappings of the attraction-repulsion dynamic of Victorian sexuality, though in highly displaced form.[28] In Adams's new model, the "mind of man" must "penetrate" the disembodied supersensual universe (487). In keeping with Victorian culture's perceptions of sexuality as precariously threatening and blissful as well as with the *Education*'s propensity for dualistic conceptualization, Adams describes this union as *either* doomed *or* fortuitous, for the "universe may be—as it has always been—either a supersensuous chaos or a divine unity, which irresistibly attracts, and is either life or death to *penetrate*" (487, emphasis mine).

Whether the mind of man will be destroyed in the chaos or restored to a new wholeness remains uncertain, but it is foolish, he indicates, to believe that such power can be resisted. In its final avatar in the *Education*, Nature as a feminized supersensual universe is thus represented as *either* tomb (supersensuous chaos) *or* womb (divine unity). This dichotomy denies and reveals its anxiety over the womb *as* tomb, a masculinist fear of women's sexuality, which in its multiplicity of pleasures seems both blissful and chaotic, and of women's procreative capacity, which requires male fertilization but upon conception has no need of men. Such anxiety is the inevitable residue of a mind/body split in which, as is the case here, mind (designated as masculine) is threatened by the body (designated as feminine and sexual). In the *Education* the individual female body is made less threatening only by displacing and abstracting its sensuality as the *super*sensual, which is "beyond the lines of force felt by the senses" (487). While Adams might find relief in escaping sensory response, his model does not relinquish the power dynamics of masculinist vision: Adams's insistence on penetration by the mind of man of the feminized universe returns agency to a now-masculinized humanity in heterosexualized intercourse with a feminized supersensual Force.

Important to the convergence of the technological and ironic modes of apocalypse in the *Education* is the way that the womb/tomb opposition within Adams's concept of the supersensual multiverse brings together what had historically been regarded as mutually exclusive elements: woman and machine. Still cast as an apocalyptic vision of the future, the feminized supersensual multiverse metamorphosizes into mechanical force. In keeping with the dual consciousness of apocalyptic thinking, which leads some to hope and others to despair, he depicts this future as being either utopian or dystopian.[29] As symbolic tomb, the dystopian supersensual multiverse is a dehumanized, mechanized, masculinized woman writ large who threatens castration, a view linked to Adams's anxiety over "machine-made, collectivist women." The *Education* thus allows us to see the trajectory of thought leading to what Marshall McLuhan described as "one of the most peculiar features of our world — the interfusion of sex and technology . . . a widely occurring cluster image of sex, technology, and death which constitutes the mystery of the mechanical bride."[30]

Over the course of the twentieth century, Adams's conceptualization has been literalized in the material reality of the cyborg, raising new possibilities for thought that have informed a variety of masculinist and feminist texts, ranging from science fiction to the history of science. From a feminist perspective, Donna Haraway has used the cyborg as a means to refute the kind of dichotomous thinking that structures the *Education* as well as other instances of the mechanical bride. Haraway argues that the ways in which cyborgs break down the boundaries between humans and machines challenge human-centric essentialism. In the cyborg, she writes, "Nature and culture are reworked; the one can no longer be the resource for appropriation or incorporation by the other" (67). But Adams's representation of women as increasingly cyborgian should make us wary of gravitating toward a form of cyborg-centric essentialism. There are no cyborgs per se, only understandings of their significance. Adams's understanding is ridden with androcentrism. And current methods of assuaging men's and women's anxieties about feminist gains — as evidenced in Hollywood films such as *Blade Runner* and *Terminator II* — indicate that such appropriation and incorporation do in fact occur with relative ease.[31]

At the same time that Adams portrays the multiverse as mechanized, he personifies it in a way reminiscent of the episode of his sister's death, in which Nature exhibits ruthless feminine power over helpless human beings. Arguing that Nature had long been harboring a vengeful force of destruction, he indicates that this force could no longer be hidden from sight. Once it "had detached itself from the unknown universe of energy" (495), Nature's hostility became apparent: "Every day Nature violently revolted, causing so-called accidents with enormous destruction of property and life, while plainly laughing at man, who helplessly groaned, and shrieked, and shuddered, but never for a single instant could stop" (495). The supersensual universe is both feminine demon and dynamo, both whorish punisher of men and sexless machine. Figuring the new women and/or the universe in such feminized terms of cruelty bespeaks the logic of a master/slave dialectic, which justifies the overcoming of the feminine or machine "masters" by their oppressed "slaves," their sons and lovers.[32]

But as I have indicated, feminine cruelty is not the exclusive logic in the *Education*. The depiction of the demon/dynamo is matched by the portrayal of the supersensual universe as a feminine redeemer. The *Education*'s dual representation of the feminine echoes apocalyptic tradition from both the Old and New Testaments. Eve as first mother and first temptress and Mary as the virginal mother and redeemer provide the paradigmatic dichotomy that has been so productive of women's oppression. New Testament apocalyptic tradition perpetuates this gender duality by pitting the abominable whore of Babylon against the holy woman forced into the wilderness. In Revelation, the holy woman, "clothed with the sun, and the moon under her feet, and upon her head a crown of twelve stars," gives birth to the messianic male child who is "destined to rule all nations with a rod of iron" (12:1-5). In Adams's apocalypse, the supersensual universe that promises to give birth to the new man combines the cunning selfishness of the temptress and the splendid selflessness of the redeemer.

Although the *Education* incorporates these dichotomous portrayals of women, it departs from the biblical representation of cities as feminine. Christ's "rightful rule" begins with the fall of Babylon and the defeat of the Antichrist, events that establish the New Jerusalem for the millennium. Modern gender metaphors of cities have tended toward assigning urban spaces as masculine, in opposition to a feminine pastoral space. Adams is in accordance with this. Also, the *Education* remains suspended in doubt about whether Babylon will fall. The final chapter summons the New York skyline as a Babylon not yet transformed:

> The outline of the city became frantic in its effort to explain something
> that defied meaning. Power seemed to have outgrown its servitude and
> to have asserted its freedom. The cylinder had exploded, and thrown
> great masses of stone and steam against the sky. The city had the air
> and movement of hysteria, and the citizens were crying, in every accent
> of anger and alarm, that the new forces must at any cost be brought
> under control. (499)

Thus casting New York as on the edge of history's final rupture, Adams prophetically observes that "the new man seemed close at hand, for the old one had plainly reached the end of his strength, and his failure had become catastrophic" (499). And yet the exhaustion endemic to ironic apocalypse thwarts assurance of the coming of the new man: "The two-thousand years failure of Christianity roared upward from Broadway, and no Constantine the Great was in sight" (500).

Despite this sense of irony, Adams remains captivated by the possibility of an elect humanity. As symbolic womb of the new era, from which the new city and the new man were to emerge, the supersensual universe holds out an Oedipalized utopian possibility. For even as this multiverse is cast as demon and dynamo, it is as well the Great Mother/lover with whom the mind might attain the bliss of union and be reborn. Adams insists that "the mind could gain nothing by flight or by fight; it must merge in its supersensual multiverse, or succumb to it" (461) and that the "mind of man" must continue to enlarge its "field of complexity . . . even into chaos, until the reservoirs of sensuous or supersensuous energies are exhausted, or cease to affect him, or until he succumbs to their excess" (487). These expressions of a desire to merge with the supersensual multiverse are less paradoxical when considered in relation to the *Education*'s early pastoral dream, signified by summer and its longing for envelopment in the nurturance of a feminine world seen to stave off mutability, responsibility, death itself.

The espousal of merging with an omnipotent Force is also part of a Puritan legacy. In Puritan theology, acknowledgment of one's helplessness before an all-powerful God was necessary for the full restoration of the soul after death, a merging with the divine for eternity. Paradoxically, according to this view, only through complete surrender could a person achieve victory over the fallen state of humanity. Although Adams retains the necessity of submission and the desire to merge, he departs from Puritan representations in the way he genders this Almighty Force as feminine. As Ivy Schweitzer has shown, Puritan discourse also appropriated the feminine, but did so by making the male sinner feminine. In this case, the sinner's desire for merging with God is figured as a "radical passivity" that was understood as feminine. God remains the Father, and the sinner seeks to become womanly and compliant, desiring "the blinding and all-powerful penetration by a superior force."[33] As Schweitzer points out, this figuration of the feminine operates to maintain a hierarchy of God over man and man over woman.

If at first sight Adams's engendering of the multiverse as feminine and his admonitions for a masculine humanity to merge with the multiverse seem to challenge this hierarchy, a closer look reveals that this is not the case after all. His advocacy of surrender is actually a means to greater power, for submission to the multiverse is precisely what is to bring forth the new man. If humanity can learn to submit to the Force of the multiverse, Adams states boldly in his version of the Nietzschean myth of the *Übermensch*, the "child born of contact between the new and the old energies" (500) will be "a sort of God compared with any former creation of nature. At the rate of progress since 1800, every American who lived to the year 2000 would know how to control unlimited power" (496). This evocation of mastery of unlimited power is profoundly inconsistent with the *Education*'s earlier condemnation of power. It is all the more striking when compared to an 1862 letter he wrote to his brother Charles about human and planetary vulnerability in the face of extensions of scientific power:

> You may think all this nonsense, but I tell you these times are great. Man has mounted science and is now run away with. I firmly believe that before many centuries more, science will be the master of man. The engines he will have invented will be beyond his strength to control. Some day science may have the existence of mankind in its power, and the human race commit suicide by blowing up the world.[34]

Whereas the initial stages of Adams's education entailed learning the destructiveness of an "instinct for power [that] was blind" (446), the *Education*'s final proposals for merging with the supersensual multiverse question the blindness while glorifying the value of the "instinct."[35] Through the Dynamic Theory of History, Adams metaphorizes the universe as a cyborgian Force that might give birth to a "new social mind" capable of thinking "in complexities unimaginable to an earlier mind" (497). Rather than envisioning this offspring as a challenger of godlike knowledge, Adams's utopian vision endorses ideals of enhanced mastery and control. Despite its mission to espouse a completely new formula of history, then, the *Education*'s Dynamic Theory of History patches handed-down clothing to suit a Cartesian manikin.[36]

The sense of apocalyptic urgency found in the *Education* is of course hardly unique to Henry Adams. It has surfaced throughout this century, in ideas of divine as well as technological apocalypse. Adams added to those modes a strain of irony that has over the century become recognizably distinct from the other two. In all three of these modes, the apocalyptic rhetoric of the end of time gains momentum when millennial designations such as the year 2000 coincide with horizons displaying nuclear plants, wasted stretches of land, famine, and a worldwide AIDS crisis. Of special importance to genealogical inquiry are the ways apocalyptic discourses are used to justify control over women's reproduction, medical surveillance, the risk of military "solutions" to global politics, and the pollution of the earth from industrial waste. In an essay entitled "Babies, Heroic Experts, and a Poisoned Earth," Irene Diamond demonstrates how this particular conjunction of expertise and power promotes an acceptance of mastery and control as desirable ends. Using an ecofeminist perspective, she relocates issues of technology from an "ethic of control and management" to an "ethics of interconnectedness [that] would take heed of the intricate webs that link the birth and well-being of all animals—human as well as nonhuman—with the well-being of the Earth's ecosystems."[37]

For the most part, Adams's appeal for a new man reasserts the old patriarchal desire for mastery over women and the earth. But his appeals for a "new type of man" (499) are not entirely without genealogical critical insight themselves, and it is worth giving those aspects some emphasis. When the *Education* argues that "the new American would need to think in contradictions" (498), it challenges the either/or dualisms of Western logic. And when it designates the universe as a multiverse, it proposes that teleological conceptualizations offer a false unity with hopes for certainty that are inevitably unavailable. The sustained repetition of "if" in the following passage demonstrates how inconclusiveness pervades Adams's propositions of a Dynamic Theory:

> If any analogy whatever existed between the human mind, on one side, and the laws of motion, on the other, the mind had already entered a field of attraction so violent that it must immediately pass beyond, into new equilibrium, like the Comet of Newton, to suffer dissipation altogether, like meteoroids in the earth's atmosphere. If it behaved like an explosive, it must rapidly recover equilibrium; if it behaved like a vegetable, it must reach its limits of growth; and even if it acted like the earlier creations of energy—the saurians and sharks—it must have nearly reached the limits of its expansion. If science were to go on doubling or quadrupling its complexities every ten years, even mathematics would soon succumb. An average mind had succumbed already in 1850; it could no longer understand the problem in 1900. (496).

In the closing pages of the *Education* doubt itself becomes thematic. Adams suggests that, along with silence and good-temper, doubt is a "mark of sense" because one could never finally ascertain "whether the force that educated was really man or nature—mind or motion" (501). Such doubt may be understood as a crisis of Cartesian certitude; in that sense, it functions as a challenge to masculinist discourses of mastery and control.

But within the apocalyptic logic that pervades the *Education*, this doubt is finally less a challenge to and more the core dilemma of twentieth-century masculinist abjection, otherwise known as epistemological crisis. Having begun with the premise of duality between men and women, masculinity and femininity, domination and submission, the *Education*'s critique remains caught in the revolving door of naturalized sex and gender polarization, at times asserting the traditional hierarchies, at other times reversing them. As a means of ending this endless circling, Adams's Dynamic Theory of History dreams the possibility of a new kind of man breaking through. But what finally bursts through the door is an all-too-recognizable figure of dominion.[38]

Behold, I stand at the door, and knock: if any man hear my voice, and open the door, I will come in to him, and I will sup with him, and he with me.

To him that overcometh will I grant to sit with me in my throne, even as I also overcame, and am set down with my Father in his throne. (Revelation 3:20-21)

Chapter 5
"Woman Got de Key":
Zora Neale Hurston and Resistance to Apocalypse

*Fear not; I am the first and the last; I am he that liveth, and was
dead; and behold, I am alive for evermore, Amen; and have the
keys of hell and of death.*

Revelation 1:17-18

*Consider that with tolerance and patience, we godly demons may
breed a noble world in a few hundred generations or so. Maybe all
of us who do not have the good fortune to meet, or meet again, in
this world, will meet at a barbeque.*

Zora Neale Hurston,
Dust Tracks on a Road[1]

I grew up five miles away from where Zora Neale Hurston grew up. In those pre-
Disney World years, the landscape between Orlando and Eatonville, Florida,
yielded little acknowledgment of geographic boundary difference. The starkly
flat stretch of land leaves anyone outdoors vulnerable to the scorching sun. But
it's also sprinkled with tiny lakes that give off a little coolness, and you can get
relief from the heat under the large oak trees draped with Spanish moss. So a
traveler would be hard put to distinguish where Orlando leaves off and Eatonville begins. Yet that five miles might as well have been five hundred. The social,
economic, and cultural boundaries between my all-white suburban neighborhood and elementary and secondary schools in Orlando and those of
Eatonville—the first all-black incorporated township in the United States—
were so rigidly drawn that I never even heard the name of Eatonville's famous
author until I attended graduate school in the Midwest in the late 1970s and
early 1980s.

But as a teenager I did cross the geographic divide between Orlando and
Eatonville. This was because I had heard so many warnings from my mother
about not getting "stranded" there. These enigmatic cautions, which I received
along with a driver's license on my sixteenth birthday, were a matter of course in
1962 in the South, pervaded as it was by white Southern anxiety about white
girls and women being raped by black men. Having grown up in the 1950s, and
therefore as one of the B-movie generation fascinated by the idea of sexual adventure and eroticized racism, my Catholic imagination (in both senses of the
term) was captivated, that is to say titillated, by the drama of risking that trip

across the town borders. So rather than heeding my mother's warnings to stay away, one steamy summer night I felt impelled to drive—with my heart racing, and with car doors locked and windows rolled tight—through the streets of Eatonville, trying to see the dangers that lurked there.

Much to my disappointment, Eatonville was not the sexual hotbed I expected. Rather than transgression on every corner, the main street had small stores, a church, and a post office. Hungerford High School looked a lot like the Catholic high school I attended in Orlando. Some people were standing about in groups talking and laughing with each other. Some couples were strolling down the street. Despite not finding what I expected, I didn't altogether reject what I had been told. I wish I could say that this experience dramatically overturned my beliefs about African American life, my mother's cautions, and images of blacks in films and television. But this was not entirely the case. For many years, and despite various civil rights activities, Eatonville remained in my imaginary a place of combined desire and fear. Nearly thirty years after my first trip to Eatonville, I returned there for the Second Annual Zora Neale Hurston Conference in 1991. One of the ironies about this for me now is that I first read Hurston because my mother sent me a copy of *Their Eyes Were Watching God* for my thirty-sixth birthday. So exactly two decades to the day after warning me away from Eatonville, my mother ushered me into that once-forbidden place— into at least the fictional version of it.

I recount this here for several reasons. One is because it wasn't until I read Zora Neale Hurston's portrayals of Eatonville and its residents that I really began to understand just how deeply set the stereotypes of race, sexuality, and gender that constituted my upbringing were. The second reason follows from the first: reading Hurston altered my knowledge context in a way that reading cultural theory had not. And the third reason follows from it: this altered context has helped me realize how difficult it is to depict stereotypes without reinforcing and perpetuating them. This is an important problematic for genealogical literary and film analysis. Hurston's prose—like Adams's—is filled with such stereotypes. What are we to make of them? Do they have an effect similar to those of *The Education of Henry Adams*? That is, do Hurston's representations of sexuality, gender, and race restore apocalyptic categories as Adams's do, especially since she, like Adams, also incorporates biblical images into her texts? I don't think so.

In this chapter I examine Hurston's use of such stereotypes as resistance to apocalypse. Thinking about Hurston's writings and their critical reception has helped me isolate the place ascribed to literature within the two misconceptions that often arise regarding resistance that I have discussed in previous chapters. One common misconception about resistance subscribes to a theory of power in which power is something held by one group or institution and withheld from another. In this case, resistance is defined as the seizure of power by the group that was under the thumb of the other (most typically seen as the state). It follows from this view that literature or art generally could never constitute resistance; from this view, literature will always be seen as either irrelevant to power, naively complicitous with it, or anemic in the face of challenging it.

This view of power is inadequate for several reasons. Although (as I argued in chapter 1 and explain more fully in chapter 3) decentralizing control is a way to alter the deployment of alliance, the centralization of power of that deployment simply no longer prevails in the United States as the only or even the primary power relation. The deployments of sexuality and hyperreality cannot be addressed through the model of revolution forged by either Enlightenment or Marxist political action. Understanding power as multiple relations of force enables us to discern the role of resistance as integral to those relations and to see the ways in which entrenched resistances can make revolutions possible. A genealogical perspective analyzes cultural documents such as literary texts as a discursive networks of power relations. That is, literary texts and other cultural documents are part of a culture's production of knowledge. The specific history and standing of certain texts—those sacralized as literature—help produce a society's regime of truth, while those that resist and challenge that regime are likely to be subjugated. Genealogical literary criticism takes both the sacralized and the subjugated within its purview.

A second misconception is the "litmus test" notion, which assumes that an act *in and of itself* either is or is not an act of resistance. Contrary to this view, I hold that an act, including a discursive act like a literary text, is an act of resistance only in relation to a network of power. Resistance is that which blocks existing power relations or enables an alteration in them. Thus, as I argued in regard to genealogical feminism, judgments about resistances can only be answered in terms of consequence. But of course consequences are not always recognized as such, nor is a consequence a one-time event, so such judgments will always be provisional. Furthermore, resistance may occur at the time of the act itself (or when a given text first appears), but it may also occur subsequently in reflection on that act (or text) within a different set of power relations. On this account, it is not in the interest of genealogical literary criticism to have the last word on a given text. An act that constitutes resistance one day is not necessarily an act of resistance the next, since power relations are continually shifting. A given act is subject to changing meaning, depending on cultural context and moment. Overturning a certain power relation may be subversive of hierarchy initially, only to reinstate hierarchy in another guise. It may also be the case that an act that intervenes against one social law may be complicitous with another. And if a given act of resistance is recognized as such, it will likely be dealt with so as to diffuse its effects by various means, from direct suppression to cooptation.

This understanding of resistance is what leads me to argue that although biblical imagery and race, sex, and gender stereotypes appear in Hurston's prose, their presence does not constitute or promote apocalyptic power/knowledge. In order to grasp relations of power, resistance, and literature, genealogical literary criticism needs to take into account several intersecting contexts: the social context out of which the text was composed, the social context from which the critic reads, the canonical context, the context of intertextuality, and the plot, as narrative context, of the text. The specific focus of this chapter is on Hurston's retellings of the biblical book of Genesis, briefly in a tale told by Mathilda Moseley in *Mules and Men*, Hurston's collection of folktales, and more fully in her best-known but not often analyzed short story, "The Gilded Six-Bits." These two pieces, both of which were initially published in the 1930s, exemplify the ways in which she subverts sexual, race, and gender stereotypes by giving them a twist that undermines them. Hurston's subversion of these stereotypes is an entertaining and astute form of literary resistance to apocalypse.

The more general focus here is on Hurston as a leading intellectual of the modernist era in the United States. As in the previous chapter, I want to show the continuing relevance of modernist texts in postmodern times. As with Adams, the themes that Hurston's texts present illuminate some of the central features of apocalyptic thought in regard to gender, reproduction, and ethics, which emerged in the first decades of the twentieth century and which have come to define apocalypse in the 1990s. But Adams has currency today for reflections on the end of the century in a way that Hurston does not. For example, in an essay for *Time* magazine called "The Year 2000: Is It the End—or Just the Beginning?," Henry Grunwald evoked Adams by saying that "were he around today, it is the computer, not the dynamo, that would impress him with its occult powers and emanations of moral force." And in keeping with Adams's ambivalence toward power, Grunwald cautions on one hand that "Americans" should "not assume that the next millennium will be the Millennium," while on the other hand he exhorts that the "year 2000 could very well open a second American Century, given a major, national effort of will."[2] It is far less likely for someone like Grunwald to draw on Hurston because she problematizes apocalyptic assumptions rather than perpetuating them as Adams does.

Hurston's irreverent stance toward apocalyptic logic is one of the reasons she was not canonized in the literary tradition as Adams was, although the academic literary battles over the canon in 1970s and 1980s have now recovered her importance for the Harlem Renaissance and have gotten her texts reprinted. In contrast to Adams's apocalyptic use of biblical allusion, which yearns for certainty and has an irony that turns dark, Hurston's intertextual weaving tolerates uncertainty and uses parody that is playful. Although this playful quality does not dull Hurston's critical edge—indeed, I hope to show how it sharpens it—it may well be the reason that critics have ignored the ironic and subversive handling of intricate, complex, and contradictory gender dynamics manifest throughout her writings. I would surmise that the tendency within literary criticism generally to privilege dark irony over parody is indicative of traditional criticism's ingrained apocalypticism. Literary criticism in U.S. academia tends to canonize the prophetic over the present-day and lamentation over critique.

By reading Mathilda Moseley's folktale and "The Gilded Six-Bits" as Genesis retold I seek to illuminate Hurston's anti-apocalyptic stance. This is not to say that her fictional and nonfictional texts refute apocalyptic thought entirely or explicitly; they reserve judgment on tenets integral to apocalypse, such as an eternal afterlife. Nor is it to claim that they are anti-Christian, although her writings do often expose the racist hypocrisy of white Christianity. It is to stress that (as is indicated in the passage from *Dust Tracks* that serves as my epigraph), without turning her back on hope for a better day, Hurston confronts the hardships of the present and embraces its pleasures. By fostering "tolerance and patience," her writings displace two pillars of the apocalyptic edifice: intolerance of differences and impatience for the future.

In the "Introduction" to *Mules and Men*, Hurston remarks that in thinking about the tales she had heard throughout her Eatonville childhood, "even the Bible was made over to suit our vivid imagination."[3] Out of the seventy tales collected in that work, one of the most arresting is the tale attributed to Mathilda Moseley, for not only is it one of the few tales told by a woman, it is also one of the few that specifically focuses on power relations between men and women.[4] As Hurston indicated, this tale is a making over of biblical discourse, in this case of one of the pivotal narratives of apocalypse—the creation of Adam and Eve and their fall. The scene for this particular tale is a familiar one for Hurston readers—the Eatonville store porch where "the gregarious part of the town's population gathered" (19). When Mathilda Moseley takes her turn in tale-telling, she does so in defense of women who have just been accused by George Thomas of having "plenty hips, plenty mouf and no brains (30)." Her turn to tell a story is set up by an exchange between her and her husband, B. Moseley:

> "Oh, yes, womens is got sense too," Mathilda Moseley jumped in. "But they got too much sense to go 'round braggin about it like y'all do. De lady people always got de advantage of men's because God fixed it dat way."
> "What ole black advantage is y'all got?" B. Moseley asked indignantly.
> "We got all de strength and all de law and all de money and you can't git a thing but whut we jes' take pity on you and give you."
> "And dat's jus' de point," said Mathilda triumphantly. "You *do* give it to us, but how come you do it?" (30)

Buoyed by the victory of having led B. Moseley unwittingly to state women's advantage over men, she then provides the history for why "woman got de key." According to the Mathilda Moseley version of Genesis, "in de very first days, God made a man and a woman and put 'em in a house together to live" (31). In those days, men and women had the same amount of strength and performed the same types of work. They fought sometimes—but "neither one could whip de other one" (31). Eventually the man begins to resent this equality, and he goes, not to the devil, but off to heaven to find God. He pleads with God to grant him more strength than the woman, and God does. What does the man do with his new strength? He returns home and beats the woman. The woman then journeys to heaven and beseeches God to "Jus gimme de same as you give him." God replies that he is unable to, because he has already granted the man's wish for *more* strength.

At that point, the woman goes straight to the devil, who instructs her to go back to heaven and ask God for the keys hanging by the mantelpiece. When she returns with the keys, the devil explains their value. The first key is for the kitchen, because, as the devil says, the man "always favors his stomach"; the second is for the bedroom, because "he don't like to be shut out from dat neither"; and the third is to the cradle because he doesn't want "to be cut off from his generations at all" (33). With the devil's advice and her new devices for directing or refusing the man's desires, the woman returns home and promptly locks all three doors. When the man discovers that his greater strength is no match for the locks, he goes back to heaven to plead his cause with God:

> "Well, Ole Maker, please gimme some keys jus' lak 'em so she can't git full control."
> "No, Man, what Ah give Ah give. Woman got de key."
> "How kin Ah know 'bout my generations?"
> "Ast de woman." (34)

And ever since this time women have been able, as Mathilda Moseley puts it in ending her tale, "to put de bridle" on men. Now, putting a bridle on a man is a way of saying that a woman is in a power relation with a man and that she has at that particular moment gained the advantage. But I want to emphasize here that, according to the folktale, such bridling is not in and of itself an overturning of the male-dominant power relations that were consolidated after the Maker grants man an unequal amount of strength. Both within this tale and in "The Gilded Six-Bits," woman's got the keys, but man owns the house. That inequality and God's refusal to return the couple to equal relations are what prompts the woman to take the devil's advice. The "key" that constitutes the bridle simultaneously signifies the dangers to the woman of the man's God-granted physical, economic, and legal dominance and the devil-granted means of reining that dominance in. The devil's gift is what converts domination into a power relation.

Describing woman as having the "de key" resonates with biblical import, but Mathilda Moseley's retelling of who has the keys and where they came from is at least playfully blasphemous, as indicated in the passage from Revelation cited at the beginning of this chapter. Even more familiar to most readers is the New Testament passage in which Christ charges Peter with the highest office of the church with the words: "And I will give unto thee the keys of the kingdom of heaven" (Matthew 16:19). In addition to serving as a symbol for divinely sanctioned power over the faithful, keys were used in the modern era to claim sanction for authorial exegesis of scripture in such seventeenth-century texts as *The key of the Bible, unlocking the richest treasury of the Holy Scriptures* and *Key of Knowledge for the Opening of the Secret Mysteries of St. Johns Mysticall Revelation.*[5] Rather than joining forces with these texts, however, Hurston's recording of Mathilda Moseley's tale is in company with a desacralizing text such as Raymond Williams's *Key Words.* Hurston's making over of the biblical account of Adam and Eve and their fall in both the tale and the short story functions as a kind of bridle too. Her retelling of Genesis reins in claims for the legitimacy of apocalyptic creation stories that justify and fortify male dominance, even as it acknowledges the continuing force of apocalyptic power/knowledge.

Like Mathilda Moseley's tale, "the Gilded Six-Bits" is what Henry Louis Gates calls a "tropological revision." Both revise—that is, retell with a "signal difference"—the biblical book of Genesis.[6] The tale itself carries forward the perplexing tradition of Genesis's twice-told creation story. The initial equality of the man and the woman in Mathilda Moseley's tale is akin to the first account of the creation of man and woman in Genesis 1:1-31, whereas the man's attaining of greater power and the woman's gaining the keys suggests the second account, in Genesis 2:5 through 3:24, in which Adam is created first and Eve from his rib and the temptation occurs. Yet, as Hurston states and Gates argues, the correlation is not meant to be a strict one in every respect, since the tale is, after all, a making over of the Bible. Both the tale and the story repeat with a "signal difference" the story of Adam and Eve, their succumbing to the devil's temptation, and their expulsion from paradise.

Because "The Gilded Six-Bits" retells the folktale *and* the biblical story of the Fall with a signal difference, it inscribes an additional level of intertextual complexity, particularly in regard to gender dynamics.[7] The short story's signifying on both the Bible and the folktale constitutes a double-voicing that forwards both tribute to the love between men and women and critique of it.[8] In other words, this intertextuality makes the gender dynamics of the story simultaneously tragic and comedic, evoking a biblical sorrow over humanity's fall from perfection and a folkloric irreverence regarding that condition. Thus Hurston portrays love itself, at least love between men and women, as both lamentable—a consequence of inequality breeding manipulation—and joyous. Read in this way, "The Gilded Six-Bits" brings to the foreground Hurston's insights into the complexities of heterosexual love in a patriarchal society.

To provide a summary of "The Gilded Six-Bits," I draw on Robert Hemenway's account because I believe it to be representative of the way the short story has generally been read.

> A young Eatonville wife, Missie May, is seduced by a traveling Lothario
> whose main appeal is a gold watch charm. He promises her this gold
> coin, but at the moment of submission they are discovered by her
> husband Joe. The cheapness of the affair and the tarnish of the
> marriage is represented by the coin left behind—instead of a ten-dollar
> gold piece it turns out to be only a gilded half-dollar. Joe cannot
> verbalize his grief and Missie May cannot articulate her sorrow, but they
> work during the next year to recapture their love, growing together
> again after the birth of their first child—who strongly resembles Joe.
> The story ends as Joe goes to the white man's store to buy his wife
> some candy kisses, a symbol of his forgiveness, paying for the purchase
> with the gilded six bits kept as a reminder of her infidelity. The clerk
> later says to a customer: "Wisht I could be like these darkies. Laughin'
> all the time. Nothin' worries 'em."[9]

Hemenway calls this story one of Hurston's best, and I agree with his assessment. But his treatment of it, which notes how the story's parodic use of the white clerk's stereotype of African Americans is subversive of racism, virtually ignores the text's gender parody. Disregarding this aspect inevitably leads to seeing the story as complicitous with sexist stereotyping. Alice Walker's expressed uneasiness about the story's gender stereotypes exemplifies the problems of such a reading. In her dedication in the Hurston reader she asks, "Is 'The Gilded Six-Bits' so sexist it makes us cringe to think Zora Neale Hurston wrote it? Or does it make a true statement about deep love functioning in the only pattern that at the time of its action seemed correct?"[10] Walker returns to this question later in the text to introduce the story by saying that it portrays a woman "convinced that her entire being is defined through her role of wife."[11] Set up this way, Walker seems to be asking, not whether the story is blatantly sexist, since it clearly is in her view, but whether we should make allowances for its sexist stereotypes because they provide a mode of realism for the story. This is borne out when she states later, "Of course, should the love ever cease, Missy May will find herself in the same miserable prison other women, unloved and unloving, have found in conventional marriage. Proving once again that stereotypes—to work harmlessly—require, at the least, perpetual good will."[12]

If we accept the terms of either of these readings, even the second one that credits her artistic rendering of Missy May for its historical realism, we are left with a peculiar affirmation on Hurston's part of Missie May's self-depiction when she draws on apocalyptic metaphors to declare to Joe, "if you burn me, you won't git a thing but wife ashes."[13] A genealogical reading of "The Gilded Six-Bits" points to ways in which the story actually undermines this stereotypical view of women. From the perspective of genealogical literary analysis, I am further arguing that the story's gender parody makes the very question of men's subordination of women and their ensuing inability to "read" women's motives within the context of that subordination a crucial problematic of the text. From this perspective, and with the retelling of Genesis in mind, Missie May's proud allusion to burning in hell for the infidelity—that at this point in the narrative seems unthinkable—is a clue to its parody and its resistance to apocalypse.

Hurston's comments on "feather-bed resistance" provide a guide to her use of parody. She argues in *Mules and Men* that, when confronted by a white questioner, the "Negro, in spite of his open-faced laughter, his seeming acquiescence, is particularly evasive," explaining that the "Negro offers a feather-bed resistance. That is, we let the probe enter, but it never comes out. It gets smothered under a lot of laughter and pleasantries" (2-3). She goes on to make her point through an allusion to a door for which the white man has no key: "The theory behind our tactics: 'The white man is always trying to know into somebody's else's business. All right, I'll set something outside the door of my mind for him to play with and handle' " (3). The white store clerk who mistakes Joe's laughter as a sign of nothing worrying him has been duped in this way. He lacks the keys of empathy, equity, and understanding that would open the door to personal insight.

By adding the category of gender to race, I want to suggest that "The Gilded Six-Bits" also presents a kind of feather-bed resistance to the man/woman hierarchy that the story's patriarchal love plot assumes. The story's parodic elements suggest that, although seemingly acquiescent—and even though she loves Joe—Missie May's actions enact feather-bed resistance to Joe's control over her. And like the white store clerk, Joe lacks the key to comprehend the connections between men's efforts to dominate women and women's efforts to manipulate men. Given the relative popularity of this story, it is worth asking why this resistance has not been commented on. I think that it is because heterosexist gender relations are so often literally played out, struggled against, denied, or displaced across an actual bed. By following the ways that Hurston links the white clerk's racism and men's patriarchal posturing through the exchange of coin, we can see the intricate network of power relations circulating around and in the store and the bed. The gilded six-bits itself is thus the cathexis of capitalism, racism, and heterosexism.

The story opens with a suggestion that the Fall has already occurred, for daily toil is necessary for survival: "It was a Negro yard around a Negro house in a Negro settlement that looked to the payroll of the G and G Fertilizer works for its support." What we are presented with here, as Hemenway also points out, is an African American community circumscribed by white society's social, legal, and economic systems. I would again stress that it is a racist, capitalist, *patriarchal* society within which and against which Missie May and Joe define themselves. In other words, their relationship bears the burden of the simultaneous and intersecting oppressions of white supremacist and patriarchal power relations.

Even so, their love brings echoes and glimpses of Eden. The next line announces, "But there was something happy about the place" (54). The key word here is "but," because it pivots the scene from postlapsarian labor to prelapsarian happiness. This is an oscillation that recurs throughout the story. As in Genesis, at the outset of the story Missie May, like Eve, enjoys unselfconscious nakedness. She is bathing herself in a galvanized washtub, her skin glistening under the soapsuds, eagerly anticipating Joe's return from work. Yet even here we find a hint of an Eve ready for battle between the sexes, with "stiff young breasts thrust forward *aggressively* like broad-based cones with the tips lacquered in black" (54-55, emphasis mine).

The scene that follows encapsulates the lesson of Mathilda Moseley's tale. It introduces a ritual of exchange that frames and informs the entire story, a ritual that could only occur after a fall from gender equality, that is, after the man has gotten greater strength from God and after the woman has gotten possession of the keys to the kitchen, the bedroom, and the cradle. "There came the ring of singing metal on wood. Nine times." Missie May knows how to read this code, because it was "this way every Saturday afternoon" (55). She "knew that it was her husband throwing silver dollars in the door for her to pick up and pile beside her plate at dinner" (55). In "mock anger" and double entendre, she shouts to Joe, who is hiding in the yard, " 'Nobody ain't gointer be chunkin' money at me and Ah not do'em nothin' " (55). They engage in a playful "rough and tumble," becoming a "furious mass of male and female energy," which ends with Missie May searching through all of Joe's pockets for the candy kisses and presents he has brought her (55-56).

Recalling Mathilda Moseley's tale at this moment differentiates this "friendly battle" from the two battles her tale describes. This is not the battle of equals with which Moseley begins her tale; nor is it the abusive battle that occurs once the man has gotten his greater strength. It is, instead, the accommodation that the man learns to make once the woman has secured the keys to the kitchen, the bedroom, and the cradle. This is not to say that the accommodation is devoid of pleasure. But it is to reiterate that Missie May and Joe are not equals. As B. Moseley had pointed out to his wife, like men in general, Joe has the physical strength, the law, and the money on his side. But as Mathilda Moseley points out in reply, he is willing to mortgage them to her in exchange for the pleasures of food, sex, and children.

These three keys to Joe's life constitute the next three movements of the story and coincide precisely with scenes involving the kitchen, the bedroom, and the cradle. Each of the scenes is punctuated by a ritual of money being exchanged. After the initial exchange in which Joe chinks the silver dollars through the door for Missie May to collect, the action of the story moves into the kitchen. Missie May has lovingly prepared a dinner anyone would envy: "Hot fried mullet, crackling bread, ham hocks atop a mound of string beans and new potatoes, and perched on the window-sill a pone of spicy potato pudding" (57). While this abundance makes a mere apple look meager, it is during this meal that the story's serpent figure is introduced. Instead of Eve telling Adam about the serpent's offer, the reverse occurs. Joe has already met and been thoroughly seduced by "Mister Otis D. Slemmons, of spots and places." "Dat heavy-set man wid his mouth full of gold teethes?" Missie May asks, having already apparently noted his arrival herself with less enthusiasm than Joe.

Their divergent responses to Slemmons are worth pausing over. They provide insight into gender power relations and desire in the societal context of male dominance of women. First of all, it is important to note Joe's motivation for wanting to introduce Slemmons and Missie May because it shows how male dominance creates male rivalry. Joe wants to parade his wife before Slemmons to show his ownership. "He talkin' 'bout his pritty womens—Ah want 'im to see *mine*," he declares, with pride of possession (59). Second, it is Joe, not Missie May, who is attracted to Slemmons. He expresses desire to be like him, to have his physical bulk, his worldliness, and his gold accessories. Missie May, in contrast, has little appreciation for the figure Slemmons cuts. She says Slemmons has a "puzzlegut" and "a pone behind his neck." But Joe replies: "He ain't puzzlegutted, honey. He jes' got a corperation. Dat make 'm look lak a rich white man" (58). Unswayed, Missie May praises Joe's appearance over Slemmons's. "God took pattern after a pine tree and built you noble," she says, but then adds a sentiment that bodes ill for their happiness: "if Ah knowed any way to make you mo' pritty still Ah'd take and do it" (58).

What sounds like an innocent expression—this willingness to make Joe prettier, at least in his own eyes—brings us back to the biblical story of Genesis. For here we have a suggestion that Missie May's infidelity stems from her desire to please her husband. When Eve accepts the serpent's offer of the apple and God-like knowledge, she doesn't keep it for herself; she shares it with Adam. Similarly, Missie May hatches a plan to get some of Slemmons's gold money, place it along the road, and then "discover" it for Joe (60). Sex with Slemmons is the means to this end. This second ritual of sex for money also returns the plotline to Mathilda Moseley's claim that women use the key to the bedroom as a means of countering men's economic control.

Significantly, the story then moves to the bedroom and the shattering of Joe's heart when he discovers Missie May and Slemmons in bed together. Like Adam, he sees in a flash his happiness being crushed. But he is also, as Hurston notes by evoking yet another biblical figure, "Like Samson awakening after his haircut. So he just opened his mouth and laughed" (62).[14] This laughter, a gesture of recognition of loss, points to Mathilda Moseley's tale again. It marks a realization on the part of the man—in this case Joe—that he must somehow accommodate himself to the fact that the woman—in this case Missie May—has the key to the bedroom, and that this is the price he must pay for his bargain with God.

Hurston's artistic control in the composition of this story is most manifest here. The comedic effect of the intertextualized folktale never overrides the deep sympathy evoked for Missie May and Joe, both of whom suffer terribly over the Slemmons affair. As in Genesis, both of them are stricken with agonizing awareness of the consequences of their actions. They seem like strangers to one another. Like Eve's encroaching self-consciousness about her naked body, Missie May feels "embarrassed to get up and dress" in front of Joe who suddenly seems like "a strange man in her bed" (63). She fully expects Joe to leave her. But he doesn't. Instead he remains, with the token of her infidelity—the gilded fifty-cent piece from Slemmons's watch—ever at hand to bring out as a taunting reminder to Missie May of her deed. It should also be noted here that the story's second ritual of exchange of sex for money is an interrupted one, since Joe rather than Missie May takes possession of the gilded coin when he knocks Slemmons through the kitchen and out of his house.

This exchange is not completed until three months later, when the couple resumes sexual relations. Having been expelled from their Edenic garden of delight, they no longer revel in their sexuality. Instead, Joe must create a scene of seduction. And his work now seems a heavier burden. One night he comes home complaining about pain in his back and asks Missie May to "rub him down with liniment." "Before morning, youth triumphed and Missie exulted" (65). But humiliation rather than reconciliation is what Joe is after at this point. The exchange of sex for money is made complete when Joe leaves the gold piece under the pillow. Missie May soon knows what Joe has known since the night when he found Slemmons with his wife, that the gold piece is nothing more than a gilded half-dollar. She also recognizes the code of exchange: "He had come home to buy from her as if she were any woman in the long house. Fifty cents for her love" (65). Despondent, and clearly devalued, she slips the gilded coin into his Sunday pants pocket.

This realization moves the story toward the theme of the power of the third key: the key to the cradle. Earlier in the story, we have been told that Joe and Missie May "had been married for more than a year" but still with no sign of a child, which seems to worry Joe. Indeed, "Creation obsessed him" (61). Hurston provides two time designations that focus the story around the question of paternity—or more precisely, around the question of certainty about paternity.

The first designation of time indicates that three months ensued after the incident with Slemmons and before Joe and Missie May resume sexual relations. Sometime after that, Joe sees the sign he had so longed for, that Missie May is, in his words, "makin' feet for shoes" (66). The following verbal exchange takes place:

"Won't you be glad to have a li'l baby chile, Joe?"
"You know dat 'thout astin' me."
"Iss gointer be a boy chile and de very spit of you."
"You reckon, Missie May?"
"Who else could it look lak?" (66)

Joe makes no reply to this question, merely fingers something deep in his pocket, presumably the gilded coin. The next explicit time reference brings us to the birth scene: "It was almost six months later Missie May took to bed and Joe went and got his mother to come wait on the house. Missie May delivered a fine boy" (66).

Given the two explicit references to the period of nine months following the night Slemmons was there, the question of whose son this is is the question Joe cannot force himself to ask. But his silence is what prompts his mother to use words similar to those of Missie May even before the birth had occurred. In each case the women encourage Joe to see his own image mirrored in the face of the male infant. "You ain't ast 'bout de baby, Joe," his mother says. "You oughter be mighty proud cause he sho' is de spittin' image of yuh, son. Dat's yourn all right, if you never git another one, dat un is yourn" (67). Of course, Joe's mother can't know with certainty that her son is this child's father. And it is equally true that Missie May herself does not know with certainty who the father of her child is.

If we read the story keeping in mind the history of U.S. slavery and the literary tradition established by the slave narratives of Frederick Douglass and Harriet Jacobs, this scene is pivotal, for it puts into question two notions maintained in contradiction within the white patriarchal slave system. The first notion involves the *uncertainty* of paternity: here the scene exposes the double denials of paternity endemic to slavery—the denial of the right of paternity to enslaved men and the denial of paternity by rape on the part of white slave masters. The twice-repeated phrase about how this child will be the spitting image of Joe suggests this contradictoriness in the first instance through its simultaneous invocation and refutation of the narcissistic, Oedipal relation inherent in the father-son bonding/bondage of the white patriarchy. And in the second instance it provides a reminder that the child born from a white master's rape of an enslaved woman bears the burden of a personal identity that mirrors that act of violence and violation against his or her mother. As Frederick Douglass pointed out, the "double relation of master and father" brought on a greater likelihood of being sold off, "out of deference to the feelings of his white wife," or greater hardships, including beatings.[15]

At the same time, in regard to the second fundamental but contradictory notion of patriarchy and slavery, this scene questions the value of establishing legitimacy via insistence on *certain* paternity—an epistemological principle used to control women's reproductive freedom. The control exacted by white masters is directed by physical seizure; though different in kind, it is akin to forms of juridical control over women's bodies in marriage. In her account, Harriet Jacobs presents a poignant decription of her decision at fifteen to make "a headlong plunge" into a sexual relationship with a white man who was not her master:

> It seems less degrading to give one's self, than to submit to compulsion. There is something akin to freedom in having a lover who has no control over you, except that which he gains by kindness and attachment. A master may treat you as rudely as he pleases, and you dare not speak; moreover the wrong does not seem so great with an unmarried man, as with one who has a wife to be made unhappy. There may be sophistry in all this; *but the condition of a slave confuses all principles of morality, and, in fact, renders the practice of them impossible.* (emphasis mine)[16]

Read in the light of Jacobs's insight into moral precepts under slavery, Missie May's actions may also be said to be "something akin to freedom," that is, an act undertaken within conditions of domination, not itself an act of freedom, yet one that is akin to it.

In addition to challenging the foundational strictures of slavery and patriarchy, this scene poses an ethical counterperspective that has relevance for questions involving paternity that have arisen since the story was written. Readers today may well speculate about such a scenario now that we have access to the reproductive technology of the 1990s. Do technological means of establishing biological paternity mean that "man's got de key" of certain knowledge about his generations? What doors get opened and closed under these circumstances?

In contrast to this shoring up of masculinist power/knowledge, Hurston's story introduces a counterposition, epistemologically and ethically. When Missie May and Joe's mother tell Joe that this is his son without any doubt, and when Joe accepts this child as his responsibility, they expose and displace the legacy of patriarchal paternity. It is enough to, as God puts it to the man in Mathilda Moseley's tale, "Ast de woman" (34). If the woman, and in the case of the story, the women, say that Joe should welcome this child as his son, then that is the ethical vision the story suggests should prevail. More than certain knowledge of paternity, what matters here is that Joe and Missie May resume their loving relations and care for their newly born child. This is an ethics based on care for a child as a valued individual rather than on the child as legitimated property of a biological father.

Although I am arguing that "The Gilded Six-Bits" posits this ethical counterview, I am not suggesting that it presents a didactic resolution to the story. That would be to disregard its humor altogether. Nor do I agree with those who read the final scene as a naive, happy-ever-after ending in which Joe forgives Missie May. There is no utopian thematic at work here. White supremacist, patriarchal structures are still intact, and the story's ending cleverly encapsulates the ways in which that ongoing power relation circumscribes Joe's and Missie May's relationship.

We witness this through the two key scenes that close the story. The first involves the claim Joe makes to the white store clerk that he had known from the outset that Slemmons was a fraud. I read this scene on two different registers. First of all, Joe's laughing suggests the subversive acquiescence of "feather-bed resistance" as Hurston defines it in *Mules and Men*. On the second register, however, Joe's response of resistance to the white store clerk shows how the clerk's racism prompts a kind of macho behavior in Joe. In this sense, Joe's lie and braggadocio parallel the white clerk's racist remarks when he says, "Wisht I could be like these darkies. Laughin' all the time. Nothin' worries 'em" (68). Just as readers can see the blatant inaccuracy of the white clerk's racism, which so circumscribes Joe's actions that it affects even this simple exchange, so too we can see Joe's claims to have outmanned Slemmons as a function of normative masculinity. This helps alert us to the story's more subtle critique of the gender relations that continue to circumscribe Joe's and Missie May's everyday lives, despite their reconciliation.

The story's final scene makes manifest the effects of patriarchal power relations on Joe and Missie May, for their love remains framed through metaphors of monetary value. After buying fifty cents worth of candy kisses with the fake gold piece, Joe returns home. "There was the ring of singing metal on wood. Fifteen times" (68). And, in this third ritual of exchange, Missie May again answers the call of the coins: " 'Joe Banks, Ah hear you chunkin' money in mah do'way. You wait till Ah got mah strength back and Ah'm gointer fix you for dat' " (68). It is significant that this is the first mention of Joe's last name—Banks—and, in further reinforcement of the economic disparity between the two of them, we might also note that he has apparently gotten a six-dollar raise since the opening sequence. In other words, this third exchange suggests that the reconciliation between Missie May and Joe will be a continuation of a patriarchal economy of love and pleasure in which men's physical, economic, and legal domination will be offset by women's manipulation of men's desires through holding the keys to the kitchen, the bedroom, and the cradle.

Thus Hurston's making over of the book of Genesis both reiterates the dominant discourse of the Bible, which mandates women's submission to men, and disrupts it through the incorporation of Mathilda Moseley's irreverent tale. What Hurston shows us through this intertextual engagement with biblical and folkloric discourses is that the child that issues from its mother's body will always be *at issue* in a patriarchal society. But she also underscores, through the ethical counterview of her new Adam and Eve figures, that we must *take issue* with patriarchal norms.

Part III
A Book of Revelry:
The Decline and Fall of the American Empire

Piss Christ, 1987, Andres Serrano

Chapter 6
Urination and Civilization: Practicing Pissed Criticism

*The downhill slide of American culture gathers momentum. . . .
America's art and culture are, more and more, openly anti-
Christian, anti-American, nihilistic.*

Patrick Buchanan[1]

*I think artists often provoke public awareness and uneasiness, and
that's just the way it goes, you know.*

Andres Serrano[2]

Untitled Film Still #47, 1979, Cindy Sherman

Becoming a Pissed Critic

Piss Christ, 1987, Andres Serrano

Warmly transparent, luminously glowing, like wet sunlight. I've always loved the look of urine. So when Congress legislated cuts in funding to punish the NEA for exhibiting Andres Serrano's *Piss Christ,* I got really pissed off. Granted, it wasn't simply the urine that put their wrath in motion; it was Serrano's depiction of a crucifix in urine. But I found this satisfying, too. Critiques of Christianity are hard to come by in the United States. The heat directed at Sinead O'Connor's papal protest is a sign of how rarely criticism of Christianity has a public forum. When such critiques are met with governmental attempts to silence them, as with the New Right's efforts to censure and suppress the Serrano photograph, freedom of expression is at stake. Blasphemy might be against theocratic law, but Jesse Helms and Alphonse D'Amato notwithstanding, the United States has a Constitution that supports both separation of church and state and freedom of speech. The debate that raged through Congress, the media, the NEA, museums, artist groups, and religious organizations was a struggle about democracy versus apocalyptic dogma.

This struggle has made me wonder about the place of anger and frustration within what sometimes seems to me the unduly reserved attitude of genealogical analysis. After all, some actions call for a sense of urgency that cannot be met solely by the meticulous gathering together of subjugated details and events. The legislation resulting from the ideological-political-economic alliance between Jesse Helms (R-N.C.) and Alphonse D'Amato (D-N.Y.) in the Senate, Dick Armey (R-Tex.) and Dana Rohrabacher (R-Calif.) in the House of Representatives, and Reverend Donald Wildmon of the American Family Association is one such example. The Helms amendment, since ruled unconstitutional, prohibited the NEA from using funds to "promote, disseminate, or produce materials considered obscene, including sadomasochism, homoeroticism, the sexual exploitation of children, or individuals engaged in sex acts and which, when taken as a whole, do not have serious literary, artistic, political, or scientific value." Genealogy can help us understand the complex forces that were put into operation in the passage of this legislation. Steven Dubin's *Arresting Images* is an excellent example and will be invaluable in ongoing struggles concerning government-supported art and civil rights.[3] But the legislative trampling on various freedoms—freedom of artistic expression, of controversial ideas, of thought— led by Helms and others necessitates all kinds of resistance, ranging from polite examinations of power/knowledge to defiantly transgressive counterattacks.

I call the combination of these resistances "pissed criticism." And though this chapter introduces the notion of pissed criticism by focusing specifically on representations of urine and urination, I do not mean to suggest that pissed criticism should be confined to so limited a field. Pissed criticism can take its aim at any topic. Camille Paglia is at least partially right when she says "To piss is to criticize"—it isn't necessarily so, but it can be. She's wrong, however, when she insists that women are inherently piss-poor critics:

> Male urination really *is* a kind of accomplishment, an arc of
> transcendence. A woman merely waters the ground she stands on. It
> can be friendly when shared but is often aggressive, as in the
> defacement of public monuments by Sixties rock stars. To piss is to
> criticize. John Wayne urinated on the shoes of a grouchy director in full
> view of cast and crew. This is one genre of self-expression women will
> never master. A male dog marking every bush on the block is a grafitti
> artist, leaving his rude signature with each lift of the leg. Women, like
> female dogs, are earthbound squatters.[4]

This isn't as much a wholesale trashing of women as it initially sounds and I take Paglia at her word when she says it was meant to be humorous.[5] The problematic assumption that limits Paglia's insight (and confuses the humor), the one pissed criticism should be skeptical about, is her ready acceptance of anatomy as epistemological destiny. Although she switches from pissing on a straw woman to a straw man, she stands firm on the ground of anatomical difference when she contends that men suffer from "delusional certitude that objectivity is possible based on the visibility of their genitals," and that women, by contrast, "accept limited knowledge as their natural condition, a great human truth that a man may take a lifetime to reach."[6] Like so many apocalyptcians, she naturalizes rather than politicizes the terms of her argument. Still, she's onto something. Pissed criticism leaves a "rude signature" because it gives vent to the anger and frustration of combating polemicists in power. From this perspective, earthbound squatting might leave a signature bolder and ruder than a John Hancock.

Pissed criticism uses a splatter-shot method, sending forth a torrent of resistances, ranging from problemizations to polemics. As a genealogist, I agree with Foucault about the merit of dialogue for the "work of reciprocal elucidation." But unlike Foucault, as a pissed critic I endorse polemics too. He may be right that no one has "ever seen a new idea come out of a polemic."[7] But pissed criticism, while dialogically striving for new ideas, also knows that the New Right polemics produced on the floors of Congress made no allowance for dialogue. Just as genealogy puts subjugated events on stage, staged counterpolemics help create a forum for the slower work of genealogy. By meeting full force D'Amato's denunciation of *Piss Christ* as a "deplorable, despicable, display of vulgarity," the polemical derision of a performance artist like the aptly named Annie Sprinkle creates space for the genealogical scrutiny of art critics such as Donald Kuspit, Lucy Lippard, and Peggy Phelan.[8] Pissed criticism is willing to acknowledge the feeling of relief in replying to Helms's self-righteous declaration that Serrano is "not an artist, he is a jerk," by flying a banner with the retort: "In Your Ear, Jesse Helms."[9]

Polemics help force an issue to greater notice, but that's not enough. It's in the interest of pissed criticism to be historically minded as well. Urination is a recurrent theme, it seems, in both apocalyptic and anti-apocalyptic discourse. The differences in meanings associated with urine and urination provide a useful gauge of power relations at work. In this chapter, I examine cultural values embodied in a variety of imagistic, philosophical, and literary representations of urine. Despite the wide splash of meanings, that range isn't afforded much leeway these days, and, as the Helms amendment demonstrates, some people have a downright fit when a given representation of urine doesn't accord with their apocalyptic values. They've written their own kind of "urinary tract": an intractable tract that detests bodily excretions. And I say, piss on them.

The Passing of Piss Prophets

And he shewed me a pure river of water of life, clear as crystal,
proceeding out of the throne of God and of the Lamb.
                                        Revelation 22:1

Piss Christ is a large work, sixty by forty inches, depicting, in Steven Dubin's words, a crucifix "suspended in a glorious yellow firmament, illuminated by an unseen light from above, and buttressed by a bright red backdrop."[10] Without knowledge of the title or the hoopla, one might read the photograph as a literal portrayal of the verse quoted above from the book of Revelation. Even apocalypticists might honor such a portrayal—until piss enters the picture. One point that the Serrano controversy makes clear is that, for apocalypticists, urine may well be *a* water of life, but it sure can't be *the* water of life. A verse from the Old Testament, 2 Kings 18:27, illustrates this attitude when it is declared to "the men which sit on the wall, that they may eat their own dung, and drink their own piss." But advising others to drink urine need not be regarded as an insult. According to John Bourke's late-nineteenth-century pamphlets, rites found in a range of cultures involved drinking human urine or eating urine-soaked food.[11] For some people it is sexually pleasurable.[12] And it can save your life, a point of information Dick Francis popularizes in his novel *Longshot* through his protagonist John Kendall, a survival handbook writer who advocates drinking distilled urine in case one is stranded without water.[13]

The more prevalent attitude toward urine is far more apocalyptic, regarding it as a repugnant reminder of the body as profane matter. But some modes of apocalyptic discourse do allow displays of urine. It is deemed entirely—even exclusively—acceptable in a medical context, for example. I bet even Jesse Helms doesn't flinch when he carts his urine sample into a lab. And since his amendment made exception for the production of materials considered "obscene" as long as they have serious scientific value, medical texts are under no threat of censorship. This acceptance of medicalized representations of urine is not an uncharacteristic tolerance so much as a compatibility of repugnances toward the body. But biopower's mechanisms are meant to distance rather than to censor the body and its excretions. The derisive label "piss prophets" for doctors who smell and taste urine as a diagnostic practice is a way to deauthorize methods of healing that resist the prevailing U.S. predilection for chemical analysis. Urinalysis—(the term coined in 1889 to authorize this chemical process)—meant that "real" doctors were to have as little contact as possible with their patients' bodily fluids. Technological and divine apocalypticism thus converge around this distaste for the body and certain of its functions. They share moral prohibitions as well as biopower prescriptions about display of and conduct toward excrement.

From this simultaneously prohibitive and prescriptive apocalyptic perspective, it's indecent to put urine on artistic display, it's vulgar to call it piss, and it's immoral to immerse a crucifix in it. According to this view, Serrano's title alone offends on all three counts. Yet, as the passage from the book of Kings indicates, the word "piss" was not always considered unacceptable for apocalyptic discourse. It was used in both the Wyclif translation of 1838 and the King James Version of 1611, and was only scorned for polite society in the eighteenth century.[14] By these biblical standards, then, Serrano's use of "piss" in his title is not inherently vulgar. And Serrano himself strongly disagrees with his deeply offended critics about the aesthetic and religious uses of urine. He has pointed out that urine gives him a "beautiful light."[15] He further insists that his work is "religious, not sacriligious," and that he is "not a heretic," adding, "I like to believe that rather than destroy icons, I make new ones."[16]

To my mind, the question of whether Serrano is religious or sacriligious is less important than why the issue should be posed around this particular polarity in the first place. And even more significant is the way that the blasphemy question was sidestepped through a focus on obscenity. In order to understand why a de-

Venus and Cupid, c. 1513-26, Lorenzo Lotto

bate that occurred in a constitutionally mandated secular nation was so readily framed around issues of blasphemy, which were in turn so easily translated into issues of obsenity, it is necessary to look at the ways that apocalyptic discourse sacralizes art. Most crucially, it is vital to see that the sacralization of art diminishes art's capacity for cultural critique.

Golden Showers at the Met

Serrano is not the first artist to have used urine as a key signifier in a visual work of art, of course, nor even the first to douse a deity with urine. Consider Lotto's *Venus and Cupid*.[17] This sixteenth-century painting by an artist known primarily for his religious subjects and portraits shows a reclining Venus, scantily adorned with a few rose petals, an earring of pearl and sapphire, and a crown of gold with a veil that drapes down her back and gathers over the crook of her left arm. An ivy-covered tree trunk bearing the artist's signature is in the background. Venus is lying on a deep red cloth that covers a stretch of grassy earth and from beneath which a small snake crawls out, edging toward her. Above her head is a conch shell; in front of her lies a rod and a rose in full bloom. With her right hand, she holds a blue ribbon from which a wreath of myrtle dangles. From it hangs a small brazier with incense burning. Standing at her feet is her son Cupid, with his bow and quiver over his left shoulder, a myrtle wreath jauntily crowning his head and a small scarf tied about his left upper arm. With his left hand he helps Venus hold her wreath. With his right hand he holds his penis to help guide its stream of urine through the center of the wreath and onto her lap. The smile on her face indicates her pleasure in this act.

The probable dates for this painting are between 1513 and 1526, but, in light of the Helms amendment, the really interesting date associated with it is 1986, the year it was placed on prominent display at the Metropolitan Museum of Art. Why doesn't the Christian conservative alliance marshal its outrage against this portrayal? The obvious reason is, of course, that it isn't anti-Christian; from an apocalyptic perspective, there is nothing blasphemous about depicting urine sprinkling on the body of a pagan deity. But the Helms amendment is aimed at obscenity, not blasphemy, and, following the logic of the New Right's protests, Lotto's painting is obscene, sadomasochistic, and sexually exploitative of children. In fact, conservatives have not always been indifferent to the painting. As the art historian Keith Christiansen indicates, the reappearance of the painting in 1984 allowed a cleaning of it that revealed certain tamperings done during the Victorian era. Some of these were additions, like a piece of cloth that had been added to drape over the right side of Venus's body. Cupid's penis had been transformed into a nosegay. Other alterations were deletions. The rose petals on Venus's body had been removed and Cupid's urine "arrested in mid-air."[18] The painting placed in the Met no longer contained the extra cloth and nosegay and made visible again the rose petals, penis, and the completed urine trajectory.

Despite its graphic depiction of a young boy in an act of urination on an adult woman, Lotto's *Venus and Cupid* is viewed by museum visitors daily yet prompts no cries of indignation. Why? One reason is because the Met's account of the painting normalizes it entirely within a heterosexist economy. Viewers are instructed that the painting was inspired by classical marriage poems, or epithalamia. In such poems and in the Lotto painting, "Venus confers her blessing upon a bride and expresses her hope that the marriage will be long-lived and hopeful." The iconography is "revealed" according to this logic: "The urine directed through the wreath by Cupid is an augury of fertility." The explanation guides visitors to other works of the era—fifteenth-century birth trays, for example, which also used the motif of the urinating child, who was sometimes depicted as producing gold and silver, as an expression of good luck. Christiansen's more extended reading of these symbols and his conclusion accords with the Museum's notes: "The emblematic accessories Lotto employs in this picture come as no surprise, for they are standard features of both his religious paintings and his portraits." But Christiansen also observes that Lotto's Venus "retains the fragile beauty and compelling personality of a real person . . . and his Cupid has the character of a precocious three-year-old infant."[19] This resonance of reality is no doubt why the Museum notes are so careful to instruct viewers on the "normalcy" of the painting. According to the official word, its eroticism is to be taken expressly as an endorsement of marriage—then and now.

> *And the best commendation that he could give her*
> *Was that she made water excellent well,*
> *With a fa la la, etc.*

Lady Mary Wortley Montagu[20]

The way that the Lotto is normalized keeps it from being castigated as "obscene." But what gets a work like Picasso's *La Pisseuse* (1965)—which could be used rather cleverly as an ad for Water Sports on the midnight sex channel—off the hook of obscenity and onto the walls of prestigious museums? Like the Lotto painting, the Picasso was exhibited in the United States with no outcry from the conservative Christian alliance.[21] *La Pisseuse* portrays a woman squatting on a beach near the water's edge. With a perceptible smile on her cubistically profiled face, she lifts her skirt to expose her spread thighs and pubic hair, and allows her urine to stream onto the sand. Although at the time of its creation some critics dismissed it as the work of one who had become "artistically senile," its 1984 New York City exhibition met with approbation. Robert Rosenblum hailed it as an exploration of "private fantasies inspired by universal myths."[22] Like the

La Pisseuse (Woman pissing), 1965, Pablo Picasso. Copyright
1993 ARS, New York/SPADEM, Paris

Met's and Christiansen's accounts of the Lotto painting, Rosenblum's interpretation appeals to universalizing truth claims in order to justify the painting's aesthetic value. In other words, the display of private fantasies is okay as long as they accord with normalized heterosexist attitudes. This is made explicit in Rosenblum's characterization of the urinating woman as "an almost laughably grotesque and clumsy animal who seemed grossly united with the forces of nature, nonchalantly displaying her sexual parts to male viewers [and] shamelessly pissing into the sea." It's debatable whether a figure whose feet are planted so squarely on the ground is best seen as clumsy, but to Rosenblum this is not meant to be critical. It is, rather, a way of hailing her, along with de Kooning's female figures of the same period, as "clumsy carnal creatures, so primordial in their contact with the elements that they swiftly become the stuff of primitive myth — remote deities of earth, sand, and water who embody the generative forces of nature."[23] The representation of women as embodiments of nature is an age-old tie that binds women to men and releases men from obligation to nature and others.

The sacralization of art involves a privileging of certain high-art assumptions as well as heterosexist values. Lotto's work has long enjoyed high-art status, which is why the Met would want "one of his most original masterpieces."[24] As part of a high-art context, it is only one of a great number of paintings depicting mythological figures engaged in behaviors that have been criminalized in the modern era. Considered tolerable in paintings from the past, such scenes cannot be depicted these days without criminalizing the artist, part of the reason that Picasso's established "genius" was put at risk — his dismissal as "artistically senile" is a backhanded version of criminalization. Whether or not *Piss Christ* qualifies as high art is a recurrent theme in the NEA debate. Opponents deride the photograph as having no real artistic merit because it lacks beauty and/or depth, key elements of high art. David Lee, for example, disdainfully describes the urine as "orange cocktail in hue," calling the color "strident, deliberately eye-attacking," and declaring that "formally and visually, all Serrano's pictures are similarly straightforward and unexceptional." He dismisses it as a "statement of juvenile rebelliousness by an unimaginative newcomer."[25] Supportive critics have made cases to the contrary by drawing on some of the same aesthetic categories to prove its qualities as art. According to Lucy Lippard, for instance, "Serrano produces objects of great seductive beauty which address some of the weightiest subject matter available to Western artists."[26]

The point here is not whether *Piss Christ* does or does not deserve recognition along traditional lines of aesthetic appreciation, but why the argument should run along those particular lines of judgment, and what the effect would be of its being redeemed as aesthetically respectable. An artist can really only get high-art status the "hard way" — by earning it from high-art patrons. What is at stake here is the effect of that sacralization: elevation as high art diminishes a work as cultural critique. The unquestioned acceptance of Lotto's work as not just art but high art stems from the valorization of painting as a transcendent medium of artistic expression. This is especially the case for Renaissance paintings, which mark the historical intersection between religious icons and the sacralization of art into high art. One could see *Venus and Cupid* as a celebration of pleasures regarded as abnormal and illegal by current psychological and juridical standards. But even if this were part of the Met's official explanation, it would very likely be diffused by reading that motif as an allegory of an eternal Truth. D'Amato, Helms, and the others don't need to be all that concerned with the Lotto painting, precisely because the conventions of high-art interpretation make it no threat to their values.

The photographic medium of *Piss Christ* rubs many high-art assumptions the wrong way. Within the canonical discourse of high art, photography's double role of documentary social critique and artistic expression delineates it as inferior to paintings in general, but especially to Renaissance paintings. For those who are interested in art as social critique, by contrast, photography wins out over painting because it operates through a reality effect. When it is seen as an aesthetic expression of social critique, photography functions to desacralize art, to jolt viewers out of their high-art assumptions by appealing to reality, itself seen as transient, but with a glimpse of it caught for the photographic moment. Serrano's own comments about his photograph's title emphasize the reality of the urine. As he put it in one interview: "I could just use piss for the beautiful light that it gives me and not let people know what they're looking at. But I do like for people to know what they're looking at because the work is intended to operate on more than one level."[27] In a different interview, he points out that without the title, "most people would be completely seduced" by the "beautiful glowing light." He also notes that "part of the reason why I'm doing these piss pictures is that I'm trying to come to terms with the difficult or disagreeable aspects of our lives."[28]

Given the desacralizing title, it is all the more significant when discussions of *Piss Christ*—even those that stress photography's critical edge—gravitate toward resacralization. One of the most eloquent interpretations of the photograph I have seen is the one Peggy Phelan offers, but her reading vacillates emphatically between desacralization and literal resacralization:

> The power of Serrano's image does not derive, as Senator D'Amato
> would have us believe, from an *equation* between excrement and Christ;
> rather it comes from the much more unsettling idea that our images
> and dreams of divinity and salvation cannot be distinguished from the
> fact of our waste and death. *Piss Christ* insists that our most frequent
> image of divine love has laced within it a consideration of love's
> evaporation, its loss, its devastating waste. In the age of AIDS where
> love and death promenade more boldly down the boulevards of our

erotic and spiritual imaginations, Serrano's photograph is a mournful lament for an authentic, personal image of the beloved's suffering body. . . . *Piss Christ* is too beautiful, too perfectly lit, too precise a balance between biological indifference and the thundering emptiness of spiritual hope, to be a pagan's bratty attack on Christ.[29]

Phelan's reading is itself a compelling lament. But it loses sight of an admittedly controversial but equally plausible reading of the photograph as just what D'Amato suspects—an attack on Christianity.

With *Piss Christ* in hand, Serrano stationed himself outside the apocalyptic tent—and pissed in. Much of the wrath unleashed toward the photograph is a counterattack on its anti-apocalyptic critique. The vehemence of the political-religious alliance is predictable, even understandable—people often fight back when their beliefs are under assault and struggle to maintain their strongholds of authority and power. *Piss Christ* attacks the logic of apocalypticism on many fronts. As Lucy Lippard observes, "Serrano plays with precast concepts of nature and culture, body and spirit. Well aware of the 'somatic discourse'—the Catholic and fundamentalist obsession with the body (that of Christ and those of sinners)—Serrano confronts the discomfort most people feel with their own bodies and their products, and the prevailing disgust for bodily fluids."[30]

And even though Serrano states emphatically that he is neither antireligious nor anti-Christian, I would argue that the photograph merits an anti-Christian reading. This does not make it a bratty attack, or merely a derisive comment on commercialized religion, but a warranted protest against institutionalized Christianity's responsibility for vast human suffering. How much piss would it take to wash away Christianity's guilt? From its slaughter of "heretics" in centuries past to today's vindictive refusals of various Christian sects to support reproductive and sexual freedom, Christianity has laid waste to individual lives and devastated whole populations. The photographic effect of the red backdrop is a blood-haunted reminder of Christian witch trials and colonial genocide, the Inquisition, back-alley abortions, and denunciation of people with AIDS. For those who do not believe in Christian deities, this reading of the photograph is less a question of sacrilege than of political-ethical resistance to a major force of domination. If such a reading is unsettling, it is because, as Senator D'Amato suspects, Christianity as a form of domination is under attack.

Pissin' on the Fire

Attempts to control the display of Serrano's art are part of a more widespread attempt to control sexuality, particularly homosexuality. Part of the New Right's anger and hysteria involves a chain of associations that link *Piss Christ* and "perverse" sexuality. This is rather odd, but, as I will show, it is comprehensible according to an apocalyptic logic that makes urine the missing link. As Donald Kuspit has pointed out, "piss evokes the genitals, and thus, indirectly, sexuality. The point is that both sexuality and urinating are viewed as lower functions, while Christ represents spiritual ones."[31] In addition, the right established a connection between Serrano and the Mapplethorpe exhibit by embroiling both in similar battles over government funding of the arts. But unlike Robert Mapplethorpe's photographs of homoeroticism and sadomasochism, *Piss Christ* contains no explicit scenes of sex and no display of genitals; the only torture suggested in the photograph is that depicted through the crucifix. Ultimately it is the urine that undoes the apocalyptic dream of a perfected, asexual, millennialized body, the resurrected and restored bodiless body promised through the signifier of a crucified savior.

One way to flush out the bits of homophobia and heterosexism floating around in the Serrano debate is to turn to Freud's arguments about urination in *Civilization and Its Discontents*. The furor over *Piss Christ* not only raised questions about which values our civilization should esteem, it also raised the question of the value of civilization itself. Freud's discussion sheds light on the current debate precisely because he focuses on the same bodily fluid that Serrano did and because some of his arguments are foundational to the New Right's stance. His definition of civilization is relevant in this regard because it is the operative one in the debate over art and culture in the United States today. The "word 'civilization,' " Freud states, "describes the whole sum of the achievements and the regulations which distinguish our lives from those of our animal ancestors and which serve two purposes—namely, to protect men against nature and to adjust their mutual relations."[32] Freud's emphasis on the totality of the human species, its precarious division from animals without and animality within, and the need for regulations are in keeping with modern apocalyptic discourse. This is not surprising, since the word "civilization" came into usage in the late eighteenth century, the time of emerging technologies of disciplinary biopower.

But Freud's conclusions about the outcome of civilization are strikingly anti-apocalyptic, and in this regard he departs from assumptions held by the New Right. Rejecting the "illusions" of those who hold that civilization "will necessarily lead to heights of unimagined perfection," he declares that he does "not have the courage to rise up before my fellow-men as a prophet." Writing within the context of Hitler's rise to power, he concludes the book on a poignant note:

> Men have gained control over the forces of nature to such an extent
> that with their help they would have no difficulty in exterminating one
> another to the last man. They know this, and hence comes a large part
> of their current unrest, their unhappiness and their mood of anxiety.
> And now it is to be expected that the other of the two "Heavenly
> Powers," eternal Eros, will make an effort to assert himself in the

struggle with his equally immortal adversary. But who can forsee with what success and with what result?[33]

Though reluctant to serve as prophet, he had less hesitation in assigning origin, revealing some shortsightedness in discerning the links between narratives of origin and end. "If we go back far enough," he says, "we find that the first acts of civilization were the use of tools, the gaining of control over fire and the construction of dwellings. Among these, the control of fire stands out as a quite extraordinary and unexampled achievement."

In a lengthy footnote he provides the following account of how men gained control over fire:

> Psycho-analytic material, incomplete as it is and not susceptible to clear interpretation, nevertheless admits of a conjecture—a fantastic-sounding one—about the origin of this human feat. It is as though primal man had the habit, when he came in contact with fire, of satisfying an infantile desire connected with it, by putting it out with a stream of urine. The legends that we possess leave no doubt about the originally phallic view taken of tongues of flame as they shoot upwards. Putting out fire by micturating—a theme to which modern giants, Gulliver in Lilliput and Rabelais' Gargantua, still hark back—was therefore a kind of sexual act with a male, an enjoyment of sexual potency in a homosexual competition. The first person to renounce this desire and spare the fire was able to carry it off with him and subdue it to his own use. By damping down the fire of his own sexual excitation, he had tamed the natural force of fire. This great cultural conquest was thus the reward for his renunciation of instinct.[34]

In a brief essay written a year after *Civilization and Its Discontents*, Freud expands on this conjecture. Reiterating that "in order to possess himself of fire, it was necessary for man to renounce the homosexually-tinged desire to extinguish it by a stream of urine," he interprets the Prometheus myth as a way of explaining why the acquisition of fire is "inseparably connected to the idea of an outrage." Within the human psyche, he says, the gods represent the "gratification of all the lusts which mankind must renounce."[35] Prometheus's theft of fire is thus a denial of gratification—hence Zeus's great outrage and hostility toward Prometheus. Applying this to psychoanalysis, Freud argues that the Prometheus myth is an expression of the psychical mechanism through which repression breeds aggression. Through a somewhat oblique line of thought that connects aggression, sexual desire, and repression, he comments further that the antithesis of fire and water found in other myths as well as early history is replicated in male physiology. As he puts it, "we might say that man quenches his own fire with his own water."[36] Although this explanation specifically addresses the physiological incompatibility of urination and ejaculation, it also provides a clue to Freud's acceptance of a normative sexual economy in which urination and sexual desire are antithetical. This view is reinforced in the DSM III categorization of undinism, or "water sports," as a psychosexual disorder, and helps account for the links between urine and obscenity that the New Right assumes without articulating in regard to *Piss Christ*.

According to Freud's theory of civilization, although the control of fire required "primal man' "s renunciation of homoerotic pleasure, that renunciation offered a compensation: cultural conquest. Regardless of whether one accepts Freud's theory of origins or his theory of renunciation of instinct as the source of hostility and aggression, there is merit in his insight about links between compulsory heterosexuality and men's use of fire power in the name of civilization. It is worth noting also that—at least as expressed in *Civilization and its Discontents*—Freud's ideas about the emergence of the use of fire do not carry an exclusive endorsement of heterosexuality. Nor does he argue that male homoerotic renunciation is necessary for contemporary civilization. In contrast to those who denounce homosexuality, he argues against such strictures in the name of civilization. The requirement that "there shall be a single kind of sexual life for everyone," he states emphatically, "disregards the dissimilarities, whether innate or acquired, in the sexual constitution of human beings; it cuts off a fair number of them from sexual enjoyment, and so becomes the source of serious injustice."[37]

What Freud discerns about Western European civilization in light of this injustice certainly holds for U.S. apocalypticism: "Fear of a revolt by the suppressed elements drives it to stricter precautionary measures."[38] That's part of the reason that the New Right raised such an uproar over the Serrano photograph. *Piss Christ* challenges their definition of civilization and their demands that all citizens submit themselves to New Right values. Instead, Serrano follows Virginia Woolf, Lillian Smith, and Adrienne Rich in urging a questioning of those values, especially the value of loyalty to an oppressive civilization.[39] As a display of a man's urine, *Piss Christ* refuses the homoerotic renunciation that Freud conjectures gave rise to heterosexist civilization. As a display of urine drenching a crucifix, *Piss Christ* douses the zeal for obedience marshaled through the promise of eternity in heaven and the threat of the everlasting flames of hell. To apocalypticists these are not minor points. Empires have been built on such hopes and fears.

Freud himself did not adhere to his admonishment against mandating "a single kind of sexual life for everyone," especially where women were concerned. His accounts of women's hostility toward civilization are in notable contrast to feminists such as Woolf, Smith, and Rich. At the end of the footnote cited above from *Civilization and Its Discontents*, he states: "It is as though woman had been appointed guardian of the fire which was held captive on the domestic hearth, because her anatomy made it impossible for her to yield to the temptation of this desire."[40] According to this view, then, women's anatomy relegates them to keeping the home fires burning. They are unable to renounce an instinct they're physically incapable of gratifying in the first place. As a result, they have to be directed by men's renunciation. Freud notes that on occasion a woman will resent being captive to the fire on the hearth; such a woman "finds herself forced into the background by the claims of civilization and she adopts a hostile attitude towards it."[41]

In the final line of the footnote, Freud links urine to women's discontent. "It is remarkable," he observes, "how regularly analytic experience testifies to the connection between ambition, fire and urethral erotism."[42] Earlier works had been less elliptical on this point. In an essay from 1908, he mentions "the burning ambition of people who earlier suffered from enuresis."[43] Before that, in his "Analysis of a Case of Hysteria," published in 1905, he discusses bed-wetting, ambition, and sexuality specifically in regard to Dora's dream about her house catching on fire and her family's escape to safety. Tellingly, in Dora's case, the antithesis of fire and water follows a different line of thought from the one about male renunciation of sexual desire and the achievement of cultural conquest. Although he alludes to the contrary between fire and water, he interprets Dora's dream as expressing a wish *for* sexual desire, for a kind of burning that is not antithetical to, but rather productive of, "water." According to his view she desires "being consumed with love," which "makes things wet." He extrapolates from this dream that both she and her brother "were addicted to bed-wetting up to a later age than is usual with children," a point that Dora confirms.

The pivotal point in his analysis is the cause of her bed-wetting: masturbation.[44] Dora's guilt over this sexual act, he suggests, is concealed by her "open accusations against her father." Freud's analysis catches Dora in a classic double bind. Despite the fact that she "denied flatly" his speculation, he interprets one of her gestures as "further step toward the confession." On her next visit, he explains, she wore a new accessory—"a small reticule of a shape which had just come into fashion; and, as she lay on the sofa and talked, she kept playing with it—opening it, putting a finger into it, shutting it again, and so on." He takes this opportunity to explain to her the "nature of a 'symptomatic act.' "[45]

Of more significance here than Dora's denial that she masturbated is Freud's symptomatic desire to "tear from her," as he puts it, the secret of her sexual pleasure. His arguments in "Some Psychical Consequences of the Anatomical Distinction Between the Sexes" (1925) help clarify his response and her possible reluctance to discuss masturbation with him. Regarding female masturbation as a "masculine activity," he argues that a girl will—and to his mind, should—relinquish her autoerotic pleasure upon realizing that "this is a point on which she cannot compete with boys." Those who don't give up masturbation become fixated in a "masculinity complex."[46] Burning ambition is thus a by-product of denial for women who refuse to acknowledge their physical, and hence cultural, inferiority. As many feminists have demonstrated, Freud's notions of sexual difference prevented him from dealing effectively with Dora's problems. This is particularly true of the way he construes her criticism of her father's double standards as a cover-up for her masturbation, including the transmission of his venereal disease to her mother. His assumptions about sexual difference made it difficult for him to even consider that Dora might well have been discontented with male-privileged civilization. Small wonder if she told him, in effect, to "piss off."

Full of Piss and Vinegar

Of course when women practice pissed criticism, they're accused of being incontinent. Intellectually rash, oversexed, incapable of controlling the discharge of urine—for women it's said to be the same thing. Women do suffer from urine trouble, but it's not because of the way their urinary tracts are designed. As Freud's theorizations indicate, part of the trouble is how their identities are constructed around representations of urination and sexual difference. This urinary technology of sexual difference is hardly limited to Freud. It is found in a number of mainstream places, from ads for bladder-control products in *Readers' Digest* to incontinence devices in medical textbooks. In the ads, where it isn't considered good taste to actually put women's urine on display, an interesting substitution is made; blue liquid is used to simulate the unwanted fluid. Unlike the golden glow that caused Serrano so much trouble, simulations of blue urine go unnoticed by the New Right. Even if they were noticed, they would pose no threat. The rhetoric of ads for items like Johnson & Johnson's "Serenity Guards," which promises "Revolutionary Bladder Control Protection" and "Surety Panties," which promise "pretty protection," are entirely consonant with heterosexist constructions of femininity. These ads heighten a sense of shame in getting caught with one's bladder guard down. "Millions of women have it," the ad for Serenity Guards asserts about "poor bladder control." "It's part of being female. And it could cause embarrassment." Their product comes with a promise of "Protection that lets you feel like a woman again." According to such ads, an incontinent woman is no longer a woman, but she's still less than a man.

Concern about urinary incontinence, male or female, is not a new phenomenon, of course. As one modern medical text states, "mechanical devices have been used for the control of incontinence from time immemorial," pointing out that Egyptian papyrus writings contain references to them. As with the ads for Serenity Guards and Surety Panties, what is worth noting is the gendered rhetoric used to describe the condition and the devices. One of the ancient Egyptian devices for women is described in a 1975 textbook on urinary incontinence, for example, as having the "form of a phallus, made of gold and retained intravaginally." As it turns out, the name of the eighteenth-century expert on the treatment of female incontinence is John Leake.[47] From Leake's 1777 work, "Medical instructions towards the prevention and cure of chronic or slow diseases peculiar to women," to more current calls for "managing" incontinence in both the medical literature and ad campaigns, one can chart the ways in which medical and media power/knowledge inscribes women's bodies with urine trouble.

But, as Judith Butler suggests in regard to gender trouble, if "trouble is inevitable," the task is "how best to make it."[48] Let pissed criticism's polemical placard turn "urine trouble" into the warning: "You're in trouble." To accomplish this spin, it's necessary to depose the symbolic order of male urination, which follows Freud in assigning superiority and privilege to penis pissers. Feminism has a long history of demystifying phallic authority, but at least three feminists deserve pissed criticism's highest commendation: their texts are full of piss and vinegar.

Like Freud, Simone de Beauvoir pondered the connections between urination and civilization, but she was less puzzled than he on what women might want and why urination might signify it. In her discussion of childhood in *The Second Sex*, she discusses the uses of urination:

> There is no doubt that the excretory functions, and in particular the urinary functions, are of passionate interest to children; indeed, to wet the bed is often a form of protest against a marked preference of the parents for another child. There are countries where the men urinate while seated, and there are cases of women who urinate standing, as is the custom with many peasants, among others; but in contemporary Western society, custom generally demands that women sit or crouch, while the erect position is reserved for males. This difference constitutes for the little girl the most striking sexual differentiation. To urinate, she is required to crouch, uncover herself, and therefore hide: a shameful and inconvenient procedure.[49]

As Beauvoir demonstrates, men invest themselves as the First Sex, endowing their penises with superiority, and dictating both a posture and a semiotics of standing versus crouching. This occurs most readily in childhood because of the greater genital pleasure and social privilege granted to male infants. She stresses the cultural rather than natural dimension of feelings of male superiority and female inferiority by pointing out that urination from a penis is convenient but "too definitely secondary to call forth directly a feeling of inferiority" in girls.[50] That happens only through concerted effort. The longstanding valuation of male bodies as superior to female bodies presents male urination as yet another instance of male superiority. At times, Beauvoir is seduced by it herself, as when she writes, for example, that "every stream of water in the air seems like a miracle, a defiance of gravity: to direct, to govern it, is to win a small victory over the laws of nature."[51] Despite this hyperbole, reiterated in her insistence that women of achievement are "mediocre" compared to the few male artists who deserve to be called "great men," her analysis of male privilege shows that the Woman Question is to a great extent the Urinating Woman Question. *The Second Sex* calls into question men's ostensible urinary prowess, and with it their natural capacity to criticize or project grand thoughts.

Nancy Miller has also written about the ways that male urination is conflated with phallic power. "My Father's Penis" is a daughter's account of her father's place in the phallic order and of the effects on her of "his entire system's disarray" from Parkinson's disease. She discusses the complexities of the phallus/penis conflation, and how they eventually led her to write an essay that was "born of the troubled intimacies of the autobiographical penis and the theoretical phallus." After having touched her father's penis in order to assist him in using a urinal, she recalls feeling, "smugly," that she would never again "confuse penis and phallus." "Phallus was the way my father could terrify me when I was growing up," she writes, the signifier of his power and authority. His penis was a signifier of his need for her help.

Yet, even though her father's penis is the site of his bodily disorder, the source of uncontrollable urination, the distinction is not so clear after all. As the disease continues its course through his body, including a "grueling seven-week stay in the hospital that followed a violent urinary tract infection," she concedes that "the penis/phallus connection remained alive, impossible to sever." Even as Miller indicates that the connection remained, the terms perceptibly shift in meaning. While her father was in the hospital, she reports, "it was war between his penis and the doctors' discourse; or rather my attempt to stand in as phallus for his penis—the rights of his body—against their authority to determine the course of his life." Ultimately, her concern for his body, and his right to determine its final moments, rather than biopower's interest in preserving its signs of life, makes it possible for him to die "at home, as he had wanted, after eating ice cream and watching public television."[52] In this instance, then, Miller's concern for her father, in keeping with an ethics of the flesh, clashes full force against an apocalyptic medical regime that would prolong life beyond the body's ability to sustain bodily pleasure, or even comfort.

The urinary technology of sexual difference is racial as well as gendered. Toni Morrison makes this evident in a scene from *Sula* that shows how white supremacist power extends its brutalities through prohibitions of space and how masculinist power maintains itself through women's humiliation. During the long train journey that Helene Wright and her daughter Nel take from their Northern town of Medallion to New Orleans, they are faced with intensifying racism. Morrison indicates how these oppressions as well as resistance to them are embodied, how power inscribes itself not only on bodily surfaces but in bodily fluids.

When they changed trains in Birmingham for the last leg of the trip,

they discovered what luxury they had been in through Kentucky and
Tennessee, where the rest stops all had colored toilets. After
Birmingham there were none. Helene's face was drawn with the need
to relieve herself, and so intense was her distress she finally brought
herself to speak about her problem to a black woman with four children
who had got on in Tuscaloosa.
  "Is there somewhere we can go to use the restroom?"
The woman looked up at her and seemed not to understand. "Ma'am?"
Her eyes fastened on the thick velvet collar, the fair skin, the high-
toned voice.
  "The restroom," Helene repeated. Then, in a whisper, "The toilet."
The woman pointed out the window and said, "Yes, ma'am. Yonder."[53]

When the train stops, Helene and her daughter are forced to join the woman in
the grass. "All of them, the fat woman and her four children, three boys and a
girl, Helene and her daughter, squatted there in the four o'clock Meridian
sun."[54] Part of the intended humiliation comes from the onlookers, the white
men who hang around the station, sentries of the white-only toilets. Yet Helene
learns to endure the oppression without succumbing to the feeling of humiliation. Over the course of the next three stops, she "could not only fold leaves as
well as the fat woman, she never felt a stir as she passed the muddy eyes of the
men who stood like wrecked Dorics under the station roofs of those towns."
Earth-squatting is not in and of itself demeaning, but it has been used as a means
of humiliation and oppression.

What these passages and this work of pissed criticism make clear are the ways
that the urinary technology of sexual difference joins forces with reproductive
and erotic technologies to produce a heterosexist, racist network of power relations. Filled with phallic urgency, the penis/phallus conflation is never completely elided, at least not in apocalypse-laden regimes of truth. Whether sput-
tering with delight about male transcendence or spitting with anger, apocalyptic
urinary tracts are revelations, but not of sacred truth as they claim. Rather, they
reveal that the present is a precarious time for the exercise of freedom. Against
such claims, Serrano, Morrison, Miller, and others offer counterrevelations to
show that the apocalyptic regime of truth is weighted with hopes and dreams of
millennial conquest. These counterrevelations and other anti-apocalyptic confrontations help us to see that the mighty phallus is, despite its self-representation as monumental, little more than piss proud.

Chapter 7
Resistance on the Home Front:
Re(con)figuring Home Space as a Practice of Freedom

*I think it is somewhat arbitrary to try to dissociate the effective
practice of freedom by people, the practice of social relations, and
the spatial distributions in which they find themselves. If they are
separated, they become impossible to understand. Each can only be
understood through the other.*

Michel Foucault,
"An Ethics of Pleasure"[1]

*I want to speak about the importance of homeplace in the midst of
oppression and domination, of homeplace as a site of resistance and
liberation struggle.*

bell hooks, "Homeplace"[2]

Look Homeward, Genealogist

The problem of combating hierarchical and oppressive social relations is intrin-
sically and intricately linked to altering the space in which people live, work,
play, and die. The practice of freedom thus calls into question relations of power
and space, or power/space, as well as relations of power/knowledge. Thus far, my
discussion of apocalyptic thought has primarily been cast in temporal terms: as
an evolution (or devolution) toward the end of history. It would be a mistake,
however, to ignore the spatial dimensions of apocalypticism: the total transformation of the world from profane earth to sacred Home. The term "world" is
itself an illustration of the way power constructs space in apocalyptic discourse.
Etymologically derived from the Germanic for "age" or "life" and "man," hence
"age of man," its usage differentiates human from divine existence and past and
present human existence from future afterlife. Yet, its application to heaven as
the divine world blurs that division.[3] Like "world," the term "home" is saturated
with apocalyptic desire. Heaven is God's "home," the final resting place of the
saved. The promise of the Millennium is a promise for an end to humanity's profane earthly existence, a promise that God will sacralize the earth. The end of
time is to bring a final alteration of space in which humanity's home and God's
home become one.

In this chapter, I explore homes as sites of power/space that play a unique role
in contemporary U.S. society. I construe homes as spatial deployments of the
three axes of power relations I outlined at the beginning of this book. The *de-*

135

ployment of alliance operates through kinship systems and marriage. Despite a wide diversity of living arrangements throughout the United States, homes are seen to be the domain of family units that have been sanctioned by law, the space where married couples reproduce themselves biologically and culturally. Just as patriarchy is maintained through this deployment, so too is the white supremacist insistence on racial "purity" within a given home space. Domestic assaults on women and children are brutal exercises of this form of power. Its presumed right of death is made shockingly evident in the fact that four out of five murdered women are murdered at home. The *deployment of sexuality* operates through disciplinary and demographic systems of biopower. As a function of this deployment, over the course of the nineteenth and twentieth centuries, homes became the primary sites for implementing technologies of health, hygiene, and respectability. One way to discern the mechanisms of this deployment is to focus on which groups are most vulnerable to homelessness, either because affordable housing is out of their reach or because they are not accorded equal access to housing. For example, one out of five families are headed by women, a third of which live below the poverty line, in daily jeopardy of becoming homeless.[4] Consider as well the housing discrimination against gays and lesbians. These are exercises of the deployment of sexuality at work, dividing and punishing populations eugenically and sexually. The *deployment of technoppression* operates through the circuitry of electronic communication systems. The well-appointed U.S. home is filled with technological devices, ranging from electrical toothbrushes to fax machines. Dangers of this deployment involve new, far more intricate levels of surveillance and home-worker exploitation. Whether competing with or reinforcing one another in terms of bodily control, all three power formations are consolidated within the place called home.

Genealogical analysis of power is inadequate if it ignores home space. In homes the apocalyptic regime of power/knowledge is deployed along all three of these axes. But resistance is there too. Recalling her sense of safety upon arriving at her grandmother's home after journeying through a white neighborhood, bell hooks shows that, for African Americans living in a white-supremacist culture, it was in the "homeplace, most often created and kept by black women, that we had the opportunity to grow and develop, to nurture our spirits."[5] Such homeplaces serve as a home front in struggles against apocalyptic power relations. Because home spaces are so fundamental to our daily lives, they can and should serve as primary sites of anti-apocalyptic transformation. This is a transformation both made possible and threatened by late capitalism's alterations of homes. It is a transformation emerging from activist resistances to institutionalized forms of physical assault, regulation, and surveillance. My analysis seeks to aid that transformation by looking at home space as a clash between apocalyptic and anti-apocalyptic forces. I argue that the activity of reconfiguring homes against the tenets and practices of apocalypse is itself a practice of freedom.

This chapter has three sections. In the first, I argue that genealogy needs to understand home space as a heterotopia, in order to comprehend how power operates in the present day. Foucault formulated the concept of the heterotopia in notes for a 1967 lecture; it was published in France a few months after his death, but was never reviewed by him.[6] There are, admittedly, a number of shortcomings or problems with this piece. It is not a fully developed argument, and there are inconsistencies in the formulation. Furthermore, it was put together in pre-genealogical days, which were also pre-personal computer days; thus the formulation doesn't address the ways in which home-based electronic technologies create possibilities for an elaborate surveillance and reclassification of individuals or show that transnational forces of late capitalism target homes as primary sites in this network of information circuitry. Finally, Foucault's brief remark on "the house, the bedroom, the bed" as "semi-closed sites of rest" is male-biased and naive. It wasn't until *The Use of Pleasure* and *The Care of the Self* that he expressed any particular interest in household spaces as sites of power relations, and his interest then was the ancient era. Despite these limitations, I find his speculations useful and the concept of the heterotopia essential for a genealogy of modern home space.[7]

In the second section of this chapter, I explore the legacy of first- and second-wave feminist challenges to dominant conceptualizations of the home as a private haven protecting the nuclear family from an alien outside world. Drawing on that discussion and the concept of the heterotopia, I argue that a conceptualization of homes *as neither public nor private* but *both local and global* better enables us to see the ways in which late capitalism is rapidly reterritorializing decentered homes. The third section argues that a genealogical reconfiguration of home space is crucial to combating the apocalyptic totalizing force of this reterritorialization. The reconfiguration of home space into a site for the exercise of freedom resists converting this spatialization of existence into an apocalyptic takeover.

There's No Place Like Home

Along with the subject, language, and power, the place called home has been decentered. This full-scale cultural decentering implies an altering of space as well. In other words, space itself should be approached genealogically to ascertain how experiences of space have changed over time. Foucault offers a provocative formulation along these lines by arguing that space in the Middle Ages was "the space of emplacement," in the seventeenth century a matter of "extension," and today "the site has been substituted for extension." More precisely, in our time, due in large part to electronic technology, space takes "the form of relations among sites," and current problems of space involve the coding, storage, and circulation of information. Electronic technology's alterations of space led him to declare that the "present epoch will perhaps be above all the epoch of space. We are in the epoch of simultaneity: we are in the epoch of juxtaposition, the epoch of the near and far, of the side-by-side, of the dispersed."[8] Techno-space thus alters the way time is experienced; electronic media and storage make it seem as if everything is happening at the same time. Although these historical changes mean that contemporary people experience space in ways profoundly different from people living in the Middle Ages, Foucault points out that "we may still have not reached the point of a practical desanctification of space."[9]

This certainly holds true for home space. Even with the current decentering of space and electronic gridding of homes, it is also the case that *the Home*, as a totalizing, centered concept bearing apocalyptic cultural meanings, remains hegemonically operative. Indeed, one of the dangers of the electronic age is a re-assertion of the totalizing and hierarchical forces of the space of emplacement, but with immense data banks replacing an omniscient, ubiquitous personified Deity. The Eurocentric idea of home carries its residual force from the medieval notion of space as a space of emplacement, in which there was "a hierarchic ensemble of places: sacred places and profane places; protected places and open, exposed places; urban places and rural places."[10] Space was localized within this hierarchy. With the diminishment of church authority, boundaries of localized space were broken up: "a thing's place was no longer anything but a point in its movement."[11] From the seventeenth century on, desanctification partially occurred through the establishment of space as extension. A secularized-sacralized concept of home emerged with and spurred on geographic extension through the forces of colonization, with the seizure of other people's lands justified in the name of the colonial homeland. Today, electronic space brings extended sites into local proximity. Through current technology home space is simultaneously a space of emplacement and a space of extension.

As a social construction, the place called home has certain properties distinguishing it from other socially constructed sites. Foucault offers the term "heterotopia" as a way of describing sites that have the "curious property of being in relation with all the other sites, but in such a way as to suspect, neutralize, or invert the set of relations that they happen to designate, mirror or reflect." Heterotopias are akin to utopias in their dreamlike resonance for a society, but unlike the "nowhere places" of utopias they are "real places" in which "all other real sites that can be found within the culture, are simultaneously represented, contested, and inverted."[12] At the close of his brief essay, he states that "the ship is the heterotopia *par excellence*. In civilizations without boats, dreams dry up, espionage takes the place of adventure, and the police take the place of pirates."[13] I have nothing against boats, but for modern U.S. society I would give pride of place to the home as the heterotopia par excellence. What Foucault points out about ships is far more pervasively true of U.S. homes: they are not only the "great instrument of economic development" but also the "greatest reserve of the imagination."[14] I would add that, without adequate theorization of home space, cultural critique dries up.

Even though homes are heterotopias, it is still the case that the ideal of the *Home* is a utopia. Evoking the heavenly dwelling of God and the faithful dead, Home claims to be "there" but also "here." Foucault discusses the mirror as having this kind of mixed utopian and heterotopian function:

> The mirror is, after all, a utopia, since it is a placeless place. In the mirror, I see myself there where I am not, in an unreal, virtual space that opens up behind the surface. . . . But it is also a heterotopia in so far as the mirror does exist in reality, where it exerts a sort of counteraction on the position that I occupy.[15]

This simultaneous utopian and heterotopian character often turns discussions of home into endlessly confusing debates, such as whether there is a distinction between "home" and "house." Such debates surfaced frequently at the conference "Home: A Place in the World," held at the New School for Social Research, in concert with five New York City museums, in October 1990. Rather than engage that question, which inevitably seems to mythologize "home" and discuss "house" as if it were a neutral term, I want to analyze the interplay of utopian and heterotopian meanings surrounding the places we call home—which includes the mundane signifier "house," the sacred signifier "Home," and a deviance signifier such as "detention home"—and hence to historicize what the New School's conference program called "the deep resonance 'home' has for all of us."

To say that home space has become U.S. society's heterotopia par excellence is to argue that particular power relations have transformed homes into uniquely endowed places "which are linked with all the others, which however contradict all other sites."[16] Foucault outlines several key points that help guide analysis of heterotopias, which I have drawn on throughout this chapter. The basic point is that all cultures construct heterotopias of some sort. Even though Foucault sees heterotopia as a transcultural formation, he also stresses the specific historical formation within any given society. In other words, existing heterotopias may undergo dramatic alteration, with such changes altering their function in their society. Another point emphasizes that heterotopias are "most linked to slices in time—which is to say that they open onto what might be termed, for the sake of symmetry, heterochronies." The complexity of heterotopic space is particularly relevant to my analysis of home space. As Foucault asserts, the heterotopia is "capable of juxtaposing in a single real place several spaces, several sites that are in themselves incompatible." In addition, heterotopias "always presuppose a system of opening and closing that both isolates them and makes them penetrable." Finally, and crucially, heterotopias "have a function in relation to all the space that remains."[17]

Home space has increasingly become an extra-ordinary space in relation to other social spaces. It is regarded as the place of greatest sustenance and renewal in this society. Yet it is often the place of greatest inversion of the principles of democratic freedom for which the United States claims to stand. It is touted as a buffer zone that protects one from outside forces, yet 98 percent of homes in the United States are equipped with televisions that bring daily stress and international distress inside.[18] As a heterotopia caught within the complex forces of change, home space today is a swirl of incompatible sites, rendering it a source of confusion as much as, if not more than, renewal. Many a given home brings together under a single roof several sites calling for highly varied if not contradictory behavior: hushed solemnity and gasps of sexual pleasure (a crucifix on a bedroom wall); concentration on the job and relaxed laughter (personal computer and television in a living room); self-scrutiny and theatrical disguise (a mirror in any room); confidentiality and disclosure (family secrets uttered in front of "invisible" nonfamily homeworkers); gratification, shame, indifference, guilt, pity, and political outrage (eating family dinner while watching televsion news of starvation in Somalia).

The juxtaposed incompatibility of these and other sites within U.S. homes has transformed homes into spaces best understood as heterotopias. The purpose of a genealogical approach to homes is to work against that transformation's reinforcement of forces of oppression. Past transformations of home space suggest how difficult this task is. Over the course of the modern era, the sanctified notion *the Home*, which divided terrestrial homes from the celestial heavenly home even as it sought to mirror it, merged with imperialistic impositions of the colonial home to justify the genocidal displacement of Native Americans and Africans from their homes. The nineteenth-century emphasis on building and endorsing middle-class family-owned homes precluded equitable wages for household labor, disadvantaged working-class families, disenfranchised non-legally sanctioned couples, and rendered women and children susceptible to hidden male violence. By exposing these processes of sacralization, extension, separation, and subordination as investments of domination and power, genealogy can uphold feminism's battles against domestic violence and gender constraints. It can bolster civil rights activism against housing discrimination and help urban activist efforts to make inner-city homes more secure.

A genealogical politicization of homes increasingly needs to examine modes of resistance to late capitalism's social-economic power formations as well. The modern social-spatial construction of home, which emerged within the social forces of early capitalism and took hold as part of industrial capitalism, is currently being altered through the workings of late capitalism's transnationalism and its information production and processing. The communications technology of late capitalism has the potential to convert homes into receiving stations for controlled intelligence and/or a vast electronic cottage-industry network.[19]

Against these overlapping and contradictory forces of control and exploitation, which intensify the heterotopic character of home space because of the way they open it up to global contact, a radical democratic politics aims to reconstruct homes as places that promote the exercise of liberty in a new era of worldwide communication and interdependence. Genealogy can aid that effort by identifying the particularities and peculiarities of the power/space we call home.

Current heterotopic operations of home space in the United States have a conceptual and architectural foundation that emerged in the modern era. In the seventeenth century, as the first republic in Europe, the Netherlands exemplified many of the features that were to characterize subsequent European nations and their colonies. Among these features of Dutch society was the small family house. Whereas the medieval house was filled with family members, apprentices, servants, and friends, sometimes numbering as many as 25 in one or two rooms, the Dutch structure was constituted as a dwelling for a single family, with room for a few servants but no tenants.[20] The children of this new "home" were raised by their mothers, educated in schools, and deemed to be the objects of parental affection. The word "home" itself, as Witold Rybczynski points out, connotes important differences from the medieval concept of the house as a communal place to meet and sleep. He observes that " 'Home' brought together the meanings of house and of household, of dwelling and of refuge, of ownership and of affection," and adds that "home,' which connotes a physical 'place' but also has the more abstract sense of 'state of being,' has no equivalent in the Latin or Slavic European languages." The English word "home," like the German "Heim" (as well as similar-sounding words in Danish, Swedish, Icelandic, and Dutch) derive from the Old Norse "heima."[21] The Dutch concept of home, and its corresponding physical construction as a dwelling for an individual family, gradually spread throughout Europe.

European colonization of North America brought with it a home undergoing transition from a communal to a family form. During that period homes functioned economically, to a greater degree than they now do, as relay points supporting a social order that overtly espoused male privilege. Part of that economy was due to colonial consolidation against Native Americans. Although British colonial homes housed non-family members, friends as well as servants, and served as workplaces, they were highly stratified sites, with sex-gender-class arrangements in alignment with the hierarchies of the overall society. As in the community at large, the head of the household was presumed to be male — the white father, the breadwinner, the insurer of the authority of the law, the maintainer of lineage.[22]

Not until the nineteenth century, when the Dutch Republic-inspired model of homes as child-centered, sentiment-based nuclear family dwellings was established as a normative ideal, did U.S. homes start to become heterotopias. Late eighteenth-century post-Revolutionary formulations concerning governance had turned attention to the role of housing in fostering values for the new Republic. Thomas Jefferson's chapter on buildings in *Notes on the State of Virginia* illustrates how issues of home design, hygiene, and privacy entered the political domain in a dramatically new way.[23] This emergence of the deployment of sexuality often conflicted with the power formation of alliance. Since the nineteenth century, two contending forces endemic to biopower made homes thoroughgoing heterotopias in U.S. society: capitalism and feminism. Over the course of the twentieth century, technology joined these interlinked, albeit quite different, social forces to make homes heterotopias par excellence.

Capitalism's part in the process of transforming middle-class U.S. homes into heterotopias stems from the urbanization, suburbanization, and industrialization of national space over the course of the nineteenth century. As industrial modes of production contributed to the rapid growth of cities and factories, capitalism's calculation that it was cheaper to pay men a family wage, combined with social reformism's outcry against unsafe work conditions as contributing to malnutrition and infant mortality, eventuated in separating home sites, as places of unpaid labor for women, from other work sites of paid labor for men. Compulsory education for children, increasingly a matter of concern for the bio-body politic, further redefined homes as places of affection for a nuclear family, which was owned by a comparatively absentee husband/father, overseen by a wife/mother, and enjoyed by "legitimate" children until their maturity.[24] The increased distances between where fathers worked and where they lived brought significant changes in home power/space.

Male sovereignty continued to be normative for society at large, but home spaces became increasingly identified as belonging to women. By maintaining the household through a division of labor that gave to them the care and moral training of children, housekeeping, and providing men with a respite from their paid labor, women redefined homes in their culturally defined image, even as they were redefined through biopower's mandates for hygiene and health. The feminization of the home was part of the deployment of sexuality's politics of health. That process also led to a feminist questioning of men's authority in areas ranging from child-rearing to abolition. Yet even as middle-class women gained power as moral teachers and domestic managers, most men who were relatively powerless in making community-wide decisions held fast to final authority in their homes, an authority maintained by their economic independence, reinforced by law, and sometimes enforced by violence.

What is most at stake here in terms of this history of home space is how these conflicting social and economic relations of power fuel a deeply ambivalent set of meanings that fire up apocalyptic longing and anxiety. To put a Freudian insight to genealogical service, the conflicts between male and female authority stemming from the intersections of the deployments of alliance and sexuality have made homes seem uncanny. Two quotations, one from Milton's "Paradise

Lost," the other from Freud's discussion of the "uncanny," encapsulate the problematic of the apocalyptic concept of home. In Milton's "Til we end In dust, our rest and native home," we find the link between the home and the sacred: home as heaven, the realm of the Father, where the Elect shall return. Freud, in contrast, associates one's originary home with the mother's womb, a place one longs to return to, but cannot. Pointing out the etymological relationship between *heim* (home) and *unheimliche* (uncanny), he notes that some of his male patients find "something uncanny about the female genital organs. This *Unheimliche* place, however, is the entrance to the former *Heim* of all human beings, to the place where each one of us lived once upon a time and in the beginning."[25] These contending perspectives incorporate deep-set ambivalence toward home space as simultaneously a utopian, sacred state of being, a metonomy of the Father's heavenly house, and a profane place, a metaphor of the mother's bodily enclosure. Suffering interminable homesickness yet fearing to be fully "at home" are ways of articulating the dilemma endemic to contemporary apocalypticism.

Rather than conjecturing about which came first—the split subject or the split home—I am suggesting that these are simultaneous constructions of the modern era. Profound ambivalence surrounding the place called home, the sense that it is an uncanny place, is part of what makes homes in U.S. society such complex heterotopias. Much of this complexity and ambivalence comes from changes in gendered power relations and the rising number of households headed by women. The materiality of mother-governed home space replicates women's place in the deployments of alliance and sexuality. The mother functions within home space as a simultaneously suppressed and suppressing agent of discipline. For apocalyptic-minded home dwellers, the home as uncanny, where the familiar turns strange, also comes from a rise in households of interracial and ethnic difference and/or gay or lesbian couples. The antagonisms of class, race, gender, and sexual practices within U.S. society are frequently embodied within individual households or by forcing people from homes. These existing antagonisms may be exacerbated—or lessened—through the vast electronic network that transports images and information from homes outside the United States into U.S. homes.

Examining home power/space is important because it is a foundational power/space of subjectivity. The production of new subjectivities is crucially linked to changes in home space. Converting homes into sites for the practice of freedom requires altering the current power/space of homes through resistance to the deployments of alliance, sexuality, and technopression. Understanding homes as heterotopias helps to defuse the sacred character of the home, the "sanctity" so often called on by those who would shore up masculinist, heterosexist dominance, while also relieving its sense of uncanniness and thwarting its susceptibility to electronic surveillance.

Struggles Over Home Design

The history of feminism shows that redefining the meanings and redesigning the physical arrangements of homes have always been integral to women's struggle for freedom in the United States. This is not surprising, since U.S. feminism emerged as part of—and because of—social divisions that were installed to differentiate home spaces according to gender and rank (husband from wife, parent from child, family from domestic worker). Home's thematic recurrence in feminist writings indicates that problematizing home as a place of women's oppression is a defining characteristic of feminism itself. The legacy of feminist discussions of homes provides a number of important resources that a genealogical approach to homes needs to draw on. Applying feminist proposals to a Foucauldian analytics of power suggests ways to avoid becoming further entrenched in the deployments of alliance, sexuality, and technoppression.

As Delores Hayden's *The Grand Domestic Revolution* demonstrates, nineteenth- and twentieth-century material feminists saw that it was necessary to redistribute the spatial arrangements for cooking, sleeping, dining, visiting friends, and so on, in order to redistribute social relations within homes, schools, churches, and government. But they sometimes did so in ways that reinforced the deployment of sexuality. Catharine Beecher, for example, who accepted women's subordination to men as a parallel of men's subordination to God but believed that the domestic sphere was one of higher morality informed by the natural moral supremacy of women, helped lay the groundwork for the feminization of homes. In *A Treatise on Domestic Economy* (1841), she sought ways to bridge home and government by improving the lot of (primarily white middle-class married) women so that they might more effectively instruct their sons in issues of societal governance.[26] This included providing better education for girls, who were to be future domestic managers. It also meant redesigning the home space to give wives easier access to a kitchen by putting it indoors. Although the indoor kitchen was a convenience, it also became a key site in biopower's requirements for a healthy family. In other words, it wasn't just that this rearrangement of home space restricted women's lives by keeping them in the kitchen. More problematic for women was what it obligated them to do for the sake of the nation. The indoor kitchen enmeshed them in biopower's insistence that family bodies be kept healthy for the welfare of the body politic.

At the turn of the century, and from a dramatically different political perspective, Charlotte Perkins Gilman formalized a socialist feminist critique of home as the space of women's economic and social exploitation. In essays and fictional accounts, Gilman demonstrated that masculinist ideals of homebound motherhood were at odds with goals of progress. Proposing the home as the matrix of the social order, she advocated a society that would privilege the well-being of mothers and children. In direct opposition to the spatial arrangements advocated by Beecher, Gilman's socialist vision included the ideas of raising children collectively and redesigning home spaces so that community kitchens and dining rooms would supplant single-family ones.[27] Even though Beecher and Gilman were diametrically opposed in many ways, Gilman's views aren't so different from Beecher's if one considers biopower's techniques for installing a politics of health and population perfectibility. Like Beecher, her proposals challenge a male-dominated form of biopower, but they also seek to advance technologies of normalization, with women as the advance guard for biopower.

A genealogical politicization of homes looks for ways to enhance the practice of freedom through spatial distributions that resist the disciplinary and managerial forces of biopower. Communal housing is a form of spatial redistribution that feminists have often found attractive because of their efforts to create gender and race equality. Many of these projects, from the nineteenth-century Oneida community to 1960s communes, failed because of the hostility of surrounding communities. Disapproval of their sexual and gender libertarianism led to economic, social, and legal penalties. One version of the communal model, Co-Housing Groups, is currently gaining in popularity, at least in part because it does not radically challenge gender and racial norms. Based on a Scandinavian model of communal living, these suburban pedestrian "villages" include property ownership with collective responsibilities for child care; each unit has its own kitchen, but it is part of the Co-Housing ethos for community members to dine together several nights a week. From a genealogical perspective, current co-housing appears to be a form of biopower oriented to the economically privileged, washed with nostalgia for small-town America, and with little to say about improving the lives of those who can't afford its prices.[28] Practices of collective living with a goal of resistance to normalizing power may be more readily found in projects such as the Iris House in New York City, established for women living with AIDS. But, like its more radical predecessors, Iris House has to confront social ostracism as well as economic difficulties.

Nineteenth- and twentieth-century feminist analyses have also illuminated the ideology of home. First- and second-wave feminist critiques of the romanticization of the home profoundly challenge that dominant construction by exposing the home as a space of systematic inequity and coercive sexuality. The antebellum Southern home was perhaps the most romanticized, in its own time and in its reappearances in popular fiction and film. Foremost among these critiques is Harriet Jacobs's riveting descriptions of hiding in her grandmother's attic for seven years in order to escape the violence of slavery, resist the sexual demands of her white slavemaster, and insure her children's safety. In *Incidents in the Life of a Slave Girl* (1861) Jacobs exposes the hidden interior of Southern plantation homes, which despite their courtly and gracious facades were sites of physical and verbal abuse and hypocrisy. Her discussion of the plantation mistress illustrates the ways that wealthy white Southern femininity began to incorporate the deployment of sexuality through the hysterization of white women's bodies. As Jacobs indicates, black women, whether slave or free, were prohibited to participate in that process but were judged by its standards. By representing the attic imprisonment of her persona Linda Brent within the space of her grandmother's house—the home of a free woman—she dramatizes how the system of slavery violated the ostensibly free homes of Southern blacks as well.[29] Jacobs's account thus points to the formation of a racial intersection within homes of the deployment of alliance and the deployment of sexuality. Contemporary racial segregation in housing is maintained by white supremacist violence, the racist enactment of the deployment of alliance. The deployment of sexuality, by contrast, manages racism, through such discriminatory formations as zoning restrictions and tax benefits for homeowners.

Second-wave U.S. feminist analyses have exposed the effects of home ideology on women living in a postwar consumer economy. Betty Friedan's powerful indictment of the feminine mystique established the detrimental effects of isolation and medicalization of suburban women.[30] Marge Piercy's novel *Woman on the Edge of Time* indicated how the working poor are especially vulnerable to threats of home surveillance and eviction. She shows the network of police and medical power relations that intersect home space to such an extent that they have authority to remove a woman from that space and hospitalize her until her conduct is deemed normal. Feminist critiques of the politics of labor have demonstrated that women are disciplined to perform a second shift of unpaid housework; married women who are full-time workers do 70 percent of this work.[31] These feminist studies need to be incorporated into genealogical analysis of the intersection of the deployments of alliance and sexuality.

One of the most important developments in feminist criticism of the male-dominant home is the campaign against domestic violence. The frequency and patterns of battering and sexual assault within homes suggest that, for women and children, homes are often induction sites for male abuse. Staggering levels of violence against women and children in homes today clearly show that the deployment of alliance continues to be exercised along with the other formations of power. Women's shelters serve as an immediate feminist resistance to this deployment, since they allow a woman to remove herself from her home. Longer term alternative homes function as combined resistance to the deployments of both alliance and sexuality. Instead of the kind of medicalization that subdues or pathologizes women, a home space like the Elizabeth Stone House in Massachusetts offers a residential mental health program, which includes an eight-week emergency shelter for battered women, a five-month residential program for women and children, and a transitional housing program providing day care and job training. Homes like these provide safety, self-help resources, and education to fend off both physical and medical abuse. The complicated task of genealogical examination of home space is to extend our understanding of how such homes counter the deployments of alliance and sexuality while also keeping tabs on media portrayals of women fighting back—as in the made-for-TV movie *The Burning Bed*, for example.

Second-wave feminists have established in myriad ways how the normalized nuclear-family ideology and the normative ideal of a single-family suburban home function to disqualify alternative home arrangements by condemning African American intergenerational households, single-mother homes, communes, and gay and lesbian households as deviant and/or "broken."[32] Some of these analyses give voice to the subjugated knowledges of alternative homes. But as the 1992 battle over the multicultural Rainbow curriculum in New York City makes clear, with the most intense objections to its use launched against the lesbian- and gay-affirmative children's books "Heather has Two Mommies" and "Daddy's Roommate," the giving of voice must be reinforced by a genealogical approach to home space that provides better understandings of the complexities and multiplicities of its physical setting and inhabitants. The most important contributions to this area are to be found in the relatively new field of feminist geography, which specifically addresses issues of architecture and public policy in regard to transforming hierarchically gendered spaces into egalitarian spaces.[33]

A genealogy of homes must also address the longstanding concept of a home as a private space. Feminist theorizing of homes makes clear that the notion of separate spheres implies a separation in power relations that simply does not hold. Second-wave feminist writings, particularly Marxist and socialist feminist analyses, have demonstrated in a variety of ways—from establishing the personal as political to providing extended analyses of reproduction of labor and consumerism in homes—that societal power relations do not line up behind a door marked "public" and retreat at the threshold of a door marked "private." Understanding homes as heterotopias traversed by physical, medicosexual, and electronic power networks is crucial for a home-front resistance to apocalyptic power relations. Given the redefinition of homes that comes out of challenges to male authority and privilege, it is not too surprising that conservative government officials and religious leaders continue to evoke the notion of home as a private and sanctified place.

More surprising, or maybe just suspect, is the continued acceptance of the ideas of public versus private in so-called liberal social theory, which purports to seek greater equity in the United States. Whatever the political and personal motivation for retaining this inadequate and highly misleading conceptualization, it can be understood as a consequence of thinking about home space as an abstraction, a universal and transcultural given rather than a specific and local construction. A kind of either/or thinking occurs from such abstractions, and certain conclusions are likely to follow. One is to privilege the private over and against the public. This stance envisions homes as places from which to battle public corruption; according to this line of thought, the public sphere might eventually be made moral by the actions of individuals properly trained within the home. The home is conceptualized as a core radiating honor and morality outward toward the larger community. Christopher Lasch's work largely takes this position, but argues that consumer society's values have brought about a breakdown of the necessary strong nuclear family with clear-cut parental order. On this line of thought, corruption from without has jeopardized the home-place's security and threatened its role as a moral center.[34]

A second scenario reverses the first by privileging the public domain as the scene of moral transformation which will eventually make its way to the private sphere. The popular *Habits of the Heart* provides a case in point. Accepting a separation between the public and private as a home/community dichotomy and documenting a recurrence of alienation from community, the authors then lament the loss of civic virtue by blaming private individualism, a mode of consciousness they see as also diminishing private experience. Ultimately, they call for community-minded social science as a public philosophy that could lead the way to an enrichment of private life.[35] A third argument places the public and the private in dialectical relation to one another, arguing for an ongoing tension that will mutually enrich each sphere. While this is an improvement on the first two positions inasmuch as it sees power relations in transaction, nonetheless, in this model too, abstract categories take precedence over empirical complications.

Abstract oppositions between *the* private and *the* public necessarily miss the workings of a vast and complex network of overlapping and exclusionary power relations.[36] The social space notion of the heterotopia allows us to see the ways in which U.S. homes are not private places either in opposition to or thoroughly infiltrated by public ones, but rather (and increasingly, with computer technology) sites of power relations both local and global. The concept of a heterotopia thus moves the analysis out of the framework of the public/private binary altogether. This does not mean that genealogical analysis relinquishes questions about the public and private, if that conceptualization is the one that has prevailed in a given society, as it has in ours. It means that genealogical analysis should ascertain the ways in which the categories of the private and the public have been used to define and regulate individuals and populations by demarcating certain behaviors as acceptable and expected within homes and excluding others as deviant. In regard to sexuality, for example, the public/private split has been used as a means of normalizing sexual activities. Bedroom privacy is secured for marital genital intercourse. But in the 25 states where antisodomy laws are in effect, there is no honoring of bedroom privacy for homosexual pleasures, as the Hardwick decision demonstrates. And although adultery and fornication are typically performed in secret places, approximately half of the states in the United States have laws making their practice a matter of public concern.[37] At the same time, sexual assaults against children and women have been harder to establish and penalize because of legal uses of the concept of home as a private sphere.

In addition to examining the legal and medical discourses and practices that divide, classify, and designate home space on the basis of a normalizing public/private dichotomy, genealogy needs to study the ways that home power/space gets rezoned through popular media. In this regard, to continue the example of sexualization, a genealogical approach to the home might consider such issues as the eroticization of kitchens during the 1970s, ranging from *The Total Woman*'s suggestions that wives adorn their otherwise naked bodies in Saran Wrap to the *Playboy* Advisor's praise of sex on the kitchen table. The entry of thanatos into the kitchen in the 1980s, with kitchen sex as an emblem of dangerous sexual passion, is pertinent as well. The kitchen sex scene in *Fatal Attraction* overlays the sexual liberation exhilaration of the seventies with the sexual panic of the eighties. Just as sexual obsession entered kitchens during the last few decades, so too did kitchen consciousness extend to bedrooms, ranging from home fashion magazines depicting sinks, refrigerators and coffeemakers as the new necessities of a well-equipped master bedroom to the ominous ice pick under the bed at the end of *Basic Instinct*.[38] In light of the contemporary spatial conjunction between bedrooms and cinema rooms à la VCRs, genealogical analysis might also consider the power/knowledge effects of watching such films on television from the "marriage bed," a striking instance of the intersecting deployments of alliance, sexuality, and technopression.

The bed itself is a site that has undergone significant alteration over time. Formerly a site of sex (consensual or coercive), childbirth, sickness, and death, beds have become more exclusively sexualized, with hospitals taking over bodily illness and death; a sexual assault that occurs in one's home, in one's own bed, is now the domain of police, various social services, the law, and media news. In terms of the commodification of beds, the satin-sheet sexy bed represented the dream of free-sex times, but in the sex-panic era, that has been replaced by an emphasis on down comforters. For a while it seemed as though death from disease or old age might be banished from the home altogether, with only its representation allowed in. Several factors are bringing bodily death back home, however. One, of course, is the soaring rise in costs of medical care and hospitalization, which also leaves many without homes, to die on the streets or in temporary shelters. Another is the alternative health movement, which argues for the familiarity of home as a more humane place for one's final period of life. Like it has with so many other aspects of our daily life, AIDS is dramatically transforming the way death is regarded, who has the right to say when it should occur, and where it should take place. A genealogy of homes would strive to ascertain the power relations that traverse the bed as a key site of the intersection of sexuality, commodification, rest, recuperation, violence, disease, and death.

A genealogical approach to home space wreaks a certain havoc on the analytical orderliness that the private-versus-public binary constructs. But just as genealogical analysis shows that modern subjectivity is neither unified nor coherent but multiple and contradictory, so too genealogy can help us analyze the home as a space of multiple and contradictory investments of power which elicit multiple and conflicting forms of resistance. It is equally important to perceive that late-capitalist, masculinist forces reterritorialize homes by denying this multiplicity. Dominant media representations renew desire for and illusions of the home as a private haven, a retreat from public scrutiny, even as communications technologies restructure it as a site of increased surveillance. Televisions, VCRs, and computers are dramatically transforming homes into local and global sites of electronic information gathering and dissemination. Thinking of homes as heterotopias enables us to see that the power deployments within homes are often at odds with each other. The opposition between deployments of alliance and sexuality, for instance, is made visible in the American Medical Association's 1992 pronouncement that violent men are a threat to women's health. Deployments of sovereign and disciplinary power, themselves competing for the bodily control of home inhabitants, are increasingly also in contention with technopression's electronic monitoring. Genealogy's task is to consider how these conflicts between deployments of power might be used to enhance resistance to them.

Homing in on Home Space

What you need today is an international business machine.

Somehow the word "foreign" seems foreign these days. The world is smaller, so people are thinking bigger, beyond borders.

Yet cultures will always be different, and that's the paradox of international business—the need to be global and local at the same time.

Ad for IBM, sole advertiser for the Time
Magazine Special Issue: Beyond the Year 2000

As the legacy of feminism makes clear, efforts to redesign home space are not new. But redesigning is not the same thing as what I am calling reconfiguring. Historically and conceptually, attempts to redesign homes have focused on a public/private formulation, which some first- and second-wave feminists accepted and some problematized. Reconfiguration takes its point of departure from the deconstruction of that split by seeing homes and the bodies that inhabit home space as a nexus of power relations that are both local and global. Because it understands homes as heterotopias, genealogical reconfiguration seeks a hybrid mode of resistance. It thus brings together electronic and aesthetic metaphors to describe a politics that refuses apocalyptic claims for an absolute end of time and place. Such a politics implies an ethical position that eschews the ideal of a completely autonomous agent whose consciousness is sui generis and for whom freedom means to be free of obligation.

Genealogical reconfiguration holds to the premise that individuals are initially and continually constituted in their homes as interdependent, interconnected social subjects. Reconfiguration seeks to arrange home space and its social relations as counters to forces of electronic reterritorialization. Reconfiguration seeks new ways to express meanings about homes as foundational spaces for the practice of freedom. Without acknowledging the conflicts that constrain freedom, both within and outside the walls of homes, there can be no such practice. Michael Cunningham's A Home at the End of the World is a poignant instance of reconfiguration. Giving an ironic twist to the apocalyptic tone of its title, Cunningham's novel portrays an anti-apocalyptic home in the making. As Bobby, one of the members of a newly defined family of friends/lovers/caretakers, puts it about his home: "This is ours; we have it to run from and we have it to return to. . . . Jonathan and I are here to maintain a present, so people can return to it when their futures thin out on them."[39] Described this way, their home is at once an acknowledgment of the societal oppressions and exclusions that emerge from the power relations within home space and an effort to transform these relations and themselves.

Contemporary media representations often draw on nostalgia to depict the home as the harmonious place it never really was. One portrayal, found everywhere from Ralph Lauren interiors to a slew of situation comedies featuring deliriously happy families and households of all sorts, recreates the home as a private retreat, safe from the slings and arrows of a threatening public life—denying the sexual assaults, murders, and illnesses that occur in homes. Such depictions have extended the once unquestioned equation of home and nuclear family to include a variety of family forms: blended, single parent, two same-sex adults, interracial and intergenerational groups (grandfathers were especially popular in the late eighties and early nineties, even though grandmothers are statistically more likely to be the surviving spouses). Other media depictions capitalize on the entertainment value of scenes of murder and sexual assault taking place inside a home. Some shows blur the lines between real life and simulation through home video footage and/or what is known oxymoronically as "real life simulations." Late capitalism can accommodate this complex of contradictory information, and thrives on it as long as homes help produce commodity-purchasers (and television's home shopping networks have made this increasingly likely).

Just as genealogy can help us see the ways in which depictions that either promote nostalgia or deny conflict conceal the decentering effects of electronic technology in homes, so too it can help curb the tendency to overemphasize the control effects of this technology. Mark Poster has argued, for example, that electronic modes of information create a "superpanopticon." Although Poster draws on Foucault for the panopticon analogy, he is not particularly Foucauldian in his disregard of resistance. He argues that, like Bentham's Panopticon, the superpanopticon instills a sense of surveillance—even when no actual watching is occurring: "Electronic monitoring of the population occurs silently, continuously, and automatically along with the transactions of everyday life."[40] Introducing the term "mode of information" to "designate social relations mediated by electronic communications systems, which constitute new patterns of language," he applies this line of thought to the family and its transformation.[41] "Through the use of television, telephones, Walkmen, and video cassette recorders," he argues, "the child, while physically in the home, receives communications from people outside the family."[42] Middle-class families, like those he surveyed in Orange County, California, are at a "crossroads." On one hand, they are committed to an egalitarian family structure that fosters self-direction for all its members. Yet, on the other hand, they have at their disposal a number of electronic technologies that may go against their own goals, both in terms of overt messages and in the surveillance mechanisms of the mode of information. Poster's concept of the mode of information is valuable for a genealogy of the home, but his analysis ignores modes of information resistance. Electronic determinism is a postmodern version of apocalyptic prophecy. Genealogists need to keep in mind that the electronic network is not a one-way system. Where there is surveillance, there is countersurveillance.

While maintaining a wary stance toward the apocalypticism that pervades theories of late capitalism, genealogy needs to join Poster in undertaking empirical research about the effects of electronic technology on home space. This is particularly important in regard to home computers. The installation of personal computers in homes in the United States is more likely for the middle- and upper-class, but even though only one-third of U.S. homes currently have personal computers, as with telephones, radios, and televisions, as prices for computers continue to fall, they may well become regular—and regulating—household fixtures.[43] In some instances, corporations equip home workers for telecommuting, though more often, workers are responsible for purchasing and repairing their own computers. Reluctance to lose managerial control has kept telecommuting from being widely adopted thus far, but if it does become the "wave of the future" as computer ads like to suggest, it will have considerable effect on home work and leisure time as well as spatial arrangements.[44] The move toward establishing electronic cottage industries extends the reaches of the electronic network. As Donna Haraway argues, drawing on Richard Gordon's notion of a "homework economy," "the concept indicates that factory, home, and market are integrated on a new scale."[45] Much more genealogical investigation needs to be done on the ways that this new integration is transforming workers and their homes and how they in turn might direct that transformation.

These integrations are rapidly altering relations between homes, families, schools, prisons, sexuality, politics, and law as well. These changes invite genealogical study of such practices as parental control over children's television viewing and the Nintendo effect on a generation attaining adulthood. The integration of homes and schools by way of interactive television needs to be assessed genealogically as a convergence of deployments of disciplinary power and technopression's use of pleasure. Implanted mechanisms that allow prisoners to live at home deserve genealogical attention for this intersection of discipline, punishment, and electronic surveillance. Genealogy faces new questions about home privacy and electronic mail, including the confidentiality of White House e-mail.[46] Other such questions emerge. How do electronic communications through "GayNet" transform the ideological space of the "closet"? How is government decision making informed by widespread home viewing of U.S. military intervention? What new definitions of friend and stranger emerge through electronic intimacy with people one never sees?

We don't know yet — cannot know in advance — what the transformations in social life will be because of these new circuitries in the power/knowledge/space home network. But it is neither too soon nor too late for cultural theory to look homeward. Far more genealogical research about the effects of the mode of information needs to be done to help us understand the extent to which the places we call homes are under negotiation between forces of electronic monitoring and forces of electronic resistance. Rather than adding to voices of doom, genealogy can aid the practice of freedom by circulating information about the democratic home-front strategies and tactics that are being used to deterritorialize homes. It can help spread the word — and send the signal — about ways to establish local/ global electronic linkages for activist groups. A genealogical approach to homes creates a forum for those who are currently fighting the forces of alliance, sexuality, and technopression on their own home fronts. After all, there are home dwellers who have been educated through feminism, civil rights struggles for equitable housing, and a wide variety of grassroots organizations who are concerned about the well-being of the earth, and who are computer-literate, who are, at this moment, reconfiguring their homes into sites of power/space that foster the practice of freedom. By examining their modes of resistance to all three deployments of power — physical seizure, disciplinary surveillance, and electronic monitoring — genealogy can help them change what it means to be a homebody.

Coda
On Waco: A Monday Morning Wake-Up Call

Writing this Coda in the weeks after the destruction of the compound in Waco, Texas, on April 19, 1993, I am struck by the way that public fascination with David Koresh and the Branch Davidians quickly soared and then almost as suddenly dropped off, not once, but twice. In the first few weeks after the Bureau of Alcohol, Tobacco, and Firearms raided the compound, the media filled its airtime with long-distance shots of the buildings huddled together in an expanse of Texas prairie land, interspersing the stillness of that image with footage of a Bible-wielding Koresh vociferously preaching to mesmerized followers. But as the seige dragged on, media coverage and public interest abated. After the F.B.I. assault that reduced the compound and its inhabitants to ashes, viewers were left exhausted from the second round of live media images of destruction and stories on the messiah who loved guns, rock and roll, sex, and scripture. By the time the NBC movie, "In the Line of Duty: Ambush in Waco," aired on May 23, some people with whom I talked reported being bored with the topic. Others simply felt that everything that could be said had been said. Even those still engaged in trying to understand its implications reported being drained by the monotony of media portrayals.

This shift from media-induced hunger to satiation illustrates the dangers of technoppression's mode of knowledge production. Hyperreal simulations of violence blur into news accounts of torture and death. A numbing sets in, dulling ethical-political responsiveness and inquiry. It happened with Jonestown as well. Jonathan Z. Smith's criticism of press sensationalism is as true for Waco in 1993 as it was for Jonestown in 1978: "The press, by and large, featured the pornography of Jonestown—the initial focus on the daily body counts, the details on the conditions of the corpses. Then, as more 'background' information became available, space was taken over by lurid details of beatings, sexual humiliations, and public acts of perversion."[1] As Smith points out about Jonestown, the problem with such sensationalism is that very little understanding of the event comes out of a repetition of startling images and 30-second interviews. How many times can one hear with interest pronouncements by "cult experts" or "former cult members," as they are typically labeled, that Koresh was a charismatic madman or that his sexuality was bizarre? Media repetition, even of lurid details, breeds a sense of overfamiliarity, if not outright boredom; it manufactures disinterest. By default, the findings of the official review board of the Justice Department become end-of-season reruns.

The dynamic of riveted attention followed by dismissive indifference also shows how apocalypse is an all-or-nothing affair, even when it's not the "real thing." Despite the general use of the term "apocalypse" to designate the destruction of the Branch Davidian compound, very few people proclaimed that this was *the* Apocalypse prophesied in the Bible. Rather than seeing the leaden smoke and explosions of flame engulfing the compound as the beginning of the End, most who witnessed the event on live television or in its numerous replays saw the devastation as either a warranted or unfortunate consequence of a justified U.S. government action to uphold the law.[2] Since so many in the United States profess belief in the Second Coming, those polled might well be reassuring themselves that the Beast has not yet left his Mark.[3] From the perspective of mainstream millennialism, Branch Davidian belief is merely millennial truth gone awry, twisted and distorted by a self-proclaimed manipulative or mad messiah. Pathologizing Koresh enables another kind of reeassurance to occur among the "true believers": his abuse of children is different in kind from the physical punishment taking place within their homes; his sexual obsessions expose the invalidity of Davidianism, but television evangelicalism and Catholicism are not to be judged by the sexual misconduct of their clergy; his stash of weapons is demented, but holdings by members of the National Rifle Association are all-American.

Such attitudes are the antithesis of genealogical investigation. They ignore or fail to heed the threat of the ways in which apocalyptic beliefs and actions have indeed left their mark not only on Waco but throughout the United States. They are as hasty and ill-advised as the response of Branch Davidian Steve Schneider who tossed the telephone out of the window at 5:55 A.M. that fateful Monday morning when federal agents called to tell of their impending assault. Three hours later, when they unfurled a white sheet bearing the message, "We Want Our Phones Fixed," it was too late for second thoughts; the F.B.I. was unwilling to halt its battering of the building and spraying of tear gas. The destruction at Waco is now of the past, but its significance is far from over. Waco is an event with important implications for democratic freedom. Immediate public and congressional approval of a federal government attack on a religious sect—before an investigation had even begun—means few throughout the United States understand the ways of apocalypse. To dismiss Koresh as an aberration and to condone the F.B.I. raid as a righteous act of justice is to fail to grasp the significance of Waco as emblematic of widespread U.S. apocalypticism. For what is so striking about Waco is that it is a convergence of all three modes of apocalypticism: divine, technological, and ironic.

> If you want to get to heaven in the good old way,
> Johnny get your gun, get your gun.[4]

David Koresh's pronouncements can be readily discerned as divine apocalypse. He espoused history as divinely ordained. He held the Bible to be the word of God and insisted that biblical prophecy was a statement of truth about how the world would end in cataclysmic struggle between forces or righteousness and evil. He taught that divine judgment would reward the elect in heaven and punish sinners in hell for eternity. Such pronouncements are consonant with divine apocalypse's mode of comprehending and narrating truth. They accord with the belief of 40 percent of U.S. citizens who avow that the Bible is the literal word of God. As Paul Boyer has pointed out, Koresh's teachings were in "important respects indistinguishable in tone and content from the presentations of other apocalyptic preachers who now crowd the airwaves."[5] What does distinguish Koresh from other fundamentalists, of course, was his claim to be Christ, chosen by God to lead others to heaven. It's not the messianic claim per se that distinguished Koresh from other fundamentalists, just the claimant. Even that distinction is slight, since Branch Davidianism is hardly alone in proclaiming the messiah to be among us.

Koresh, or anyone else, clearly has a right to believe and make public such claims, just as anti-apocalypticists have a right to argue back, to point out the intolerances and hatred they see within in apocalyptic discourses, as well as the historical consequences of putting apocalyptic values into social practice. It would be simpler, of course, if expressions of divine apocalypse were readily distinguishable from the secular. But one of the main points of *Anti-Apocalypse* is to demonstrate the extent to which an apocalyptic regime of truth permeates contemporary life in the United States. Our ostensibly secular mainstream media itself used divine apocalyptic discourse to portray Koresh as a prophetic and possibly supernatural figure. Take, for example, the lead article in the *Time* magazine issue that featured on its cover a rapturous close-up of David Koresh engulfed in flames, captioned by Revelation 6:8: "His name was Death, and Hell followed with him." The entire cover story follows suit. Interspersing dramatic descriptions of the final hours leading up to the demolition of the compound with biblical passages from Revelation, the news story literalizes Koresh as a demonic figure, ending with the words: "And the devil who had deceived them was thrown into the lake of fire and sulfur, where the beast and false prophet were, and they will be tormented day and night forever and ever."[6] However one judges the quality of this story—as a sermon, or possibly as parody of Koresh—it is egregious reporting. But it is not puzzling when seen in light of the discursive dynamic of contemporary apocalypticism. Once the more than 100 agents from the Bureau of Alcohol, Tobacco, and Firearms moved in on Koresh's compound on February 28, 1993, "Waco" was no longer to be understood as a town in Texas. Like the term "apocalypse," the meanings of "Waco" began to proliferate, becoming immediately enmeshed in an already existing network of apocalyptic discourses. The *Time* reporter's biblical exegesis of Waco exemplifies, albeit more explicitly than usual, the ways that media productions of knowledge frame and infuse "news" with an apocalyptic regime of truth.

Hollywood gospel abounds as well these days, and may be part of the reason that the *Time* story's blend of reporting and scripture could be deemed acceptable by its editorial staff. Like Hollywood, news magazines have learned to play it both ways, selling their wares to believers and skeptics alike. As Pat Broeske indicates, a striking number of film and television screenwriters have turned to scripture for inspiration. Broeske's interviews with several such writers disclose their allegiance to divine apocalypse, ranging from traditional fundamentalism to the New Age mode of spirituality. Others seem to be capitalizing on the public's eagerness for apocalyptic truth in all its glory and all its gory details.[7] One reason that divine apocalypse is a hot commodity in the era of sex panic is because of its focus on transgression and punishment. It is part of the logic of divine apocalypse to recite or rehearse graphic manifestations of evil so that potential sinners can have adequate knowledge of what to shun. Details of punishment need to be elaborated, too, to give a full enough sense of what transgression will bring. Icons of lust like David Koresh become the fetish objects of this mode of apocalypticism, his fiery death the justified punishment for his evil ways. Through portrayals of apocalypse, film and television can have its sexualized body and beat it too. The point I want to stress here is that by portraying apocalypse, media proliferates it.[8] Regardless of authorial motive or belief, as these scripts are converted into films over the next few years, they are likely to fuel apocalyptic fits of panic already witnessed in responses to global warfare, African famine, AIDS, and the approach of the year 2000. In that sense, Waco as a key event of 1993 may well be a sign of the coming of seven years of incited tribulation.

> Mine eyes have seen the glory of the coming of the Lord
> He is trampling out the vintage where the grapes of wrath are stored
> He has loosed the fateful lightning of his terrible, swift sword
> His truth is marching on.[9]

Just as Waco was produced from and produces these forms of divine apocalypse, so too the 51-day siege began and ended through expanding operations of technological apocalypse. Both sides, the Branch Davidians and the invading government personnel alike, set in motion forces of technological death and devastation. It is easy enough to see how Koresh's biblically inspired reasoning meshed readily with a technological means to fight the enemy. It makes apocalyptic sense for soldiers in God's army to fight Satan's fire with God's fire; in our era that means AK-47s. For the government it seems to have worked the other way around: technological prowess gained momentum and favor as it took meaning from divine apocalypse. The initial raid by the Bureau of Alcohol, Tobacco, and Firearms, which left 4 agents dead and 16 wounded, involved storming the compound in full daylight, as open targets, and despite knowing that the Davidians knew they were coming. Did the Bureau think its agents were invincible?[10]

The agents planning the second raid did not make the same mistake. They erred, literally, on the side of overkill by launching a full-scale military operation. As an editorial in *The Nation* entitled "The War in Waco" pointed out, the "militarization of law enforcement derives from past campaigns of federal and local police against bootleggers, the Mafia, drug dealers (and users) and poor minority criminals. In those 'wars' the targets were converted into 'enemies,' with all the dehumanizing and demonizing that entails."[11] Justifying the military defeat of such "enemies" within our own borders spells out a messianic mission for the U.S. government. During the last two decades, confrontations between local and federal officials and these "enemies" serve as the bold markers to a militarization that is becoming increasingly routine. Even when they represent the worst kind of bungling by officials, the drama of events like those surrounding the 70-day occupation of South Dakota's Pine Ridge Reservation in 1973, or the bombing of the Move house in 1985, and Waco, tends to legitimize the more wide-scale use of troops and military as a means of law enforcement. Since the uprising following the first trial of the police officers who beat Rodney King, the routine of cordoning off certain neighborhoods in anticipation of controversial verdicts is being represented as necessary to law enforcement. The deployment of government troops in areas where violence might spring up threatens the safety and rights of all citizens, even if it is done on their behalf. As Waco demonstrates, the death count and destruction of messianic government actions are often indistinguishable from messianic "criminal" or "deviant" actions.

Foucault's discussion of biopower illuminates the mutual reinforcement between the regulation and control of the entire population and the genocidal impulse to eradicate portions of it. Although biopower exerts force by managing and disciplining life, death remains one of its means of enforcement. Biopower's techniques for fostering health and securing longevity have been developing in scope and intricacy over the last two centuries, yet "wars were never as bloody as they have been since the nineteenth century, and all things being equal, never before did regimes visit such holocausts on their own populations."[12] Technological apocalypse intertwines with biopower's promises to insure the well-being of the good citizens by using its machinery to destroy the evil ones. At the same time that biopower promotes the life of the civil body by enforcing genocide, it is confounded by suicide. As Foucault indicates, the personal "determination to die" was "one of the first astonishments of a society in which political power has assigned itself the task of administering life."[13] In regard to Waco, government expressions of shock about mass suicide, especially in the face of extensive deliberation about how to avoid another Jonestown, are a record of that astonishment. Whereas divine apocalypse hails the determination to die for God as martyrdom, technological apocalypse has no provision for the kind of agency involved in ending one's own life.

"Hey, did you hear the one about . . . ?"

Jokes about Waco began circulating as soon as the dead and wounded bodies from the first assault were cleared away. Although it takes a certain amount of cynicism to joke about such things, the dark humor of Waco also reveals just how anxiety-ridden the discourse of ironic apocalypse is. Despite its pose of world-weary exhaustion and its stance of political-ethical inertia, the discourse of ironic apocalypse should not be construed as untroubled about the catastrophe it regards as inevitable. As with those that followed Jonestown and the explosion of the Challenger, Waco jokes allowed for expressions of fear about cultural disorder, disempowerment, and life's contingency through a rhetoric of denial and trivilization. Jokes in general provide outlets for distasteful ideas. "Sick" jokes thrive on shock value. But that does not mean that their utterances are nonnormative. What is particularly revealing about Waco jokes as a form of ironic apocalypse is the way that they permit expressions of racism, sexism, homophobia, and hostility toward certain religious groups. Because they are "only" jokes, their articulation throughout homes, schools, military bases, and work places, on morning radio talk shows, and over e-mail, is more readily tolerated or condoned.[14]

The first round of jokes pathologized the name "Waco" by punning on the sound-alike term "Wacko" and playing on Waco as an acronym for "We Ain't Coming Out!" Such jokes put in bold relief not only the predominance but also the economy of medicalized discourse in contemporary U.S. society. The encapsulation of Branch Davidian behavior as both ridiculously insane and ludicrously defiant is characteristic of the way deviance is pathologized around a duality that simultaneously dismisses and accuses. This duality framed much of the serious discussion about the religious sect as well. Referring to the Davidians as a "cult" reduces their religious practice to a mental health problem. With the bursting flames of the compound came a flurry of acronyms that replicated this conflation of mental illness and defiant deviance, such as "We Are Christianity's Outcasts" and "We Are Clinical Outpatients." The predictable "mad messiah" equation between Koresh and Jim Jones was expressed in a question-and-answer format: "Why did the Branch Davidians commit mass suicide? To keep up with the Jonses!"

Waco humor was a theater of mutually reinforcing stereotypes. Dismissive links between the Davidians and other religious groups were found in jokes like "What do you call a Scientologist with a flamethrower? A copycat," or "Did you hear the Pope canonized David Koresh? He's a Friar!" The most virulent of these were aimed at Judaism: "The events in Waco could have been foreseen, had anyone in the F.B.I. understood that David Koresh was encapsulating Jewish history. First they reenacted the Passover, then there was the reenactment of the Warsaw ghetto uprising." Other jokes ridiculing the Davidians exhibit thinly veiled hostility toward women, blacks, and gays. This is the case, for example, with "How do you pick up a Branch Davidian woman? With a Dust-Buster"; "What do Rodney King and David Koresh have in common? They're both black"; and "Did you hear that David Koresh was a closeted gay? He was flaming, but he didn't come out." Using stereotypes to denigrate certain groups is a way of differentiating oneself from them, and insult is a means of dissociating further. In this respect, Waco jokes provide a sharply focused picture of social combat in which anti-Semitism, misogyny, white supremacy, and homophobia are seen as acceptable weapons against democratic activists.

In a startling repetition compulsion, cannibalism recurred throughout Waco jokes. The deaths of the Davidians—a quintessential event of disorder—was reordered and contained through the familiar and everyday: food preparation. The engulfing and hellishly power flames were brought under control through motifs of cooking. From "How is Waco like a Snickers bar? Roasted nuts," and "What was David Koresh's favorite breakfast cereal? Crispy Critters!" to a new round of acronyms like "What a Cook Out" and "We Are Crispy Outside," we can discern efforts to stave off fears of contingency and death. On e-mail, one of these jokes aimed specifically at the deaths of the children was followed by a rare admission of perhaps crossing the line of acceptable sick humor. A parenthetical "Gross" followed "Did you hear about the new restaurant opening in Waco? It's a new Sizzler. / What's their first special to be? Baby back ribs." What I find most telling about these jokes is their use of a taboo to license barbaric hostility. This is the function of cannibalism in imperialist discourse, in which such accusations against a group's leader justify the massacre of the group. Whereas divine and technological apocalypse are made more compelling through the drama of the End, ironic apocalypse gains its cynicism from regarding as unpreventable the many endings that human misjudgments and cruelties have brought about. The jokes themselves reinforce cynicism by domesticating forces of destruction. The contemptuousness endemic to ironic apocalypticism fosters a particular kind of danger. As the Waco jokes indicate, this mode allows hatred to proliferate by appearing to be both beyond metaphysical superstition and above the political fray.

Apocalypticism in each of its modes fuels discord, breeds anxiety or apathy, and sometimes causes panic. Decision-making suffers when it takes apocalyptic form — whether at the level of individual, everyday personal choices or of local, national, and international government, military, and peace-keeping deliberations. What makes apocalypse so compelling is its promise of future perfection, eternal happiness, and godlike understanding of life, but it is that very will to absolute power and knowledge that produces its compulsions of violence, hatred, and oppression.

An event like Waco should jolt us out of apocalyptic slumber, but it should not end our dreams. Understanding Waco can help transform dreams of everyday freedom into genealogical truth. A wake-up call should not be confused with a clarion call. Rather than the sound of trumpets proclaiming the End, a wake-up call is a reminder that there is a day ahead, someone to meet, or work to do. Its ring can sound urgent. In the poem "Lennox Avenue Mural," Langston Hughes sounds such a tone when he ponders what happens to a dream deferred: "Does it dry up / like a raisin in the sun? / Or fester like a sore," or "stink like rotten meat," or "crust and sugar over"? "Maybe it just sags / like a heavy load. *Or does it explode?*" But urgency and passion are not the same as apocalyptic threat. Against the shrillness of end-time alarms or the blaring trumpets of millennial triumph, let Waco serve as a more humble reminder that there is a great deal of work to do in exposing the costs of apocalypse. Or as Hughes puts it at the end of his poem: "Good morning, daddy! / Ain't you heard?"

Notes

Introduction

1. Michel Foucault, "The Masked Philosopher," in *Michel Foucault: Politics, Philosophy, Culture, Interviews and Other Writings, 1977-1984*, ed. Lawrence D. Kritzman (New York: Routledge, 1988), p. 329.

2. The Foucauldian concept of truth: "Truth is a thing of this world: it is produced only by virtue of multiple forms of constraint. And it induces regular effects of power. Each society has its regime of truth, its 'general politics' of truth." Michel Foucault, "Truth and Power," in *Power/Knowledge* (New York: Pantheon, 1980), p. 131.

3. Francis Fukuyama, *The End of History and the Last Man* (New York: Macmillan, 1992). Kathy Dobie, "Lord of the Trees: Jesus Appears in New Haven," *Village Voice* (December 29, 1992), pp. 33-37.

4. Quoted in Bill Lawren, "Are You Ready for Millennial Fever?," *Utne Reader*, reprinted from *Psychology Today* (March/April 1990), 96-97.

5. The argument that apocalypticism is ingrained in American culture has had currency over the century, enjoying special vogue in the 1960s with Vietnam and the struggle for civil rights as a cultural context. Nathan A. Scott, Jr., provides a particularly useful analysis of the apocalyptic rhetoric of that decade in his " 'New Heav'ns, New Earth': The Landscape of Contemporary Apocalypse," *Journal of Religion* 53 (January 1973), pp. 1-35. I am indebted to such studies, but also want to differentiate my approach from one that assumes an American mentality. Discourse analysis shows how unities are forged and mandated, that is, how they operate as constraints on other forms of knowledge, whereas mentality tends to accept an idea as unified outside of power relations (or as passed on by "influence," an entirely beneficent form of power relation). Two more recent books that I really wish I had had while writing mine are: Harold Bloom, *The*

American Religion (New York: Simon and Schuster, 1992); and Paul Boyer, *When Time Shall Be No More: Prophecy Belief in Modern American Culture* (Cambridge, Mass.: Harvard University Press, 1992). Boyer's study of fundamentalist prophecy writers is invaluable.

6. "A Statistical Portrait of the 'Typical' American," *New York Times*, July 26, 1992, section E, p. 5.

7. Cornel West, "Learning to Talk of Race," *New York Times Magazine*, August 2, 1992, p. 26. West's use of an "Either we learn . . . / or the fire" is in keeping with the jeremiad, a form of prophecy that focuses on the possibility of staving off the calamity on the horizon even as it uses apocalyptic images to gain participation.

8. Ibid.

9. Amos Funkenstein, "A Schedule for the End of the World: The Origins and Persistence of the Apocalyptic Mentality," in *Visions of Apocalypse: End or Rebirth?* ed. Saul Friedlander et al. (New York: Holmes and Meier, 1985), p. 57.

10. Michel Foucault, *The Archaeology of Knowledge*, trans. A. M. Sheridan Smith (New York: Harper and Row, 1972), p. 38.

11. Ibid., p. 27.

12. In *The Archaeology of Knowledge* Foucault provides five tasks to undertake in examining discourse which guide my approach throughout this book: 1) "To show how quite different discursive elements may be formed on the basis of similar rules"; 2) "To show to what extent these rules do or do not apply in the same way, are or are not arranged in accordance with same model in different types of discourse"; 3) "To show how entirely different concepts . . . occupy a similar position in the ramification of their system of positivity"; 4) "To show, on the other hand, how a single notion . . . may cover two archaeologically distinct elements"; 5) "Lastly, to show how, from one positivity to another, relations of subordination or complementarity may be established." Ibid., pp. 160-61. Also see Foucault, "Two Lectures" in *Power/Knowledge* (New York: Pantheon, 1980); in particular, see pages 93-108 for his methodological precautions regarding analysis of discourses.

13. Norman O. Brown, *Apocalypse and/or Metamorphoses* (Berkeley: University of California Press, 1991), p. 6. This assertion was made in 1960. Brown's more recent pronouncements about Dionysus are somewhat more circumspect. For example, in "Dionysus in 1990," the final essay of this collection, he concedes that it "may well be that human beings can tolerate Dionysian truth only if it is held at a distance, projected onto human or divine scapegoats, admitted under the sign of negation. Reality may be too much for us. We may, like Job, have uttered what we cannot understand" (p. 198).

14. Swami Nostradamus Virato, "11:11 Doorway to the Cosmos: Interview," *New Frontier Magazine* 101 (December 1991), pp. 11-13. Quoted by Ted Daniels, *Millennium Watch* 1 (May 1992), pp. 1-3.

15. See Andre Reszler, "Man as Nostalgia: The Image of the Last Man in Twentieth-Century Postutopian Fiction," in *Visions of Apocalypse: End or Rebirth?*, ed. Friedlander et al. (New York: Holmes & Meier, 1985), pp. 196-215.

16. For discussions of the tenets and key features of apocalypse, see Amos Funkenstein, "A Schedule for the End of the World: The Origins and Persistence of the Apocalyptic Mentality," in *Visions of Apocalypse: End or Rebirth?* ed. Friedlander et al. p. 57. Friedlander's "Introduction" is also excellent.

17. Thomas Jefferson, *Notes on the State of Virginia*, ed. William Peden (New York: Norton, 1972), p. 163. This apocalyptic anxiety is uncharacteristic of Jefferson's writings. I discuss his nonapocalyptic aesthetics of liberty in *Freedom, Foucault, and the Subject of America* (Boston: Northeastern University Press, 1991).

18. A succinct and insightful overview of millennialism in the United States may be found in Catherine L. Albanese, *American Religions and Religion* (Belmont, Calif.: Wadsworth, 1992). This far more abreviated description is drawn from her account. I thank Susan Henking for giving me a copy of this book.

The apocalyptic tendency of American culture as expressed in national literature has been explored by a number of critics. See, in particular, R. W. B. Lewis, "Days of Wrath and Laughter," in his *Trials of the Word* (New Haven: Yale University Press, 1965), pp. 184-235. Lewis establishes the historical context for literary apocalypticism from Puritan millennialism and traces a dramatic shift from that view to Melville's "savagely comical apocalypse" in *The Confidence-Man*. Ihab Hassan explores the gloomier expressions of literary apocalypticism, which veers into annihilative silence, in his *Literature of Silence* (New York: Knopf, 1967). For more recent analyses of apocalypticism in American literature, see David Ketterer, *New Worlds for Old: The Apocalyptic Imagination, Science Fiction, and American Literature* (Bloomington: Indiana University Press, 1975); Zbigniew Lewicki, *The Bang and the Whimper: Apocalypse and Entropy in American Literature* (Westport, Conn.: Greenwood Press, 1984); and Douglas Robinson, *American Apocalypses: The Image of the End of the World in American Literature* (Baltimore: Johns Hopkins University Press, 1985).

19. Melville also brought an intense sense of irony to narratives of human destruction, but the causes for it in his works oscillate between divine vengeance and nature's destructive forces. Adams extends this irony explicitly to technological achievement. As I will show in chapter 4, his irony combines the comic that R. W. B. Lewis discusses and the annihilative that Hassan deals with.

20. This segment appeared in Bill Jersey's "Fighting Back," the first of three segments of the PBS series "The Glory and the Power: Fundamentalism Observed," June 15, 1992.

21. L. S. Klepp, "Heaven Can Wait: Prophets Hope for the Worst," *Voice Literary Supplement* (February 1993), p. 10; Robert Jay Lifton and Charles B. Strozier, "Waiting for Armageddon," *The New York Times Book Review* (August 12, 1990), p. 25. See Hal Lindsey, *The Late Great Planet Earth* (Grand Rapids, Idaho: Zondervan, 1970).

22. Lifton and Strozier, "Waiting," pp. 1, 24-25.

23. Anne Primavesi, *From Apocalypse to Genesis: Ecology, Feminism and Christianity* (Minneapolis: Fortress, 1991), p. 71.

24. Bill McKibben, *The End of Nature* (New York: Random House, 1989).

25. Jean Baudrillard, "The Anorexic Ruins" in *Looking Back on the End of the World* (New York: Semiotext(e), 1989), p. 34. Also see the use of millennialism in Arthur Kroker, Marilouise Kroker, and David Cook, *Panic Encyclopedia: The Definitive Guide to the Postmodern Scene* (New York: MacMillan, 1989).

26. Foucault, *Archaeology of Knowledge*, p. 27.

27. Michel Foucault, "Nietzsche, Genealogy, History," in *Language, Counter-Memory, Practice: Selected Essays and Interviews*, trans. Donald F. Bouchard and Sherry Simon (Ithaca: Cornell University Press, 1977), p. 148.

28. Ibid.

29. Michel Foucault, "Two Lectures," in *Power/Knowledge*, ed. Colin Gordon (New York: Pantheon, 1980), pp. 82-83.

30. Henry Adams, *The Education of Henry Adams*, ed. Ernest Samuels (Boston: Houghton Mifflin, 1973), p. 496.

31. Bush quoted in William Safire's "On Language" column, *New York Times Magazine* (June 21, 1992), p. 10.

1. Eu(jean)ics: The New Fashion in Power

1. For a fashion-magazine history of jeans, from working wear to jeans couture, see Joe Keenan, "It's All in the Jeans," *Vogue* (August 1992), pp. 222-27, 296.

2. Mike Snider, "Many Favor Gene Therapy to Enhance Babies," *USA Today*, September 29, 1992.

3. Jean Baudrillard, *Forget Foucault*, trans. Nicole Dufresne (New York: Semiotext(e), 1987).

4. For Foucault's discussion of the archive see in particular chapter 5 of *The Archaeology of Knowledge*, trans. A. M. Sheridan Smith (New York: Harper and Row, 1972).

5. R. C. Lewontin, Steven Rose, and Leon Kamin, *Not in Our Genes: Biology, Ideology, and Human Nature* (New York: Pantheon, 1984), pp. 26-27.

6. Michel Foucault, *History of Sexuality* (New York: Vintage, 1978), p. 118.

7. Ibid., pp. 42-43.

8. Foucault calls this subjectivity an "empirico-transcendental doublet" to signify how the human sciences which constituted it "are directed towards that which, outside man, makes it possible to know, with a positive knowledge, that which is given to or eludes his consciousness." Foucault, *The Order of Things: An Archaeology of the Human Sciences* (New York: Vintage, 1973), p. 378.

9. For analysis of sexual difference in scientific discourse, see Evelyn Fox Keller, *Reflections on Gender and Science* (New Haven: Yale University Press, 1985). For race difference, see Stephen Jay Gould, *The Mismeasure of Man* (New York: W.W. Norton, 1981). And for an extended discussion of these issues, see Lewontin et al., *Not in Our Genes*.

10. Michael Warner, "Introduction: Fear of a Queer Planet," *Social Text* 29 (1991), pp. 3-17.

11. Foucault, *History of Sexuality*, p. 106.

12. See, for example, the essays in *Feminism and Foucault: Reflections on Resistance*, ed. Irene Diamond and Lee Quinby (Boston: Northeastern University Press, 1988).

13. The translations for "Cuando Estamos Juntos" ("When We're Together") and "Detente" ("Wait") appear in *Harper's*, in, respectively, the November 1986 issue and the October 1987 issue.

14. Jean Baudrillard, "The Ecstasy of Communication," in *The Anti-Aesthetic: Essays on Postmodern Culture*, ed. Hal Foster (Port Townsend, Wash.: Bay Press, 1983), pp. 126-27.

15. Jean Baudrillard, "The Order of Simulacra," *Simulations*, trans. Philip Beitchman (New York: Foreign Agents Series, Semiotext(e), 1983), p. 150.

16. Baudrillard, "Rituals of Transparency," in *The Ecstasy of Communication*, trans. Bernard and Caroline Schutze (New York: Foreign Agents Series, Semiotext(e), 1988),

pp. 36-37; Paul Simon, "The Boy in the Bubble," *Graceland*, Warner Bros. Records, 1986.

17. Arthur and Marilouise Kroker, "Theses on the Disappearing Body in the Hyper-Modern Condition," in *Body Digest, Canadian Journal of Political and Social Theory* 11:1-2 (1987), pp. i-xvi; Arthur Kroker and Michael Dorland, "Panic Cinema: Sex in the Age of the Hyperreal," *CineAction!* (Fall 1987), pp. 3-5.

18. My analyses are aided by Erving Goffman, *Gender Advertisements* (London: Macmillan, 1979); Judith Williamson, *Decoding Advertisements: Ideology and Meaning in Advertising* (London: Marion Boyers, 1978); Torben Vestergaard and Kim Schroder, *The Language of Advertising* (Oxford: Basil Blackwell, 1985). Also see the essays by Julia Emberley, "The Fashion Apparatus and the Deconstruction of Postmodern Subjectivity"; Kim Sawchuk, "A Tale of Inscription/Fashion Statements"; Gail Faurschou, "Fashion and the Cultural Logic of Postmodernity"; Berkeley Kaite, " 'Obsession' and Desire: Fashion and the Postmodern Scene" in *Body Digest, Canadian Journal of Political and Social Theory* 11:1-2, (1987).

19. For a history of the leading jeanswear corporation, see Ed Cray, *LEVIs* (Boston: Houghton Mifflin, 1978).

20. Stuart and Elizabeth Ewen, *Channels of Desire: Mass Images and the Shaping of American Consciousness* (New York: McGraw-Hill, 1982), pp. 110, 112.

21. Cray, *LEVIs*, p. 90.

22. Ibid., p. 125, and Ewen and Ewen, *Channels*, pp. 114-15.

23. Joan Saltalamachia, Levi's jeans division advertising manager, quoted in Cray, *LEVIs*, p. 150.

24. John Carlos Rowe, "Modern Art and the Invention of Postmodern Capital," *American Quarterly*, 39 (Spring 1987), p. 156.

25. Jean Baudrillard, "The Precession of the Simulacra," trans. Paul Foss and Paul Patton, in *Simulations* (New York: Foreign Agents Series, Semiotext(e), 1983), p. 11.

26. Cynthia Enloe, *Bananas, Beaches, and Bases* (Berkeley, University of California Press: 1990), pp. 155-56.

27. Also see Andrew Sullivan, "Flogging Underwear: The New Raunchiness of American Advertising," *The New Republic* (January 18, 1988): pp. 20-24.

28. The semiotics of the triangle on clothing are increasingly complex, bringing together symbols for female genitals, the Nazi triangles, and the challenge of the pink triangle of AIDS activism. It would probably be impossible to discern the effect this combination has on how people read the Guess? insignia, but in my own (extremely nearsighted) case I have sometimes mistaken the Guess? triangle for an AIDS activist button.

29. Jacob Davis applied the practices of riveting and reinforcing seams in horse blankets to clothing and received the patent for these improvements (also assigned to Levi Strauss, who paid the patent fee) in 1873. See Cray, *LEVIs*, pp. 16-22.

30. Baudrillard, "The Ecstasy of Communication," in *The Anti-Aesthetic: Essays on Postmodern Culture*, ed. Hal Foster (Port Townsend, Wash.: Bay Press, 1983), p. 133.

31. Danae Clark, "Commodity Lesbianism," *Camera Obscura* 25-26 (January/May 1991), p. 183.

32. Reported by J. Madeleine Nash and Dick Thompson, "The Gene Hunt," *Time*

(March 20, 1989), pp. 62-67.

33. Larry Casalino, "Decoding the Human Genome Project: an Interview with Evelyn Fox Keller," *Socialist Review* 2 (April-June 1991), pp. 111-28.

34. Baudrillard, "Precession," p. 2.

35. Nash and Thompson, "Gene Hunt," p. 67. Watson resigned as head of the genome project in 1992, in part, according to reports, over disagreement with the NIH plan to patent the DNA fragments as they are mapped.

36. An article in *The Christian Century*, while voicing concern that original sin will lead to hubris in this matter, argues that human beings are cocreators with God and that the Human Genome Project may be seen as "human creativity" bringing about the fulfillment of God's design. See Ann Lammers and Ted Peters, "Genethics: Implications of the Human Genome Project," *The Christian Century*" (October 3, 1990), pp. 868-72.

37. William F. Allman, "The Amazing Gene Machine," *U.S. News and World Report* (July 16, 1990), pp. 53-54.

38. Donna Haraway, "Situated Knowledges: The Science Question in Feminism and the Privilege of Partial Perspective," *Feminist Studies* 14 (Fall 1988), p. 581.

39. Ibid., p. 583.

40. Evelyn Fox Keller, *A Feeling for the Organism: The Life and Work of Barbara McClintock* (New York: W.H. Freeman, 1983).

41. Baudrillard, "Rituals of Transparency," p. 38.

42. Baudrillard, "Precession," p. 77, n. 7.

43. Foucault, *History of Sexuality*, p. 159.

44. This 90-minute film was produced and directed by Sandra Elgear, Robyn Hutt, and David Meiran, for Testing the Limits, 1992.

45. Michel Foucault, "What is Enlightenment?" in *The Foucault Reader*, ed. Paul Rabinow (New York: Pantheon, 1984), pp. 43-44.

46. Ibid., p. 50.

47. Quotations from Barbara McClintock, Meaghan Morris, Cornel West, and Michel Foucault, respectively.

2. Genealogical Feminism: A Politic Way of Looking

1. Michel Foucault, "How Much Does It Cost for Reason to Tell The Truth?" in *Foucault Live*, trans. Mia Foret and Marion Martius, ed. Sylvere Lotringer (New York: Semiotext(e), 1989), p. 251.

2. Michel Foucault, "Two Lectures," *Power/Knowledge*, ed. Colin Gordon (New York: Pantheon, 1972), p. 85.

3. Michel Foucault, "Nietzsche, Genealogy, History," *Language, Counter-Memory, Practice*, ed. Donald F. Bouchard (Ithaca: Cornell University Press, 1977), pp. 152-53.

4. Genealogical research is in keeping with Donna Haraway's concept of situated knowledges. As I construe it, genealogical feminism would have what Haraway calls "feminist objectivity" as a goal. This would distinguish it from the masculinist tradition of objectivity that claims a transcendent perspective. See Haraway, "Situated Knowledges: The Science Question in Feminism and the Privilege of Partial Perspective," *Feminist Studies* 14 (1988).

5. Margaret Fuller, *Woman in the Nineteenth Century* (New York: Norton, 1971);

Starhawk, *Dreaming the Dark* (Boston: Beacon Press, 1982); and *The Spiral Dance: A Rebirth of Ancient Religion of the Great Goddess* (San Francisco: Harper and Row, 1986).

6. Scholarly output on apocalyptic literature is vast, but for succinct yet thorough analyses see the discussions in Katherine R. Firth, *The Apocalyptic Tradition in Reformation Britain, 1530-1645* (New York: Oxford University Press, 1979); T. Wilson Hayes, *Winstanley the Digger: A Literary Analysis of Radical Ideas in the English Revolution* (Cambridge, Mass.: Harvard University Press, 1979); and Charles Webster, *The Great Instauration: Science, Medicine and Reform, 1626-1660* (London: Duckworth, 1975).

7. The fast-growing Christian Coalition, which promotes grassroots education and politics to battle homosexuality, abortion, and multicultural education, illustrates the importance of feminist coalitional politics. See Robert Sullivan, "An Army of the Faithful," *New York Times Magazine*, April 25, 1993: 32-36, 40-44. As Diana Fuss has argued, it is "politics which feminism cannot do without, politics that is essential to feminism's many self-definitions." "Reading Like a Feminist," *differences* 1 (Summer 1989), p. 90.

8. Despite the deconstructive insight Jacques Derrida brings to his discussion of Nietzsche's enigmatic jotting, "I have forgotten my umbrella," by arguing that it serves as a reminder that all texts are equally enigmatic and partial, it was possibly a tactical error when Nietzsche forgot his. Jacques Derrida, *Spurs: Nietzsche's Styles*, trans. Barbara Harlow (Chicago: University of Chicago Press, 1979), pp. 133-35.

9. Some working definitions: by "perspective" I mean a way of looking at something, but "way of looking" also suggests the spectator's embodiment. I use the term "practice" in the way that Sara Ruddick has defined it: "Practices are collective human activities distinguished by the aims that identify them and by the consequent demands made on practitioners committed to those aims. The aims or goals that define a practice are so central or 'constitutive' that in the absence of the goal you would not have the practice." See Ruddick, *Maternal Thinking: Toward a Politics of Peace* (New York: Ballantine, 1989), pp. 14-15. A movement would be a large-scale consolidation of a particular practice.

10. Susan Faludi, *Backlash: The Undeclared War Against American Women* (New York: Crown, 1991).

11. This is part of the tradition initiated by Joachim of Fiore. See Frank Kermode, "Apocalypse and the Modern," in *Visions of Apocalypse: End or Rebirth?*, ed. Friedlander et al .(New York: Holmes and Meier, 1985), p. 89.

12. Catherine Keller, "Women Against Wasting the World," in *Reweaving the World: The Emergence of Ecofeminism*, ed. Irene Diamond and Gloria Feman Orenstein (San Francisco: Sierra Club Books, 1990), p. 262.

13. Diana Fuss, *Essentially Speaking* (New York: Routledge, 1989), p. xii.

14. bell hooks, "Black Women and Men: Partnership in the 1990s," in *Yearning: Race, Gender, and Cultural Politics* (Boston: South End Press, 1990), p. 207.

15. Denise Riley, *"Am I That Name?" Feminism and the Category of "Women" in History* (Minneapolis: University of Minnesota Press, 1987), p. 113.

16. See, for example, Constance Jordan, "Feminism and the Humanists: The Case of Sir Thomas Elyot's *Defence of Good Women*," in *Rewriting the Renaissance: The Discourses of Sexual Difference in Early Modern Europe*, ed. Margaret W. Ferguson, Maureen Quilligan, and Nancy J. Vickers (Chicago: University of Chicago Press, 1986), pp. 242-58.

17. The concept of power/knowledge is analytically distinguishable from both a ju-

ridical notion of power and a "spirit of the age" concept. Rather than assuming that power resides exclusively in the law and/or the state and that individuals exist before ideas and centralized power, this approach assumes that "power is everywhere," is "exercised at innumerable points," and has "a directly productive role." Michel Foucault, *History of Sexuality*: Vol. 1. trans. Robert Hurley (New York: Vintage, 1980), pp. 93-95.

18. Although essentialist assumptions may be traced in earlier discourse, the question of essentialism, its status as a category of thought and as a concern for identity politics, is a twentieth-century concept. Thanks to Pat Mann, Mary Katherine Wainwright, and Margaret Walker for engaging in such lively debate over issues of essentialism and universalism.

19. Theresa de Lauretis, *Alice Doesn't: Feminism, Semiotics, Cinema* (Bloomington: Indiana University Press, 1984), p. 182.

20. Judith Butler, *Gender Trouble: Feminism and the Subversion of Identity* (New York: Routledge, 1990), p. 5.

21. Ibid., pp. 5-6.

22. Michel Foucault, "Michel Foucault: An Interview," *Edinburgh Review* (1986), p. 59.

23. Michelle Rosaldo, "Toward an Anthropology of Self and Feeling," in *Culture Theory*, ed. R. Shweder and R. Levine (New York: Cambridge University Press, 1984), p. 143. Thanks to José de Vinck for bringing this passage to my attention.

24. Foucault, *The History of Sexuality*, trans. Robert Hurley (New York: Vintage, 1980), pp. 92-96.

25. Leonie Caldecott and Stephanie Leland, eds., *Reclaim the Earth: Women Speak Out for Life on Earth* (London: Women's Press, 1983); Anne Witte Garland, *Women Activists: Challenging the Abuse of Power* (New York: Feminist Press, 1988).

26. Michel Foucault, "Polemics, Politics, and Problemizations: An Interview," in Paul Rabinow, ed., *Foucault Reader* (New York: Pantheon, 1984), p. 385.

27. Wilmette Brown, "Roots: Black Ghetto Ecology," in Caledcott and Leland, eds., *Reclaim the Earth*, p. 73.

28. Ibid., p. 84.

29. Gayatri Chakravorty Spivak, "Feminism and Critical Theory," in *In Other Worlds: Essays in Cultural Politics* (New York: Routledge, 1987), p. 89.

30. Gayatri Chakravorty Spivak with Ellen Rooney, "In a Word: Interview," *differences* 1 (Summer 1989), pp. 126-27. Also see Diana Fuss's overview of the critics who have argued for taking the "risk" of essence, *Essentially Speaking* (New York: Routledge, 1989), pp. 18-21.

31. Wangari Maathai, *The Green Belt Movement: Sharing the Approach and the Experience* (Nairobi: Environment Liaison Centre International, 1988), p. 12.

32. I am grateful to Njoke Njehu for bringing this movement to my attention.

33. Donna Haraway, *Simians, Cyborgs, and Women: The Reinvention of Nature* (New York: Routledge, 1991), p. 199.

34. Dick Hebdige, "Postmodernism and the 'The Other Side,' " *Journal of Communication Inquiry* 10 (Summer 1986), p. 78.

35. By "strategies and tactics" I have in mind the distinction made by Michel de Certeau. He states: "I call a 'strategy' the calculus of force-relationships which becomes pos-

sible when a subject of will and power (a proprieter, an enterprise, a city, a scientific institution) can be isolated from an 'environment.' A strategy assumes a place that can be circumscribed as *proper* (*propre*) and thus serves as the basis for generating relations with an exterior distinct from it (competitors, adversaries, 'clienteles,' 'targets,' or 'objects' of research). Political, economic, and scientific rationality has been constructed on this strategic model." In contrast to a strategy, he argues, a tactic is "a calculus which cannot count on a 'proper' (a spatial or institutional) localization, nor thus on a borderline distinguishing the other as a visible totality. The place of a tactic belongs to the other. A tactic insinuates itself into the other's place, fragmentarily, without taking it over in its entirety, without being able to keep it at a distance. . . . It must constantly manipulate events in order to turn them into 'opportunities.' " Michel de Certeau, *The Practice of Everyday Life*, trans. Steven Rendall (Berkeley and Los Angeles: University of California Press, 1984), p. xix.

36. Meaghan Morris, "Politics Now," in *The Pirate's Fiancée: Feminism, Reading, Postmodernism* (New York: Verso, 1988), p. 185. Laura Donaldson also points to the importance of semiotics for a materialist feminism (and vice versa) by examining the ideological implications of the "idealist construct of 'woman' " in "(ex)Changing (wo)Man: Towards a Materialist-Feminist Semiotics," *Cultural Critique* (Winter 1988-89), p. 8.

3. Philosophy Today: Not-for-Prophet Thought

1. Michel Foucault, "How Much Does It Cost for Reason to Tell the Truth?" trans. Mia Foret and Marion Martius, in *Foucault Live*, ed. Sylvere Lotringer (New York: Semiotext(e), 1989), p. 251.

2. Some analysts, following Buber, distinguish between prophecy and apocalypse. Buber sees prophecy's engagement with history as being in opposition to apocalypticism's abstraction and withdrawal from history. Rather than viewing apocalypse as a decadent form of the prophetic tradition, as Buber does, I view prophecy as a more historically attuned version of apocalyptic discourse, one that retains its links to notions of transcendent Truth but expresses its great concern with humanity's failures to grasp that truth. In this sense, the prophet might be analogous to a universal intellectual. Carrying the analogy one more step, genealogical approaches would be the contribution of what Foucault calls the specific intellectual. See Martin Buber, "Prophecy, Apocalyptic, and the Historical Hour," in *Pointing the Way*, trans. Maurice Friedman (New York: Harper and Bros., 1957).

3. Michel Foucault, *The Use of Pleasure*, trans. Robert Hurley (New York: Pantheon, 1985), p. 9.

4. From a Foucauldian perspective, the discipline of academic philosophy is largely responsible for preventing philosophy from exploring the determinants of its own thought. This is not exclusively the case, however. For example, for a critique of philosophy's requirements of impartiality from within academic philosophy, see Margaret Urban Walker, "Partial Consideration," *Ethics* 101 (July 1991), pp. 758-74. Feminist philosophy has long critiqued philosophy from within its own thought. One of the ways that traditional philosophy has defused the impact of that critique is by maintaining feminist philosophy's base on the border zone between academic departments of philosophy and women's studies programs.

5. Jacques Derrida, "Of an Apocalyptic Tone Recently Adopted in Philosophy," trans. John P. Leavey, Jr., *Oxford Literary Review* 6 (1984), p. 29.

6. Foucault, "The Art of Telling the Truth," in *Michel Foucault: Politics, Philosophy, Culture: Interviews and Other Writings, 1977-84*, ed. Lawrence D. Kritzman (New York: Routledge, 1988), p. 95.

7. In other words, nonapocalyptic philosophy exists. In the academy, the practice of philosophy as an ontology of the present may be found in the domain of feminist philosophy and some radical social theory. As I have shown elsewhere, philosophical questions about the conditions of subjectivity abound in a work such as Maxine Hong Kingston's *The Woman Warrior* and June Jordan's essays in *On Call*. See Lee Quinby, *Freedom, Foucault, and the Subject of America* (Boston: Northeastern University Press, 1991). But these works are not generally seen as philosophy. The discipline of philosophy has been far more devoted to the analytics of truth as a defining discourse. Texts that explicitly approach the question of "what we are today" tend to be placed in other fields—in women's studies, political science, education, literature, or cultural studies—in terms of their use in classrooms or the category labels on their covers (and hence their placement in bookstores).

8. Foucault cites these three axes of genealogy in "On the Genealogy of Ethics," in Hubert Dreyfus and Paul Rabinow, *Michel Foucault: Beyond Structuralism and Hermeneutics* (Chicago: University of Chicago Press, 1983), pp. 237-38.

9. Ibid.

10. Michel Foucault, "Technologies of the Self," in *Technologies of the Self: A Seminar with Michel Foucault*, eds. Luther H. Martin, Huck Gutman, Patrick H. Hutton (Amherst: University of Massachusetts Press, 1988), p. 18.

11. Michel Foucault, "On the Genealogy of Ethics: An Overview of Work in Progress" in Dreyfus and Rabinow, *Michel Foucault*, pp. 245, 251.

12. Ibid., p. 233.

13. Ibid., p. 230.

14. Foucault, "Technologies of the Self," p. 20.

15. Ibid., p. 22.

16. Ibid., p. 35.

17. Ibid.

18. Foucault, *Use of Pleasure*, p. 5.

19. Frances Bartkowski, "Epistemic Drift in Foucault," in *Feminism and Foucault*, ed. Irene Diamond and Lee Quinby (Boston: Northeastern University Press, 1988), pp. 53-54.

20. For example, *Foucault: A Critical Reader*, ed. David Hoy (New York: Basil Blackwell, 1986).

21. Cameron McCarthy, "Marxist Theories of Education and the Challenge of a Cultural Politics of Non-Synchrony," in *Becoming Feminine: The Politics of Popular Culture*, ed. Leslie G. Roman, Linda K. Christian-Smith, with Elizabeth Ellsworth (New York: Falmer Press, 1988), pp. 185-203. Also see *Cultural Studies*, ed. Lawrence Grossberg, Cary Nelson, Paula Treichler (New York: Routledge, 1992).

22. For a poststructuralist defense of experiential education, see David Thornton Moore, "Experiential Education as Critical Discourse," in *Combining Service and Learning:*

A Resource Book for Community and Public Service, vol. 1, ed. Jane C. Kendall and Associates (National Society for Internships and Experiential Education), pp. 273-83.

23. For example, see *Inside/Out: Lesbian Theories, Gay Theories*, ed. Diana Fuss (New York: Routledge, 1991); John D'Emilio and Estelle Freedman, *Intimate Matters: A History of Sexuality in America* (New York: Harper and Row, 1988).

24. I prefer the phrase "multiply discursive subjectivity" to "subject position." I have heard people discussing their various subject positions as if, as they switch from one site of enunciation to another, they can leap at will from one mode of subjectivity to another. Such a view loses sight of the ways in which we are subjected by dominant power/knowledge formations. Also, it doesn't account for the way we experience ourselves as continuous even when we do take up contradictory discourses.

25. I'd like to thank Kate Mehuron for helping me think about this philosophical discussion.

26. Feminist philosophy is a bold exception. See, for example, Sandra Lee Bartky, *Femininity and Domination: Studies in the Phenomenology of Oppression* (New York: Routledge, 1990); and Judith Butler, *Gender Trouble: Feminism and the Subversion of Identity* (New York: Routledge, 1990). For a theory of situated social power, also see Thomas E. Wartenberg, *The Forms of Power: From Domination to Transformation* (Philadelphia: Temple University Press, 1990).

27. Michel Foucault, *History of Sexuality, Volume I: An Introduction*, trans. Robert Hurley (New York: Vintage, 1980) p. 92.

28. Michel Foucault, "Power and Strategies," *Power/Knowledge*, ed. Colin Gordon (New York: Pantheon, 1980), p. 142.

29. Michel Foucault, "The History of Sexuality," in *Power/Knowledge*, ed. Colin Gordon, pp. 140-41.

30. Ibid., p. 186.

31. This is not to say that resistance is never possible under domination, but rather to emphasize that the exercise of freedom is not built in to the social relations of domination. For Foucault's discussion of the distinction between domination and power relations, see Foucault, "The Ethic of Care for the Self as a Practice of Freedom," in *The Final Foucault*, pp. 122-23.

32. Michel Foucault, "Power and Strategies," *Power/Knowledge*, ed. Colin Gordon, p. 142.

33. Ibid.

34. Michel Foucault, "The Subject and Power," Afterword in Hubert L. Dreyfus and Paul Rabinow, *Michel Foucault: Beyond Structuralism and Hermeneutics* (Chicago: University of Chicago Press, 1983), p. 210.

35. Ibid., p. 211.

36. Examples of the practice of a philosophy of the present in the United States that consider some of these questions may be found in the following: bell hooks, *Yearning: Race, Gender, and Cultural Politics* (Boston: South End Press, 1990); Sarah Lucia Hoagland, *Lesbian Ethics: Toward New Value* (Palo Alto: Institute of Lesbian Studies, 1988); Patricia S. Mann, *Micro-Politics: Agency in a Postfeminist Era* (Minneapolis: University of Minnesota Press, 1994); *Foucault and Education: Disciplines and Knowledge*, ed. Stephen J. Ball (New York: Routledge, 1990).

37. Two particularly insightful approaches to this question may be found in Michele Barrett, *The Politics of Truth: From Marx to Foucault* (Stanford: Stanford University Press, 1991) and John Rajchman, *Truth and Eros: Foucault, Lacan, and the Question of Ethics* (New York: Routledge, 1991).

38. Foucault, "Two Lectures," p. 81.

39. Foucault distanced his project from deconstruction in this way: "It is clear how far one is from an analysis in terms of deconstruction (any confusion between these two methods would be unwise)." Michel Foucault, "Polemics, Politics, and Problemizations: An Interview," in *The Foucault Reader*, ed. Paul Rabinow (New York: Pantheon, 1984), p. 389. I'm not arguing that the two methods are analytically similar, but rather that deconstruction may be used against apocalypse.

40. Jacques Derrida, "No Apocalypse, Not Now (full speed ahead, seven missiles, seven missives)," *Diacritics* 14 (Summer 1984), p. 27.

41. Patricia Hill Collins, *Black Feminist Thought: Knowledge, Consciousness, and the Politics of Empowerment* (Boston: Unwin Hyman, 1990), p. 231.

42. Joan Nestle, ed. *The Persistent Desire: A Femme-Butch Reader* (Boston: Alyson, 1992).

43. See, for example, Cindy Patton, *Inventing AIDS* (New York: Routledge, 1990); and *AIDS: Cultural Analysis, Cultural Activism*, ed. Douglas Crimp (Cambridge, Mass.: MIT Press, 1988).

44. Foucault, *Use of Pleasure*, p. 5.

45. For discussions of Greek and Christian traditions of a hermeneutics of desire, see the collection of essays in *Technologies of the Self: A Seminar with Michel Foucault*, ed. Luther H. Martin, Huck Gutman, and Patrick H. Hutton (Amherst: University of Massachusetts Press, 1988). The essay by William E. Paden, "Theaters of Humility and Suspicion: Desert Saints and New England Puritans," points out that the Puritans began to refer to the body or flesh as the "self," and strove to renounce the self in its turning away from God.

46. Foucault, *Use of Pleasure*, p. 244.

47. An ethics of the flesh is in countertradition to what Mary Daly has called "necrophilia." My exploration overlaps with and is indebted to her discussion of gyn/ecology, but an ethics of the flesh is not necessarily separatist, though it might at times be politically so. See Daly, *Gyn/Ecology: The Metaethics of Radical Feminism* (Boston: Beacon, 1978).

48. Foucault's references to an ethics of the flesh are specifically in regard to Christianity and conceptually in opposition to the ancient Greek ethics of pleasure. Although I agree with this opposition beween the Christian ethics that allows certain acts and prohibits others and the Greek system's problemization of pleasure, I am departing from his use of the term "flesh" as an oppositional one to an aesthetics of existence per se. In other words, I am interested in appropriating the meanings of flesh to describe contemporary practices that resist apocalyptic moral codes. Another approach to changing the meanings of flesh in philosophical discourse is by ironizing the use of the term in specific philosophical texts. See Kate Mehuron, unpublished dissertation, *Metamorphoses: Thinking in the Crisis of Speculative Reflection* (Nashville: Vanderbilt University Press, 1989).

49. This discussion is indebted to Carol Gilligan's differentiation between the differ-

ent gendered voices of justice and compassionate responsibility, but it does not follow that particular differentiation. See *In a Different Voice* (Cambridge, Mass.: Harvard University Press, 1982). I am also influenced by the arguments that Nancy Chodorow and Dorothy Dinnerstein have made regarding the importance of men and women sharing child care. But an ethics of the flesh is not limited to the issue of child care and shared parenting is not the only means of fostering this ethics.

50. On the role of self-control and austerity, see Foucault, "The Concern for Truth," in *Michel Foucault: Politics, Philosophy, Culture*, ed. Lawrence D. Kritzman (New York: Routledge, 1988), pp. 261-62.

51. Jean Baudrillard, "Why Theory," in *The Ecstasy of Communication*, trans. Bernard and Caroline Schutze, ed. Sylvere Lotringer (New York: Semiotext(e), 1988), p. 101

52. Sarah Lucia Hoagland, *Lesbian Ethics: Toward New Value* (Palo Alto: Institute of Lesbian Studies, 1988), p. 126; see in particular chapter 3, "Power, Paternalism, and Attending."

53. Gilligan, *In a Different Voice*.

54. Barbara Johnson, "Apostrophe, Animation, and Abortion," in *Feminisms*, ed. Robyn Warhol and Diane Price Herndl (Brunswick: Rutgers University Press, 1991), p. 635.

55. Sara Ruddick, *Maternal Thinking: Toward a Politics of Peace* (New York: Ballantine, 1989), p. 187. See in particular the chapter called "Histories of Human Flesh."

56. Sucheng Chan, "You're Short Besides!" in *Making Face, Making Soul: Haciendo Caras*, ed. Gloria Anzaldua (San Francisco: Aunt Lute Foundation Books, 1990), p. 167.

57. Douglas Crimp, "Portraits of People With AIDS," in *Cultural Studies*, ed. Grossberg, Nelson, and Treichler, pp. 117-33.

58. Paul Monette, *Borrowed Time: An AIDS Memoir* (New York: Avon, 1988).

4. Conceiving the New Man: Henry Adams and the Birth of Ironic Apocalypse

1. Henry Adams, *The Education of Henry Adams*, ed. Ernest Samuels (Boston: Houghton Mifflin, 1973), p. 500. Subsequent references to this text will appear parenthetically.

2. For discussions of women's lives in the United States during the Victorian period, see the anthologies edited by Martha Vicinus, *Suffer and Be Still: Women in the Victorian Age* (Bloomington: Indiana University Press, 1972); and *A Widening Sphere: Changing Roles of Victorian Women* (Bloomington: Indiana University Press, 1977).

3. For an excellent full-length treatment of how genealogy may be used for literary analysis, see Simon During, *Foucault and Literature: Towards a Genealogy of Writing* (New York: Routledge, 1992).

4. Kimmel points to three gender discourses in the earlier period that may also be witnessed in the contemporary one: an antifeminist backlash that seeks to reestablish male dominance, a promale reassertion of traditional masculinity, and a profeminist redefinition of gender and support for woman's participation in the public sphere. See Kimmel, "The Contemporary Crisis of Masculinity in Historical Perspective" in *The Making of Masculinities*, ed. Harry Brod (Boston: Allen and Unwin, 1987), p. 123.

5. John Patrick Diggins takes up the issue of Adams's turn from the Virgin to the

Dynamo in terms of the opposition between feminine power and authority and masculine power and authority, yet, despite his perceptiveness about the workings of this opposition in the *Education*, Diggins seems to hold to designations of masculinity and femininity as innate rather than culturally constructed. For example, in explaining why "masculine will and self-control seemed the last remnant to cling to when [Adams] felt feminine impulses within himself," Diggins states, "Modern man fears the irrationality and destructive tendencies of feminine power as much as classical man, represented by Adams's ancestors, feared the arbitrariness and corruption of political power" (p. 167). He argues further, "In worshipping the Dynamo, man worships the power drive within himself, and whether this 'primal force' be matter or mind, the only thing he knows is that it is blind and unresponsive to prayer. Man whores after the energies of nature yet cannot wrest the secret of the atom, and knowledge remains helpless to control its own creation" (p. 191). Such metaphors of gender polarity replicate the sex/gender dualisms that I am trying to deconstruct in Adams's text. See Diggins, " 'Who Bore the Failure of the Light': Henry Adams and the Crisis of Authority," *New England Quarterly* 64 (June 1985), pp. 165-92.

By "gender polarity" I wish to indicate the social meanings that have been attributed to anatomical differences. The assumption throughout this analysis is that there is no given, fixed meaning to anatomical differences but that patriarchal culture polarizes traits and assigns them to binaried categories, relegating the feminine to the status of a deviance or deficiency in relation to the masculine. It follows from this assumption that terms such as masculinity, femininity, and heterosexuality have no biological status.

6. Throughout my discussion I refer to both the author and the narrator of the *Education* as Adams, not out of assumptions of authorial intention, but rather as a way of accepting both the narrator and the author as constructed personae who go by the designation "Henry Adams."

7. For an extended discussion of the ways in which this movement between conflict and resolution occurs in modernist art, in this case between transgression and compliance with the dominant order, see Tom Hayes and Lee Quinby, "The Aporia of Bourgeois Art: Desire in Thomas Mann's *Death in Venice*," *Criticism* (Spring 1989), pp. 159-77.

8. For discussions of the "New Woman," see, for example, Rosalind Rosenberg, *Beyond Separate Spheres: Intellectual Roots of Modern Feminism* (New Haven: Yale University Press, 1982); Carroll Smith-Rosenberg, *Disorderly Conduct: Visions of Gender in Victorian America* (New York: Oxford University Press, 1985); Martha Banta, *Imaging American Women: Idea and Ideals in Cultural History* (New York: Columbia University Press, 1987), chapters 1-2; and Louise Cogan, *All-American Girl: The Ideal of Real Womanhood in Mid-Nineteenth-Century America* (Athens: University of Georgia Press, 1989), pp. 257-62.

9. John D'Emilio and Estelle Freedman, *Intimate Matters: A History of Sexuality in America* (New York: Harper and Row, 1988), p. 174.

10. Ibid.

11. Ernest Samuels, *Henry Adams* (Cambridge, Mass.: Harvard University Press, 1989), p. 201.

12. Eugenia Kaledin's biography of Marian "Clover" Adams indicates that Henry Adams had long held the view that women were losing their unique moral qualities: "Clover must have frequently heard Henry rail against women with intellectual pretensions. Sympathetic as he often was with the cause of education for women, he also saw it as a reason

for the loss of their emotional strength" (169). See Kaledin, *The Education of Mrs. Henry Adams* (Philadelphia: Temple University Press, 1981).

13. Also see Hayden White's discussion of the *Education* as a demonstration of the importance of semiotics for historical analysis. White argues that the "intellectual historical artifact viewed semiologically permits us to see the system of meaning production operating directly in a way that other kinds of historical artifacts do not—because these other kinds of artifacts (weapons, treaties, contracts, account books) inevitably appear to us more as the effects of such operations, or at best as instruments of them, rather than as causes of them" (210). *The Content of Form: Narrative Discourse and Historical Representation* (Baltimore: Johns Hopkins University Press, 1987).

14. Henry Adams to Whitelaw Reid, Paris, Sept. 9, 1908, in Appendix A, *The Education of Henry Adams*.

15. Henry Adams to Barrett Wendell, Washington, March 12, 1909, in Appendix A, *The Education of Henry Adams*.

16. A discursive analysis following Bakhtin would render a far more extensive number of literary genres and modes, but for the purposes of this essay, I am specifically interested in the ways in which these meanings are informed by and inform gender categorization and have therefore limited my analysis to this. For examples of analysis of discourse as multivoiced, see M. M. Bakhtin, "Discourse in the Novel," in *The Dialogic Imagination* (Austin: University of Texas Press, 1981), pp. 259-422.

17. Leo Marx cites the *Education* as a prime example of Richard Chase's analysis of the singularly American tendency to define "reality as a contradiction between radically opposed forces." See Marx, *The Machine in the Garden* (New York: Oxford University Press, 1964), pp. 344-45; also Chase, *The American Novel and its Tradition* (New York: Anchor Books, 1957). But, as Russell Reising argues, this practice is neither unique to nor monolithically the case in America. In *The Unusable Past*, Reising makes the important point that the major critics of American literature have focused on and favored texts that depict reality as dualized. What Chase calls the American tradition is only one strain within the culture—the one that has been privileged in American literary history. Reising argues that we should attend to texts that forward alternatives to dualistic thinking. I fully agree but would add that it is equally important to deconstruct the hierarchies within these privileged texts. See Reising, *The Unusable Past* (New York: Methuen, 1986).

18. According to Wayne Lesser, Adams's "self-conscious representation—the blending of multinational and cultural interests"—strives for a "modification of power" (p. 393). Lesser's insight about the *Education's* "rhetoric of positive anticipation" (p. 388) is an important corrective to the tendency to accept its dualisms as a failure to create a new vision. However, his discussion stops short of investigating the role of gender polarity in that "final imagining." My analysis of the *Education's* gender politics implies a critique of Lesser's proposal about this "final imagining" that derives "from within love's field of perception" (391). An examination of the *Education's* inscriptions of gender isolates the ways in which the representations of power and love sometimes subvert but largely reinforce masculinist hierarchies—*despite* the work's expressed challenges to domination. See Lesser, "Criticism, Literary History, and the Paradigm: *The Education of Henry Adams*," *PMLA* 97 (May 1982), pp. 378-92.

19. These stated oppositions, which are informed and reinforced by the unstated op-

position of sexual difference, structure the first half of the *Education* and may be indicated in summary form by the titles of the first nine chapters: "Quincy" (vs.) "Boston," "Washington" (vs.) "Harvard," "Berlin" (vs.) "Rome," "Treason" (vs.) "Diplomacy," and "Foes or Friends." John Carlos Rowe also points to these Dionysian-versus-Apollonian chapter divisions but argues that the "structure of the *Education* . . . finally suggests the failure of any consistent dialectical method. The first six chapters set up an opposition of forces that poses a tentative order for the work as a whole" (p. 100). John Carlos Rowe, *Henry Adams and Henry James: The Emergence of a Modern Consciousness* (Ithaca: Cornell University Press, 1976).

20. For a critique of the nostalgia integral to depictions of the Mother as an originary moment outside of patriarchal discourse and practice, see Jane Gallop's review of the collection entitled *The (M)other Tongue*. The conclusion of the editors' introduction, she argues, employs the image of the mother as one in whom "we are not divided" (p. 318), an image that loses sight of the insight of the designation (M)other, which makes visible the other inscribed within the self. See Gallop, "Reading the Mother Tongue: Psychoanalytic Feminist Criticism," *Critical Inquiry* 13 (Winter 1987), pp. 314-29.

21. For discussion of discourses of self, see the collection of essays *Technologies of the Self: A Seminar with Michel Foucault*, ed. Luther H. Martin, Huck Gutman, and Patrick H. Hutton (Amherst: University of Massachusetts Press, 1988).

22. Nina Auerbach, *Woman and the Demon: The Life of a Victorian Myth* (Cambridge, Mass.: Harvard University Press, 1982).

23. Ibid., p. 186.

24. For discussions of men's psychosexual, misogynistic fears of women, see chapter 6 in Dorothy Dinnerstein's *The Mermaid and the Minotaur: Sexual Arrangements and Human Malaise*, (New York: Harper and Row, 1976) and Klaus Theweleit's discussions of men's depictions of women under fascism in *Male Fantasies*, trans. Stephen Conway in collaboration with Erica Carter and Chris Turner (Minneapolis: University of Minnesota Press, 1987). Theweleit's discussion of the castrating woman, pp. 70-79, is particularly relevant here.

25. As Dorothy Dinnerstein has pointed out, adult ambivalence toward mortality "is preceded and performed by an ambivalence that takes shape in infancy." Feelings of resentment over the loss of oneness associated with the pleasures from the mother's body come to be regarded as "flesh's treachery" and are scapegoated onto feminized personifications of nature and death (Dinnerstein, *Mermaid and Minotaur*, p. 121).

26. This period is also the time of his marriage to Marian "Clover" Hooper and her suicide in 1885. Most critics have dealt with the conspicuous absence of discussion of this tragedy by simply acknowledging Adams's own statement that it had broken his life "in halves." In her biography, *The Education of Mrs. Henry Adams*, Eugenia Kaledin argues that the *Education*, "with its pointed omission, may remain the greatest monument to Clover Adams. As a criticism of our culture, it honored the vitality and imagination of all the women Henry Adams knew who did not want to imitate men and who stood for something more than technological progress. To Adams, the instinctive sensibilities that Clover represented surpassed anything a man could learn at Harvard" (pp. 257-58). On one level, I accept this view, believing that Adams deeply loved his wife. On another level, however, Kaledin's characterization of Adams's definition of proper womanhood

encapsulates the dilemma the "new women" faced in their efforts to enter the public domain as decision makers.

27. Sacvan Bercovitch argues that Adams registers "condemnation of the Dynamo" (p. 195). This is too strong a claim in light of Adams's admission that the Virgin had no force in America whereas the Dynamo did and that, moreover, the Dynamo's multiplicity was more in keeping with the multiverse. See Bercovitch, *The American Jeremiad* (Madison: University of Wisconsin Press, 1978).

28. By "return of the repressed" I mean to focus on the problemization of gender polarity that psychoanalytic discourse provides, without accepting as explanation a given psychosexual formation of gender and sexuality. Rather, my assumption is that in a text that polarizes sexual difference, such "irruptions" are always already constructed.

29. Catherine Keller discusses this entrenched duality in light of current ecological concerns in "Women Against Wasting the World," *Reweaving the World: The Emergence of Ecofeminism*, ed. Irene Diamond and Gloria Feman Orenstein (San Francisco: Sierra Club Books, 1990), p. 251.

30. See both Marshall McLuhan, *The Mechanical Bride: Folklore of Industrial Man* (Boston: Beacon Press, 1951), pp. 98, 101; and Jane Caputi, "Seeing Elephants: The Myths of Phallotechnology," *Feminist Studies* 14 (Fall 1988), pp. 487-524.

31. Donna Haraway, "A Manifesto for Cyborgs," *Socialist Review* 15 (1985), pp. 65-108.

32. Juliet Flower MacCannell notes, in regard to Hegel, in what could apply equally to Adams and the Dynamo, that "Lacan asks, did we ever concern ourselves about masters and slaves until we had a powerful machine to compare human labor with, to compute it against? And a machine more powerful than the master" (p. 932). See MacCannell, "Oedipus Wrecks: Lacan, Stendhal, and the Narrative Form of the Real," *Lacan and Narration: The Psychoanalytic Difference in Narrative Theory*, ed. Robert Con Davis (Baltimore: Johns Hopkins University Press, 1983), pp. 910-40.

33. Ivy Schweitzer, *The Work of Self-Representation: Lyric Poetry in Colonial New England* (Chapel Hill: University of North Carolina Press, 1991), p. 96.

34. Quoted in Leo Marx, *Machine in the Garden*, p. 350.

35. Although there are moments when the *Education* is overtly disdainful of both men and women, sharing the view expressed in Ezra Pound's poem, "The female is a chaos / the male / is a fixed point of stupidity," such opinions are typically followed by less misanthropic and even complimentary assertions about women and men. See Carolyn Burke's discussion of Pound, in "Getting Spliced: Modernism and Sexual Difference," *American Quarterly* 39 (Spring 1987), pp. 98-121, p. 103 in particular.

36. See Susan Bordo's critique of the Cartesian formula, in particular her final chapter entitled "The Cartesian Masculinization of Thought and the Seventeenth Century Flight from the Feminine" (pp. 97-118), in *The Flight to Objectivity* (Albany: SUNY Press, 1987).

37. Irene Diamond, "Babies, Heroic Experts, and a Poisoned Earth," in *Reweaving the World* ed. Diamond and Orenstein, pp. 204, 209.

38. Lois Hughson's discussion of Adams's challenges to the Emersonian conception of "history as biography" provides an excellent reading of his work as political history. Equally insightful is her remark that the "picture of man in the *Education* confronting

multiplicity and humbled by his failure to understand or dominate his experience is moving. The image of power restored through the new theory of history is chilling in its abstraction and inhumanity" (p. 2). See Hughson, *From Biography to History: The Historical Imagination and American Fiction, 1880-1940* (Charlottesville: University of Virginia Press, 1988).

5. "Woman Got de Key": Zora Neale Hurston and Resistance to Apocalypse

1. Zora Neale Hurston, *Dust Tracks on a Road*, (1942; New York: J.B. Lippincott, 1971).

2. Henry Grunwald, "The Year 2000: Is It the End—Or Just the Beginning?" *Time* (March 30, 1992), pp. 73-76.

3. Zora Neale Hurston, *Mules and Men* (1935; New York: Harper and Row, 1990), p. 3. Hereafter cited parenthetically in the text.

4. For an extended analysis of female folktelling and the subversive use of voice in *Mules and Men*, see Mary Katherine Wainwright, "Subversive Female Folktellers in *Mules and Men*," in *Zora in Florida*, ed. Steve Glassman and Kathryn Seidel (Gainesville: University of Florida Press, 1991).

5. For an excellent review of this use of "keys" in the context of Roger Williams's *A Key into the Language of America*, see Ivy Schweitzer, *The Work of Self Representation: Lyric Poetry in Colonial New England* (Chapel Hill: University of North Carolina Press, 1991), p. 192.

6. Henry Louis Gates, Jr., *The Signifying Monkey: A Theory of Afro-American Literary Criticism* (New York: Oxford University Press, 1988), p. xxv.

7. Gates argues that African-American literary history is characterized by this kind of "tertiary revision, by which I mean that three elements tend to be involved in the relationship of ancestry. These elements include texts that provide models of form, texts that provide models of substance, and the text at hand" (*Signifying Monkey*, p. 122).

8. For the theory of the double-voiced text, also see Bakhtin's *The Dialogic Imagination*, ed. Michael Holquist, trans. Caryl Emerson and Michael Holquist (Austin: University of Texas, 1981).

9. Robert Hemenway, *Zora Neale Hurston: A Literary Biography* (Urbana: University of Illinois Press, 1977), 188.

10. Alice Walker, "On Refusing to Be Humbled By Second Place in a Contest You Did Not Design: A Tradition By Now," *I Love Myself When I am Laughing . . . And Then Again When I am Looking Mean and Impressive* (Old Westbury, Conn.: Feminist Press, 1979), p. 2.

11. Alice Walker, "Introductory Note for Hurston's Fiction," in *I Love Myself When*, p. 175.

12. Ibid., p. 176.

13. Zora Neale Hurston, "The Gilded Six-Bits," *Spunk* (1933; Berkeley, Turtle Island Foundation, 1985), p. 57. Hereafter cited parenthetically in the text.

14. In *Their Eyes Were Watching God*, Hurston uses the Samson motif three times in building up to the scene in which Janie kills Tea Cake to save her own life.

15. Frederick Douglass, *Narrative of the Life of Frederick Douglass* (1845; New York: Signet, 1968), p. 23.

16. Harriet Jacobs, *Incidents in the Life of a Slave Girl*, ed. with introduction by Jean Fagan Yellin (1861; Cambridge, Mass.: Harvard University Press, 1987), p. 55.

6. Urination and Civilization: Practicing Pissed Criticism

1. Patrick Buchanan, editorial in *Washington Times*, quoted in Nicols Fox, "NEA Under Seige," *New Art Examiner* (Summer 1989), p. 18.

2. Interview with Degen Pener, "Egos and Ids," *New York Times*, Section V, February 7, 1993, p. 4.

3. Steven C. Dubin, *Arresting Images: Impolitic Art and Uncivil Actions* (New York: Routledge, 1992).

4. Camille Paglia, *Sexual Personae* (New York: Vintage, 1991), p. 21.

5. Interview on the *McLaughlin Report*, January 2, 1993.

6. Paglia, *Sexual Personae*, p. 22.

7. Michel Foucault, "Polemics, Politics, and Problemizations: An Interview," in *The Foucault Reader*, ed. Paul Rabinow (New York: Pantheon, 1984), pp. 381, 383.

8. Alphonse D'Amato, Senate speech of May 18, 1989, quoted in Peggy Phelan, "Serrano, Mapplethorpe, the NEA, and You," *The Drama Review* (Spring 1990), p. 6.

9. Jesse Helms quoted in Charles Hagen, "After the Storm," *Art News* (September 1991), p. 61. The banner appeared at a Santa Cruz event; see Dupin, p. 251.

10. Steven C. Dubin, *Arresting Images: Impolitic Art and Uncivil Actions* (New York: Routledge, 1992), p. 98.

11. "1881 Water Sports," in *About Time: Exploring the Gay Past*, ed. Martin Duberman (New York: Meridian, 1991), p. 54.

12. Pat Califia states that there are "no recorded cases of people getting AIDS from ingestion or being splashed by urine. However, urine can contain HIV." She advises people with impaired immune systems "not to take other's people's piss into [one's] mouth or anus" because of exposure to hepatitis, which could be dangerous under the circumstances. "Boiling urine will kill any HIV that might be present, but it won't kill other viruses like hepatitis. . . . piss is safe for 'external use only.' " Califia, *The Advocate Advisor* (Boston: Alyson, 1991), p. 174.

13. Dick Francis, *Longshot* (New York: Ballantine, 1990), p. 92. Special thanks to Mary Katherine Wainwright for bringing this to my attention.

14. Hugh Rawson, *Wicked Words* (New York: Crown, 1989), p. 301-2.

15. Dupin, *Arresting Images*, p. 98.

16. Coco Fusco, "Andres Serrano Shoots the Klan: An Interview with Andres Serrano," *High Performance* (Fall 1991), pp. 42-43.

17. I wish to thank Lennard Davis for calling this painting to my attention.

18. Keith Christiansen, "Lorenzo Lotto and the Tradition of Epithalamic Paintings," *Apollo* (September 1986), pp. 166-73.

19. Ibid., p. 173.

20. From an eighteenth-century verse by Lady Montagu, quoted in Rawson, *Wicked Words*, p. 302.

21. *La Pisseuse* was donated to the Musée National d'Art Moderne, Centre Georges Pompidou, in 1984. It was exhibited in New York that year as well.

22. Robert Rosenblum, "The Fatal Women of Picasso and de Kooning," *Art News*

(October 1985), p. 103.

23. Ibid., pp. 100-103.

24. The label "original masterpiece" is from Christiansen, cited above.

25. David Lee, "Urine Test," *The British Journal of Photography* (November 1991), p. 16.

26. Lucy R. Lippard, "Andres Serrano: The Spirit and the Letter," *Art in America* (April 1990), p. 239.

27. Serrano quoted in Dupin, *Arresting Images*, p. 98.

28. Interview with Derek Guthrie, "Taboo Artist: Serrano Speaks," *New Art Examiner* (September 1989), p. 45.

29. Peggy Phelan, "Money Talks, Again," *The Drama Review* (Fall 1991), p. 132-33.

30. Lippard, "Serrano," p. 243.

31. Donald Kuspit, "Sexual Censorship and the New Authoritarianism," *New Art Examiner* (September 1989), p. 43.

32. Sigmund Freud, *Civilization and Its Discontents*, trans. James Strachey (New York: Norton, 1989), p. 42.

33. Ibid., p. 111.

34. Ibid., pp. 42-43. I would like to thank the members of the NYC Bakhtin reading group and Bob Stamm, in particular, for encouraging me to explore this passage further.

35. Freud, "The Acquisition of Power Over Fire (1932)," *Character and Culture*, ed. Philip Rieff (New York: 1963), pp. 295-96.

36. Ibid., pp. 299-300.

37. Freud, *Civilization and Its Discontents*, p. 60.

38. Ibid.

39. Adrienne Rich, "Disloyal to Civilization: Feminism, Racism, Gynephobia (1978)," in *On Lies, Secrets, and Silence* (New York: Norton, 1979), pp. 275-310.

40. Freud, *Civilization and Its Discontents*, p. 43.

41. Ibid., p. 59.

42. Ibid., p. 43.

43. Freud makes this brief mention of urethral erotism in his 1908 essay devoted to the questions of character formation and anality. Males as well as females may be subject to both the burning ambition and the urethral erotism. See Freud, "Character and Anal Erotism," in *The Freud Reader*, ed. Peter Gay (New York: Norton, 1989), p. 297.

44. Freud, "Fragment of an Analysis of a Case of Hysteria," in *The Freud Reader*, pp. 211-14.

45. Ibid., p. 215.

46. From *The Freud Reader*, p. 676.

47. Dr. Lynn Edwards, "Mechanical and Other Devices," in *Urinary Incontinence*, ed. Dr. K. P. S. Caldwell (London: Sector, 1975), p. 117.

48. Judith Butler, *Gender Trouble: Feminism and the Subversion of Identity* (New York: Routledge, 1990), p. ix.

49. Simone de Beauvoir, *The Second Sex*, trans. H. M. Parshley (New York: Vintage, 1989), p. 273.

50. Ibid., p. 276.

51. Ibid., p. 274.

52. Nancy Miller, "My Father's Penis," in *Getting Personal: Feminist Occasions and Other Autobiographical Acts* (New York: Routledge, 1991), pp. 145-47.

53. Toni Morrison, *Sula* (New York: New American Library, 1973), p. 23.

54. Ibid., p. 24.

7. Resistance on the Home Front: Re(con)figuring Home Space as a Practice of Freedom

1. Michel Foucault, "An Ethics of Pleasure," in *Foucault Live*, trans. Steven Riggins (New York: Semiotext(e), 1989), p. 266.

2. bell hooks, "Homeplace: A Site of Resistance," *Yearning: Race, Gender, and Cultural Politics* (Boston: South End Press, 1990), p. 43.

3. For discussion of the totalizing and imperialistic usage of the term "world," see Dietmar Kamper and Christoph Wolf, "Preface," *Looking Back on the End of the World*, ed. Dietmar Kamper and Christoph Wolf (New York: Semiotext(e), 1989), p. 1.

4. *WAC STATS: THE FACTS ABOUT WOMEN* (New York: Women's Action Coalition, 1992).

5. hooks, "Homeplace," pp. 41-42.

6. Michel Foucault, "Of Other Spaces," *Diacritics* 16 (Spring 1986), p. 22.

7. In his overview of geography in relation to critical social theory, Edward Soja points to Foucault's analysis of space as an exception to the overriding tendency to privilege time over space. See Edward Soja, *Postmodern Geography: The Reassertion of Space in Critical Social Theory* (New York: Verso, 1989). Soja includes housing in his discussion of postmodern urban spatiality, but not the interior spaces of homes.

8. Foucault, "Of Other Spaces," pp. 22-23.

9. Ibid., p. 23.

10. Ibid., p. 22.

11. Ibid., p. 23.

12. Ibid., p. 24.

13. Ibid., p. 27. The absence of theorization about power relations and homes by male theorists in general is a continuing failure of critical thought. Ironically, it replicates the second shift women perform in the house, since, despite the fact that men presumably spend a fair amount of their time in their homes, only feminist theory consistently addresses the problematic of home space.

14. Ibid.

15. Ibid., p. 24.

16. Ibid.

17. Ibid., pp. 24-27. Although my argument draws on these principles, I'm not suggesting that genealogy should be bound to them. As I said earlier, Foucault fails to reflect adequately on homes.

18. "Your Money," GMAC newsletter, vol. 3, no. 5 (1992), p. 2.

19. For discussion of the formation of a new subjectivity resulting from late capitalism's "homework economy," see Donna Haraway, "A Manifesto for Cyborgs: Science, Technology, and Socialist Feminism in the 1980s," *Socialist Review* 80 (1985), pp. 85-92.

20. Witold Rybczynski, *Home: The Short History of an Idea* (New York: Penguin, 1986), pp. 28, 51-59.

21. Ibid., pp. 61-62.

22. This discussion focuses on the homes of the English colonizers rather than the dwelling places of Native Americans because it was the European model that colonization made hegemonic. Native American concepts of shelter—then and now—function counterhegemonically and as such work as part of the current politicizing of homes.

23. Jefferson, *Notes on the State of Virginia* (New York: Norton, 1972), pp. 152-53. Foucault focuses on this shift in terms of architecture's new role in government. He comments, for example, that "from the eighteenth century on, every discussion of politics as the art of government of men necessarily includes a chapter or a series of chapters on urbanism, on collective facilities, on hygiene, and on private architecture. Such chapters are not found in the discussions of the art of government of the sixteenth century." See "An Ethics of Pleasure," pp. 258-59.

24. Despite its polemic for a conservatively gendered society, Ivan Illich's *Gender* (New York: Pantheon, 1982) remains a valuable source for these changing social-economic conditions.

25. Sigmund Freud, "The Uncanny," *Collected Writings*, vol. 17 (London: Hogarth Press), p. 245. David Adams quotes this passage from Freud in a fascinating discussion of home as an "absolute metaphor" in philosophy and on the importance of resisting that monotheistic position. See David Adams, "The Divine Art of Forgetfulness: Benjamin, Blumenberg, and Pyncheon," unpublished dissertation (Graduate Center, CUNY, 1990), pp. 203, 214-15. I wish to thank Gerhard Joseph for bringing the dissertation to my attention.

26. Catharine Beecher, *A Treatise on Domestic Economy* (New York: Schocken Books, 1977).

27. Charlotte Perkins Gilman, *Women and Economics* (New York: Harper and Row, 1966); and *Herland* (New York: Pantheon, 1978).

28. For a brief discussion of Co-Housing, see Claudia Wallis, "The Nuclear Family Goes Boom!" *Time* (Special Issue, Fall 1992), p. 44.

29. Harriet Jacobs, *Incidents in the Life of a Slave Girl*, ed. with Introduction by Jean Fagan Yellin (1861; Cambridge, Mass.: Harvard University Press, 1987).

30. Betty Friedan, *The Feminine Mystique* (New York: W.W. Norton, 1963). Also see Elaine Tyler May, *Homeward Bound: American Families in the Cold War Era* (New York: Basic Books, 1988).

31. *WAC STATS: The facts about women* (New Work: Women's Action Coalition, 1992), p. 52.

32. Biddy Martin and Chandra Talpade Mohanty, "Feminist Politics: What's Home Got to Do with It?" in *Feminist Studies / Critical Studies*, ed. Theresa de Lauretis (Bloomington: Indiana University Press, 1986).

33. See, for example, Marion Roberts, *Living in a Man-Made World: Gender Assumptions in Modern Housing Design* (New York: Routledge, 1991); Leslie Kanes Weisman, *Discrimination by Design: A Feminist Critique of the Man-Made Environment* (Chicago: University of Illinois Press, 1992); and Joni Seager, "Blueprints for Inequality," *The Women's Review of Books* 10 (January 1993), pp. 1, 3-4.

34. Christopher Lasch, *Haven in a Heartless World: The Family Besieged* (New York: Basic Books, 1977); *The Culture of Narcissism: American Life in an Age of Diminishing Ex-*

pectations (New York: Norton, 1979); and *The Minimal Self: Psychic Survival in Troubled Times* (New Haven: Yale University Press, 1988).

35. Robert Bellah et al., *Habits of the Heart: Individualism and Commitment in American Life* (New York: Harper and Row, 1986).

36. See Mark Poster's critique of Lasch by way of a social science study on families in Orange County, California. Poster states: "Lasch's pronouncement is too sweeping in its claims, generalizing too easily from psychoanalytic diagnoses of narcissism to sociological conditions; it overlooks many of the advances in contemporary families over the limitations of the Oedipal family (limitations Lasch does not acknowledge); and it fails to distinguish excesses in cultural patterns, which may be harmful to individuals, from the cultural patterns themselves, which may offer new possibilites for genuine gratification." *Critical Theory and Poststructuralism: In Search of Context* (Ithaca: Cornell University Press, 1989), pp. 145-46.

37. An article in *Time* magazine notes the recent use of such laws in divorce cases as a way of punishing and/or publicly humiliating spouses. See Andrea Sachs, "Handing Out Scarlet Letters," *Time* (October 1, 1990), p. 98.

38. A genealogist with an "inquiring mind" might also want to gauge the effect of having Michael Douglas constitute the link between the kitchen and the bedroom in both films.

39. Michael Cunningham, *A Home at the End of the World* (New York: Farrar Straus Giroux, 1990), p. 336.

40. Poster, *Critical Theory and Poststructuralism*, p. 122.

41. Ibid., p. 126. And also see his second book which furthers these arguments, *The Mode Of Information: Poststructuralism and Social Context* (Chicago: University of Chicago Press, 1990).

42. Poster, *Critical Theory and Poststructuralism*, p. 168.

43. "Your Money," GMAC Newsletter, p. 23.

44. Barbara J. Risman and Donald Tomaskvic-Devey, "The Social Construction of Technology: Microcomputers and the Organization of Work," *Business Horizons* (May-June 1989), pp. 71-74).

45. Donna Haraway, "A Manifesto for Cyborgs," *Socialist Review* 15 (1985), pp. 85-86.

46. In January 1993, a federal judge ruled that the Bush administration could not erase e-mail computer tapes. The information in question included memos regarding Iran-contra and Iraqgate. Philip Elmer-Dewitt, "Who's Reading Your Screen?" *Time* (January 18, 1993), p. 46.

Coda

1. Jonathan Z. Smith, *Imagining Religion: From Babylon to Jonestown* (Chicago: University of Chicago Press, 1982), p. 109.

2. An ABC News poll taken two days after the destruction of the compound indicated that 72 percent of the 530 adults surveyed thought the FBI had done the right thing and that 95 percent held David Koresh responsible for the deaths. "Reno Wins Praise at Senate Hearing," *New York Times*, April 23, 1993: A20.

3. Paul Boyer cites a 1988 Gallup poll indicating that 80 percent of the respondents

believed that they will appear before God on Judgment Day. A 1986 poll reported a smaller proportion of U.S. citizens identifying themselves as evangelical or born-again: 32 percent. Paul Boyer, *When Time Shall Be No More* (Cambridge, Mass.: Harvard University Press, 1992), pp. 2-3.

4. "Johnny Get Your Gun," written by Monroe Rosenfeld in 1886, was a popular favorite in the late nineteenth century, and later adapted by George M. Cohan for his World War I song "Over There."

5. Paul Boyer, "A Brief History of the End of Time," *The New Republic*, May 17, 1993: 31.

6. Nancy Gibbs, "Fire Storm in Waco," *Time*, May 3, 1993: 26-42.

7. Pat H. Broeske, "What in Heaven's Name is Going On?" *New York Times*, April 25, 1993: H27.

8. Ten years after writing his important article on contemporary apocalypse, Michael Barkun's observation that apocalyptic ideas have flourished rather than waned is more accurate than ever. In 1983, he suggested the possibility that the "number of [apocalyptic] believers may become so large that their very numbers and influence [might] produce a fundamental change in the social order." Given the volume and dispersal of the discourses of apocalypse over the past decade, I would say that such a change is in the making. Michael Barkun, "Divided Apocalypse: Thinking About the End in Contemporary America," *Soundings* 66, no. 3 (Fall 1983): 276.

9. Julia Ward Howe drew on the Book of Revelation for inspiration for her enormously popular "Battle Hymn."

10. The made-for-television film "In the Line of Duty: Ambush in Waco" makes a similar point by paralleling the portrayals of the Davidians and the ATF agents during the build-up of the raid.

11. "The War in Waco," *The Nation*, May 10, 1993: 616.

12. Michel Foucault, *The History of Sexuality*, vol. I, pp. 136-37.

13. Ibid., p. 139.

14. I would like to thank Ben Clardy and Peter Cummings for providing me with approximately fifty Waco jokes, many of which they received through e-mail.

Bibliography

Adams, David. "The Divine Art of Forgetfulness: Benjamin, Blumenberg, and Pynchon." Unpublished dissertation. Graduate Center, CUNY, 1990.

Adams, Henry. *The Education of Henry Adams.* Ed. Ernest Samuels. Boston: Houghton Mifflin, 1973.

Albanese, Catherine L. *American Religions and Religion.* Belmont, Calif.: Wadsworth, 1992.

Allman, William F. "The Amazing Gene Machine." *U.S. News and World Report,* July 16, 1990: 53-54.

Auerbach, Nina. *Woman and the Demon: The Life of a Victorian Myth.* Cambridge, Mass.: Harvard University Press, 1982.

Bakhtin, M. M. "Discourse in the Novel." *The Dialogic Imagination.* Ed. Michael Holquist, trans. Caryl Emerson and Michael Holquist. Austin: University of Texas Press, 1981.

Ball, Stephen J., ed. *Foucault and Education: Disciplines and Knowledge.* New York: Routledge, 1990.

Banta, Martha. *Imaging American Women: Idea and Ideals in Cultural History.* New York: Columbia University Press, 1987.

Barrett, Michele. *The Politics of Truth: From Marx to Foucault.* Stanford: Stanford University Press, 1991.

Bartky, Sandra Lee. *Femininity and Domination: Studies in the Phenomenology of Oppression.* New York: Routledge, 1990.

Baudrillard, Jean. "The Ecstasy of Communication." *The Anti-Aesthetic: Essays on Postmodern Culture.* Ed. Hal Foster. Port Townsend, Wash.: Bay Press, 1983.

_____. *The Ecstasy of Communication.* Trans. Bernard and Caroline Schutze, ed. Sylvere

Lotringer. New York: Semiotext(e), 1988.

_____. *Forget Foucault*. Trans. Nicole Dufresne. New York: Semiotext(e), 1987.

_____. *Looking Back on the End of the World*. NewYork: Semiotext(e), 1989.

_____. *Simulations*. Trans. Philip Beitchman. New York: Foreign Agents Series, Semiotext(e), 1983.

Beecher, Catharine. *A Treatise on Domestic Economy*. New York: Schocken, 1977.

Bellah, Robert, et al. *Habits of the Heart: Individualism and Commitment in American Life*. New York: Harper and Row, 1986.

Bercovitch, Sacvan. *The American Jeremiad*. Madison: University of Wisconsin, 1978.

Bloom, Harold. *The American Religion: The Emergence of the Post-Christian Nation*. New York: Simon and Schuster, 1992.

Bordo, Susan. *The Flight to Objectivity*. Albany: SUNY Press, 1987.

Boyer, Paul. *When Time Shall Be No More: Prophecy Belief in Modern American Culture*. Cambridge, Mass.: Harvard University Press, 1992.

Brown, Norman O. *Apocalypse and/or Metamorphoses*. Berkeley: University of California Press, 1991.

Brown, Wilmette. "Roots: Black Ghetto Ecology." *Reclaim the Earth: Women Speak Out for Life on Earth*. Ed. Leonie Caldecott and Stephanie Leland. London: Women's Press, 1983.

Buber, Martin. *Pointing the Way*. Trans. Maurice Friedman. New York: Harper and Bros., 1957

Burke, Carolyn. "Getting Spliced: Modernism and Sexual Difference." *American Quarterly* 39 (Spring 1987): 98-121.

Butler, Judith. *Gender Trouble: Feminism and the Subversion of Identity*. New York: Routledge, 1990.

Caldecott, Leonie, and Stephanie Leland, eds. *Reclaim the Earth: Women Speak Out for Life on Earth*. London: Women's Press, 1983.

Califia, Pat. *The Advocate Advisor*. Boston: Alyson, 1991.

Caputi, Jane. "Seeing Elephants: The Myths of Phallotechnology." *Feminist Studies* 14 (Fall 1988): 487-524.

Casalino, Larry. "Decoding the Human Genome Project: an Interview with Evelyn Fox Keller." *Socialist Review* (1991): 111-128.

Certeau, Michel de. *The Practice of Everyday Life*. Trans. Steven Rendall. Los Angeles: University of California Press, 1984.

Chan, Sucheng. "You're Short Besides!" *Making Face, Making Soul: Haciendo Caras*. Ed. Gloria Anzaldua. San Francisco: Aunt Lute Foundation Books, 1990.

Chase, Richard. *The American Novel and its Tradition*. New York: Anchor Books, 1957.

Christiansen, Keith. "Lorenzo Lotto and the Tradition of Epithalamic Paintings." *Apollo* (September 1986): 166-73.

Clark, Danae. "Commodity Lesbianism." *Camera Obscura* 25-26 (January/May 1991): 181-201.

Cogan, Louise. *All-American Girl: The Ideal of Real Womanhood in Mid-Nineteenth-Century America*. Athens: University of Georgia Press, 1989.

Collins, Patricia Hill. *Black Feminist Thought: Knowledge, Consciousness, and the Politics of Empowerment.* Boston: Unwin Hyman, 1990.

Cray, Ed. *LEVIs.* Boston: Houghton Mifflin, 1978.

Crimp, Douglas, ed. *AIDS: Cultural Analysis, Cultural Activism.* Cambridge, Mass.: MIT Press, 1988.

_____. "Portraits of People with AIDS." *Cultural Studies.* Ed. Lawrence Grossberg, Cary Nelson, and Paula Treichler. New York: Routledge, 1992. 117-133.

Cunningham, Michael. *A Home at the End of the World.* New York: Farrar Straus Giroux, 1990.

Daly, Mary. *Gyn/Ecology: The Metaethics of Radical Feminism.* Boston: Beacon Press, 1978.

Daniels, Ted. *Millennium Watch.* May 1992.

de Beauvoir, Simone. *The Second Sex.* Trans. H. M. Parshley. New York: Vintage, 1989.

D'Emilio, John, and Estelle Freedman. *Intimate Matters: A History of Sexuality in America.* New York: Harper and Row, 1988.

de Lauretis, Theresa. *Alice Doesn't: Feminism, Semiotics, Cinema.* Bloomington: Indiana University Press, 1984.

Derrida, Jacques. "No Apocalypse, Not Now (full speed ahead, seven missiles, seven missives)." *Diacritics* 14 (Summer 1984): 20-31.

_____. "Of an Apocalyptic Tone Recently Adopted in Philosophy." Trans. John P. Leavey, Jr., *Oxford Literary Review* 6 (1984): 3-37.

_____. *Spurs: Nietzsche's Styles.* Trans. Barbara Harlow. Chicago: University of Chicago Press, 1979.

Diamond, Irene. "Babies, Heroic Experts, and a Poisoned Earth." *Reweaving the World: The Emergence of Ecofeminism.* Ed. Irene Diamond and Gloria Feman Orenstein. San Francisco: Sierra Club Books, 1990. 201-10.

Diamond, Irene, and Lee Quinby, eds. *Feminism and Foucault: Reflections on Resistance.* Boston: Northeastern University Press, 1988.

Diggins, John Patrick. " 'Who Bore the Failure of Light': Henry Adams and the Crisis of Authority." *New England Quarterly* 64 (June 1985): 165-92.

Dinnerstein, Dorothy. *The Mermaid and the Minotaur: Sexual Arrangements and Human Malaise.* New York: Harper and Row, 1976.

Dorland, Michael, and Arthur Kroker. "Panic Cinema: Sex in the Age of the Hyperreal." *CineAction!* (Fall 1987): 3-5.

Douglass, Frederick. *Narrative of the Life of Frederick Douglass.* 1845; New York: Signet, 1968.

Dreyfus, Hubert, and Paul Rabinow. *Michel Foucault: Beyond Structuralism and Hermeneutics.* Chicago: University of Chicago Press, 1983.

Duberman, Martin, ed. *About Time: Exploring the Gay Past.* New York: Meridian, 1991.

Dubin, Steven C. *Arresting Images: Impolitic Art and Uncivil Actions.* New York: Routledge, 1992.

During, Simon. *Foucault and Literature: Towards a Genealogy of Writing.* New York: Routledge, 1992.

Edwards, Lynn. "Mechanical and Other Devices." *Urinary Incontinence.* Ed. K. P. S. Caldwell. London: Sector, 1975. 115-27.

Elmer-Dewitt, Philip. "Who's Reading Your Screen?" *Time* (January 18, 1993): 46.

Enloe, Cynthia. *Bananas, Beaches, and Bases*. Berkeley: University of California, 1990.

Ewen, Stuart, and Elizabeth Ewen. *Channels of Desire: Mass Images and the Shaping of American Consciousness*. New York: McGraw-Hill, 1982.

Faludi, Susan. *Backlash: The Undeclared War against American Women*. New York: Crown, 1991.

Fighting Back. Written and directed by Bill Jersey. "The Glory and the Power: Fundamentalism Observed." PBS (June 15, 1992).

Firth, Katherine R. *The Apocalyptic Tradition in Reformation Britain, 1530-1645*. New York: Oxford University Press, 1979.

Foucault, Michel. *The Archaeology of Knowledge*. Trans. A. M. Sheridan Smith. New York: Harper and Row, 1972.

———. "The Ethic of Care for the Self as a Practice of Freedom: An Interview." Trans. J. D. Gautier, S. J. special issue, *The Final Foucault, Journal of Philosophy and Social Criticism* 12 (Summer 1987): 112-131.

———. *Foucault Live*. Trans. Mia Foret and Marion Martius, ed. Sylvere Lotringer. New York: Semiotext(e), 1989.

———. *The Foucault Reader*. Ed. Paul Rabinow. New York: Pantheon, 1984.

———. *The History of Sexuality: Vol. I*. Trans. Robert Hurley. New York: Vintage, 1980.

———. *Language, Counter-Memory, Practice: Selected Essays and Interviews*. Trans. Donald F. Bouchard and Sherry Simon. Ithaca: Cornell University Press, 1977.

———. "The Masked Philosopher." *Michel Foucault: Politics, Philosophy, Culture, Interviews and Other Writings, 1977-1984*. Ed. Lawrence D. Kritzman. New York: Routledge, 1988.

———. "Michel Foucault: An Interview." *Edinburgh Review*. 1985: 59.

———. "Of Other Spaces." *Diacritics* 16 (Spring 1986): 22-27.

———. *The Order of Things: An Archaeology of the Human Sciences*. New York: Vintage, 1973.

———. *Power/Knowledge: Selected Interviews and Other Writings, 1972-77*. Ed. Colin Gordon. New York: Pantheon, 1980.

———. *The Use of Pleasure*. Trans. Robert Hurley. New York: Pantheon, 1985.

Fox, Nicols. "NEA under Siege." *New Art Examiner* (Summer 1989): 18-23.

Francis, Dick. *Longshot*. New York: Ballantine, 1990.

Freud, Sigmund. "The Acquisition of Power Over Fire (1932)." *Character and Culture*. Ed. Philip Rieff. New York: Macmillan, 1963.

———. *Civilization and Its Discontents*. Trans. James Strachey. New York: Norton, 1989.

———. *The Freud Reader*. Ed. Peter Gay. New York: Norton, 1989.

Friedan, Betty. *The Feminine Mystique*. New York: W.W. Norton, 1963.

Fuller, Margaret. *Women in the Nineteenth Century*. New York: Norton, 1971.

Fukuyama, Francis. *The End of History and the Last Man*. New York: Macmillan, 1992.

Funkenstein, Amos. "A Schedule for the End of the World: The Origins and Persistence of the Apocalyptic Mentality." *Visions of Apocalypse: End or Rebirth?* Ed. Saul Friedlander et al. New York: Holmes and Meier, 1985.

Fusco, Coco. "Andres Serrano Shoots the Klan: An Interview with Andres Serrano." *High Performance* (Fall 1991): 42-43.

Fuss, Diana. *Essentially Speaking*. New York: Routledge, 1989.

———. "Reading Like a Feminist." *differences* 1 (Summer 1989).

_____, ed. *Inside/Out: Lesbian Theories, Gay Theories*. New York: Routledge, 1991.

Gallop, Jane. "Reading the Mother Tongue: Psychoanalytic Feminist Criticism." *Critical Inquiry* 13 (Winter 1987): 314-29.

Garland, Anne Witte. *Women Activists: Challenging the Abuse of Power*. New York: Feminist Press, 1988.

Gates, Henry Louis, Jr., *The Signifying Monkey: A Theory of Afro-American Literary Criticism*. New york: Oxford University Press, 1988.

Gilligan, Carol. *In a Different Voice*. Cambridge, Mass.: Harvard University Press, 1982.

Gilman, Charlotte Perkins. *Herland*. New York: Pantheon, 1978.

_____. *Women and Economics*. New York: Harper and Row, 1966.

Goffman, Erving. *Gender Advertisements*. London: Macmillan, 1979.

Gould, Stephen Jay. *The Mismeasure of Man*. New York: W. W. Norton, 1981.

Grossberg, Lawrence, Cary Nelson, and Paula Treichler, eds. *Cultural Studies*. New York: Routledge, 1992.

Grunwald, Henry. "The Year 2000: Is It the End—Or Just the Beginning?" *Time* (March 30, 1992): 73-76.

Guthrie, Derek. "Taboo Artist: Serrano Speaks." *New Art Examiner* (September 1989): 45-46.

Hagen, Charles. "After the Storm." *Art News* (September 1991): 61-62.

Haraway, Donna. "A Manifesto for Cyborgs." *Socialist Review* 15 (1985): 65-108.

_____. *Simians, Cyborgs, and Women: The Reinvention of Nature*. New York: Routledge, 1991.

_____. "Situated Knowledges: The Science Question in Feminism and the Privilege of Partial Perspective." *Feminist Studies* 14 (Fall 1988): 581.

Hassan, Ihab. *The Literature of Silence*. New York: Knopf, 1967.

Hayes, Tom, and Lee Quinby. "The Aporia of Bourgeois Art: Desire in Thomas Mann's *Death in Venice*." *Criticism* (Spring 1989): 159-77.

Hayes, Wilson T. *Winstanley the Digger: A Literary Analysis of Radical Ideas in the English Revolution*. Cambridge, Mass.: Harvard University Press, 1979.

Hebdige, Dick. "Postmodernism and 'The Other Side'." *Journal of Communication Inquiry* 10 (Summer 1986).

Hemenway, Robert. *Zora Neale Hurston: A Literary Biography*. Urbana: University of Illinois Press, 1977.

Hoagland, Sarah Lucia. *Lesbian Ethics: Toward New Value*. Palo Alto: Institute of Lesbian Studies, 1988.

hooks, bell. "Black Women and Men: Partnership in the 1990's." *Yearning: Race, Gender, and Cultural Politics*. Boston: South End Press, 1990.

Hughson, Lois. *From Biography to History: The Historical Imagination and American Fiction, 1880-1940*. Charlottesville: University of Virginia Press, 1988.

Hurston, Zora Neale. *Dust Tracks on a Road*. 1942; New York: J. B. Lippincott, 1971.

_____. *I Love Myself When I Am Laughing . . . And Then Again When I Am Looking Mean and Impressive*. Ed. Alice Walker. Old Westbury, Conn.: Feminist Press, 1979.

_____. *Mules and Men*. 1935; New York: Harper and Row, 1990.

_____. *Spunk*. 1933; Berkeley: Turtle Island Foundation, 1985.

_____. *Their Eyes Were Watching God*. 1937; repr. Urbana: University of Illinois Press,

1978.

Illich, Ivan. *Gender*. New York: Pantheon, 1982.

Jacobs, Harriet. *Incidents in the Life of a Slave Girl*. 1861; Cambridge, Mass.: Harvard University Press, 1987.

Jefferson, Thomas. *Notes on the State of Virginia*. Ed. William Peden. New York: Norton, 1972.

Johnson, Barbara. "Apostrophe, Animation, and Abortion." *Feminisms*. Ed. Robyn Warhol and Diane Price Herndl. New Brunswick, N.J.: Rutgers University Press, 1991.

Jordan, Constance. "Feminism and the Humanists: The Case of Sir Thomas Elyot's *Defence of Good Women*." *Rewriting the Renaissance: The Discourses of Sexual Difference in Early Modern Europe*. Ed. Margaret W. Ferguson, Maureen Quilligan, and Nancy J. Vickers. Chicago: University of Chicago Press, 1986.

Kaledin, Eugenia. *The Education of Mrs. Henry Adams*. Philadelphia: Temple University Press, 1981.

Kamper, Dietmar, and Christolph Wolf, eds. *Looking Back on the End of the World*. New York: Semiotext(e), 1989.

Keller, Catherine. "Women Against Wasting the World." *Reweaving the World: The Emergence of Ecofeminism*. Ed. Irene Diamond and Gloria Feman Orenstein. San Francisco: Sierra Club Books, 1990.

Keller, Evelyn Fox. *A Feeling for the Organism: The Life and Work of Barbara McClintock*. New York: W. H. Freeman, 1983.

_____. *Reflections on Gender and Science*. New Haven: Yale University Press, 1985.

Kendall, Jane C., and Associates, eds. *Combining Service and Learning: A Resource Book for Community and Public Learning*. National Society for Internships and Experimental Education, vol. 1.

Kermode, Frank. "Apocalypse and the Modern." *Visions of Apocalypse: End or Rebirth*. Ed. Friedlander et al. York: Holmes and Meier, 1985.

Ketterer, David. *New Worlds for Old: The Apocalyptic Imagination, Science Fiction, and American Literature*. Bloomington: Indiana University Press, 1975.

Kimmel, Michael. "The Contemporary Crisis of Masculinity in Historical Perspective." *The Making of Masculinities*. Ed. Harry Brod. Boston: Allen and Unwin, 1987.

Kritzman, Lawrence D., ed. *Michel Foucault: Politics, Philosophy, Culture: Interviews and Other Writings, 1977-84*. New York: Routledge, 1988.

Kroker, Arthur, and Marilouise Kroker. *Body Digest: Special Issue of the Canadian Journal of Political and Social Theory* 11 (1987).

Kroker, Arthur, Marilouise Kroker, and David Cook. *Panic Encyclopedia: The Definitive Guide to the Postmodern Scene*. New York: Macmillan, 1972.

Kuspit, Donald. "Sexual Censorship and the New Authoritarianism." *New Art Examiner* (September 1989): 42-44.

Lammers, Ann, and Ted Peters. "Genethics: Implications of the Human Genome Project." *The Christian Century* (October 3, 1990): 868-72.

Lasch, Christopher. *The Culture of Narcissism: American Life in an Age of Diminishing Expectations*. New York: Norton, 1979.

_____. *Haven in a Heartless World: The Family Besieged*. New York: Basic Books, 1977.

_____. *The Minimal Self: Psychic Survival in Troubled Times*. New Haven: Yale University

Press, 1988.

Lawren, Bill. "Are You Ready for Millennial Fever?" *Utne Reader* (March/April 1990): 96-97.

Lee, David. "Urine Test." *The British Journal of Photography* (November 1991): 16.

Lesser, Wayne. "Criticism, Literary History, and the Paradigm: *The Education of Henry Adams.*" *PMLA* 97 (May 1982): 378-92.

Lewicki, Zbigniew. *The Bang and the Whimper: Apocalypse and Entropy in American Literature.* Westport, Conn.: Greenwood, 1984.

Lewis, R. W. B. *Trials of the Word.* New Haven: Yale University Press, 1965.

Lewontin, R. C., Steven Rose, and Leon Kamin. *Not in Our Genes: Biology, Ideology, and Human Nature.* New York: Pantheon, 1984.

Lifton, Robert Jay, and Charles B. Strozier. "Waiting for Armageddon." *The New York Times Book Review* (Aug. 12, 1990): 25.

Lippard, Lucy, R. "Andres Serrano: The Spirit and the Letter." *Art in America* (April 1990): 239-45.

Maathai, Wangari. *The Green Belt Movement: Sharing the Approach and the Experience.* Nairobi: Environment Liason Centre International, 1988.

MacCannell, Juliet Flower. "Oedipus Wrecks: Lacan, Stendhal, and the Narrative Form of the Real." *Lacan and Narration: The Psychoanalytic Difference in Narrative Theory.* Ed. Robert Con Davis. Baltimore: Johns Hopkins University Press, 1983: 910-40.

McKibben, Bill. *The End of Nature.* New York: Random House, 1989.

McLuhan, Marshall. *The Mechanical Bride: Folklore of Industrial Man.* Boston: Beacon, 1951.

Mann, Patricia S. *Micro-Politics: Agency in a Postfeminist Era.* Minneapolis: University of Minnesota Press, 1994.

Martin, Biddy, and Chandra Talpade Mohanty. "Feminist Politics: What's Home Got to Do with It?" *Feminist Studies/Critical Studies.* Ed. Theresa de Lauretis. Bloomington: Indiana University Press, 1986: 191-212.

Martin, Luther H., Huck Gutman, and Patrick H. Hutton, eds. *Technologies of the Self: A Seminar with Michel Foucault.* Amherst: University of Massachusetts Press, 1988.

Marx, Leo. *The Machine in the Garden.* New York: Oxford University Press, 1964.

May, Elaine Tyler. *Homeward Bound: American Families in the Cold War Era.* New York: Basic Books, 1988.

Miller, Nancy. "My Father's Penis." *Getting Personal: Feminist Occasions and Other Autobiographical Acts.* New York: Routledge, 1991: 143-47.

Monette, Paul. *Borrowed Time: An AIDS Memoir.* New York: Avon, 1988.

Morris, Meaghan. *The Pirate's Fiancée: Feminism, Reading, Postmodernism.* New York: Verso, 1988.

Morrison, Toni. *Jazz.* New York: Knopf, 1992.

_____. *Sula.* New York: New American Library, 1973.

Nash, Madeleine J., and Dick Thompson. "The Gene Hunt." *Time* (Mar. 20, 1989): 62-67.

Nestle, Joan, ed. *The Persistent Desire: A Femme-Butch Reader.* Boston: Alyson, 1992.

Paglia, Camille. *Sexual Personae.* New York: Vintage, 1991.

Patton, Cindy. *Inventing AIDS.* New York: Routledge, 1990.

Phelan, Peggy. "Money Talks, Again." *The Drama Review* (Fall 1991): 131-41.

_____. "Serrano, Mapplethorpe, the NEA, and You." *The Drama Review* (Spring 1990): 4-15.

Poster, Mark. *Critical Theory and Poststructuralism: In Search of Context.* Ithaca: Cornell University Press, 1989.

_____. *The Mode of Information: Poststructuralism and Social Context.* Chicago: University of Chicago Press, 1990.

Primavesi, Anne. *From Apocalypse to Genesis: Ecology, Feminism and Christianity.* Minneapolis: Fortress, 1991.

Quinby, Lee. *Freedom, Foucault, and the Subject of America.* Boston: Northeastern University Press, 1991.

Rajchman, John. *Truth and Eros: Foucault, Lacan, and the Question of Ethics.* New York: Routledge, 1991.

Rawson, Hugh. *Wicked Words.* New York: Crown, 1989.

Reising, Russell. *The Unusable Past.* New York: Methuen, 1986.

Rezler, Andre. "Man as Nostalgia: The Image of the Last Man in Twentieth-Century Post-utopian Fiction." *Visions of the Apocalypse: End or Rebirth?* Ed. Friedlander et al. New York: Holmes and Meier, 1985: 196-215.

Rich, Adrienne. *On Lies, Secrets, and Silence.* New York: Norton, 1979.

Riley, Denise. *"Am I That Name?" Feminism and the Category of "Women" in History.* Minneapolis: University of Minnesota Press, 1987.

Risman, Barbara J., and Donald Tomaskvic-Devey. "The Social Construction of Technology: Microcomputers and the Organization of Work." *Business Horizons* (May-June 1989): 71-74.

Roberts, Marion. *Living in a Man-Made World: Gender Assumptions in Modern Housing Design.* New York: Routledge, 1991.

Robinson, Douglas. *American Apocalypses: The Image of the End of the World in American Literature.* Baltimore: Johns Hopkins University Press, 1985.

Roman, Leslie G., Linda K. Christian-Smith, with Elizabeth Ellsworth, eds. *Becoming Feminine: The Politics of Popular Culture.* New York: Falmer, 1988.

Rosaldo, Michelle. "Toward an Anthropology of Self and Feeling." *Culture Theory.* Ed. R. Shweder and R. Levine. New York: Cambridge University Press, 1984.

Rosenberg, Rosalind. *Beyond Separate Spheres: Intellectual Roots of Modern Feminism.* New Haven: Yale University Press, 1982.

Rosenblum, Robert. "The Fatal Women of Picasso and de Kooning." *Art News* (October 1985): 98-103.

Rowe, John Carlos. *Henry Adams and Henry James: The Emergence of a Modern Consciousness.* Ithaca: Cornell University Press, 1976.

_____. "Modern Art and the Invention of Postmodern Capital." *American Quarterly* 39 (Spring 1987): 156.

Ruddick, Sara. *Maternal Thinking: Toward a Politics of Peace.* New York: Ballantine Books, 1989.

Rybczynski, Witold. *Home: The Short History of an Idea.* New York: Penguin, 1986.

Sachs, Andrea. "Handing out Scarlet Letters." *Time* (October 1, 1990): 98.

Safire, William. "On Language." *New York Times Magazine* (June 21, 1992): 10.

Samuels, Ernest. *Henry Adams*. Cambridge, Mass.: Harvard University Press, 1989.

Schweitzer, Ivy. *The Work of Self Representation: Lyric Poetry in Colonial New England*. Chapel Hill: University of North Carolina Press, 1991.

Scott, Nathan A., Jr. " 'New Heav'ns, New Earth'—The Landscape of Contemporary Apocalypse." *Journal of Religion* 53 (January 1973): 1-35.

Seager, Joni. "Blueprints for Inequality." *The Women's Review of Books* 10 (January 1993): 1, 3-4.

Smith-Rosenberg, Carroll. *Disorderly Conduct: Visions of Gender in Victorian America*. New York: Oxford University Press, 1985.

Soja, Edward. *Postmodern Geography: The Reassertion of Space in Critical Social Theory*. New York: Verso, 1989.

Spiegelman, Art. *Maus II: A Survivor's Tale. And Here My Troubles Began*. New York: Pantheon, 1991.

Spivak, Gayatri Chakravorty. *In Other Worlds: Essays in Cultural Politics*. New York: Routledge, 1987.

_____. with Ellen Rooney. "In a Word, *Interview*," *differences* 1 (Summer 1989): 124-56.

Starhawk. *Dreaming the Dark*. Boston: Beacon Press, 1982.

_____. *The Spiral Dance: A Rebirth of Ancient Religion of the Great Goddess*. San Francisco: Harper and Row, 1986.

"A Statistical Portrait of the 'Typical' American." *New York Times* (July 26, 1992): E5.

Sullivan, Andrew. "Flogging Underwear: The New Raunchiness of American Advertising." *The New Republic* (Jan. 18, 1988): 20-24.

Sullivan, Robert. "An Army of the Faithful." *New York Times Magazine* (April 25, 1993): 32-36, 40-44.

Theweleit, Klaus. *Male Fantasies*. Trans. Steven Conway in collaboration with Erica Carter and Chris Turner. Minneapolis: University of Minnesota Press, 1987.

Vestergaard, Torben, and Kim Schroder. *The Language of Advertising*. Oxford: Basil Blackwell, 1985.

Vicinus, Martha, ed. *Suffer and Be Still: Women in the Victorian Era*. Bloomington: Indiana University Press, 1972.

_____, ed. *A Widening Sphere: Changing Roles of Victorian Women*. Bloomington: Indiana University Press, 1977.

WAC STATS: The facts about women. New York: Women's Action Coalition, 1992.

Wainwright, Mary Katherine. "Subversive Female Folktellers in *Mules and Men*." *Zora in Florida*. Ed. Steve Glassman and Kathryn Seidel. Gainesville: University of Florida Press, 1991.

Walker, Margaret Urban. "Partial Consideration." *Ethics* 101 (July 1991): 758-74.

Wallis, Claudia. "The Nuclear Family Goes Boom!" *Time* Special Issue (Fall 1992): 44.

Warner, Michael. "Fear of a Queer Planet." *Social Text* 29 (1991): 3-17.

Wartenberg, Thomas E. *The Forms of Power: From Domination to Transformation*. Philadelphia: Temple University Press, 1990.

Webster, Charles. *The Great Instauration: Science, Medicine and Reform, 1626-1660*. London: Duckworth, 1975.

Weisman, Leslie. *Discrimination by Design: A Feminist Critique of the Man-Made Environment*. Chicago: University of Illinois Press, 1992.

West, Cornel. "Learning to Talk of Race." *New York Times Magazine* (Aug. 2, 1992): 26.

White, Hayden. *The Content of Form: Narrative Discourse and Historical Representation.* Baltimore: Johns Hopkins University Press, 1987.

Williamson, Judith. *Decoding Advertisements: Ideology and Meaning in Advertising.* London: Marion Boyers, 1978.

Index

Lee Quinby is associate professor of English and American Studies at Hobart and William Smith Colleges. She is the author of *Freedom, Foucault, and the Subject of America* (1991) and the coeditor (with Irene Diamond) of *Feminism and Foucault: Reflections on Resistance* (1988). Her publications include articles in the *American Historical Review, Criticism,* and *Signs.*